ONE WEEK LOA

'Violent creature, brute, beast, wild b.; dragon, tiger,
wolf, mad dog; demon, devil, hell-hound, fury, monster;
savage, barbarian, Vandal, iconoclast, destroyer; man of
blood, butcher, murderer; homicidal maniac, madman;
rough, ruffian, Herod, tyrant; fire-eater, bravo, boaster;
fire-brand, agitator; revolutionary, ANARCHIST,
nihilist, terrorist, revolutionist; virago, termagant,
Amazon; spitfire, scold, shrew.'
(From *Roget's Thesaurus* (Harmondsworth, Penguin,
1957), pp. 65–6)

Modern Ideologies

ANARCHISM

David Miller
Nuffield College, Oxford

J.M. Dent & Sons Ltd
London and Melbourne

First published 1984
© David Miller, 1984

All rights reserved
This book is set in 10/12 pt VIP Plantin by
Inforum Ltd, Portsmouth
Made in Great Britain by
Biddles Ltd, Guildford, Surrey for
J.M. Dent & Sons Ltd
Aldine House, 33 Welbeck Street, London W1M 8LX

British Library Cataloguing in Publication Data

Miller, David, *1946–*
    Anarchism.—(Modern ideologies series)
    1. Anarchism and anarchists
    I. Title
    335'.83   HX833

ISBN 0–460–10093–9
ISBN 0–460–11093–4 Pbk

Preface

This book is a study of anarchism as an ideology, as a set of beliefs about human nature, society and the state that attempts both to explain the world and to help to change it. It is intended mainly as an introduction for readers new to the subject. Part I surveys the major schools of anarchist thought; Part II explores the relationship between theory and practice in anarchism; and Part III offers a critical assessment of the ideology as a whole. The book is not a history of anarchism, although it analyses various historical events from the point of view of anarchist theory, and the discussion of different anarchist revolutionary strategies in Part II is arranged roughly according to historical sequence. It might usefully be read alongside one of the excellent histories of anarchism that are currently available, for instance James Joll's or George Woodcock's.

Although I have tried to reserve my own opinions as far as possible for the final chapter, the reader should be warned that this is a critical study by a non-anarchist. I have noticed recently a tendency on the part of certain reviewers to claim that anarchism can only properly be understood by people with inside knowledge of the movement. Saying this seems to me to run the risk of devaluing anarchism as a purportedly consistent and realistic set of beliefs about man and society, and regarding it instead as an indefinable experience, rather like the taste of pineapple to those who have never eaten the fruit. It may nevertheless be as well to reveal my own ideological commitments explicitly. I should describe myself as a market socialist, from which point of view I have some sympathy both with the anarcho-individualist idea of conducting economic life on the basis of contract and with the anarcho-communist idea of co-operative production. For reasons that are spelt out in the last chapter, however, I believe that even a decentralized social system will require authoritative central regulation, and hence the continued existence of an institution that is recognizably a state.

I have incurred a number of substantial debts in the course of writing this book. The first is to R.N. Berki, who originally suggested that I should attempt the project, and has been a constant source of encouragement and advice ever since. April Carter and James Joll both read the manuscript and made many valuable suggestions for improvement. Huw Richards saved me a good deal of labour by agreeing to undertake a thorough review of the literature on Spanish anarchism. John Eisenhammer, David Goldey and Philip Williams all made helpful suggestions about reading in areas where my own knowledge was woefully thin. Gareth Howlett advised me on translations from French. I must also record my gratitude to the British Academy for making me a grant towards the costs of research for the book.

Jocelyn Burton has taken a close interest in the book throughout its period of gestation, and has been the most supportive of editors. Ann Franklin and Jenny Roberts have cheerfully shared the thankless task of typing up drafts. My last and greatest debt is to my wife Sue who has encouraged and sustained me throughout the period of writing: *Nunc scio quid sit Amor*.

Nuffield College, Oxford, 1984 David Miller

Contents

Part I Varieties of Anarchism

1 What is Anarchism? 2
2 Philosophical Anarchism 15
3 Individualist Anarchism 30
4 Communist Anarchism 45

Part II Anarchism as a Revolutionary Ideology

5 Human Nature and Historical Progress 62
6 Anarchism and Marxism 78
7 Revolutionary Organization and Strategy 94
8 Anarchism, Violence and Terror 109
9 Anarchism and Syndicalism 124
10 Anarchism and the New Left 141

Part III Assessing Anarchism

11 Constructive Achievements 154
12 Critical Questions 169

Notes 184

Select Bibliography 209

Index 213

Part I Varieties of Anarchism

1 What Is Anarchism?

Of all the major ideologies confronting the student of politics, anarchism must be one of the hardest to pin down. It resists straight-forward definition. It is amorphous and full of paradoxes and contra-dictions. Consider just a couple of these. The prevalent image of the anarchist in the popular mind is that of a destructive individual prepared to use violent means to disrupt social order, without having anything constructive to offer by way of alternative – the sinister figure in a black cape concealing a stick of dynamite. Similarly 'anarchy' is used to mean chaos, social breakdown, loss of the usual amenities of life (a weather forecaster recently described a particularly virulent spell of bad weather as 'anarchic'). But most anarchists would repudiate this image completely, and argue that their aims were eminently constructive; that they were attempting to build a society free from many of the chaotic and disfiguring features of the present one – war, violence, poverty and so forth. Again many anarchists have rejected violence, or admitted it only as a defensive measure against what they see as the violence of the state, and some at least have been saintly individuals, adhering to moral principles in their personal lives in a way that puts their critics to shame. So why is the popular image so wide of the mark? Or does it tell half of the truth about anarchism and anarchists, and omit the other half?

Next, consider in what sense anarchists are individualists. From one point of view, it may look as though anarchism elevates the individual above all social restraints, claiming that each person has the right to act exactly as he pleases without necessarily paying attention to the rights and interests of others. From another point of view, however, anarchists will maintain that their aim is to produce fully social individuals who are much more aware of their communal obligations than people are today; and indeed many anarchists have insisted that they are socialists, even perhaps the only true socialists. So we are left perplexed as to whether the real goal of anarchism is individual freedom or communal solidarity, or whether anarchists may possibly try to reconcile these apparently incompatible aims, and if so how.

2

Faced with these paradoxes and contradictions, we may begin to wonder whether anarchism is really an ideology at all, or merely a jumble of beliefs without rhyme or reason. Of course an ideology is never a fully coherent doctrine; every ideology is open-ended, capable of being developed in different directions, and therefore of generating contradictory propositions. But generally speaking we can at least find a coherent core, a consistent set of ideas which is shared by all those who embrace the ideology in question. Take Marxism, in some respects the ideology most obviously comparable to anarchism. Although, as is well known, Marxists have often disagreed bitterly about the implications of Marxist doctrine – say about whether Marx's idea of proletarian dictatorship licenses Lenin's idea of the vanguard party of the proletariat – all at least share a number of central assumptions, about history, economics, politics and so forth (we can also point to a definitive set of texts, the works of Marx himself, though this feature is peculiar to Marxism). It is by no means clear that we can find such a set of core assumptions in the case of anarchism. We must face the possibility that anarchism is not really *an* ideology, but rather the point of intersection of several ideologies. This idea forms the guiding thread for the first part of my study. I shall look at different versions of anarchism and try to assess how deep their resemblance goes. But first I must say something about anarchism in general, to locate those features which have allowed anarchists, at least superficially, to be grouped together.

We may trace the origins of anarchism to the outbreak of the French Revolution in 1789. Although it is possible, by searching diligently enough, to find precursors of anarchism as far back as the ancient Greeks – and perhaps even the Chinese – this shows only that there have always been men willing to challenge authority on philosophical or political grounds. This might be described as the primitive anarchist attitude: but for anarchism to develop beyond a stance of defiance into a social and political theory that challenged the existing order and proposed an alternative, such wholesale reconstruction needed to become thinkable. This reorientation of thought was the work largely of the Revolution, which, by challenging the old regime in France on grounds of basic principle, opened the way for similar challenges to other states and other social institutions. Henceforth all institutions were vulnerable to the demand that they should be justified from first principles – whether of natural right, social utility, human self-realization, or whatever. From this source sprang the major ideologies – conservatism, liberalism and socialism as well as

3

anarchism – in recognizably their modern form. It is therefore appropriate that the first major work which indubitably belongs in the anarchist tradition – Godwin's *Enquiry Concerning Political Justice* – should have been produced in the immediate aftermath of the Revolution (in 1793) and with that event as its direct inspiration.

Thereafter anarchism enjoyed a sporadic life. Individual thinkers produced treatises which attracted attention and in some cases disciples, but there was little continuity of thought, and nothing in the way of an anarchist *movement* until the later part of the nineteenth century. Even then, talk of an anarchist movement is liable to mislead. Anarchists were certainly active in the working-class movement that developed throughout Europe in that period, and in some places managed to gain a leading role in working-class organizations, but it is unlikely that many of their rank and file followers were anarchists themselves. So it is better to speak of the workers' movement acquiring an anarchist tint, as in other places it acquired a Marxist or a liberal tint. The movement was not continuous. It broke down or was suppressed in one place (as in France after the Paris Commune) only to reappear in another. We can therefore find eruptions of anarchist activity occurring throughout Europe from the 1860s onwards – more prominently in the Latin countries than in Germany or Britain – with France acquiring pride of place again in the early 1900s (with the Syndicalist movement), and Spain witnessing the finale with the anarchist-inspired union movement that fought and perished in the Civil War.

A history of anarchism that pays primary attention to numerical strength is therefore likely to conclude that anarchism should be treated as a sub-category of socialism, as one branch of the socialist movement that acquired mass support during these years. This is to ignore all those anarchists who were critical of mainstream socialism, especially the individualists, mainly American in origin, who produced an alternative version of anarchism that was as coherent as that of the socialists. During the nineteenth century their ideas made little impact outside of a small circle of intellectuals; but the recent revival of individualist anarchism in the U.S.A. – anarchists have combined with minimal-statists to form the Libertarian Party which polled 920,800 votes in the 1980 Presidential election – makes it easier to do justice to their claims. The tendency of the standard histories of anarchism, by contrast, is to give considerable attention to the early non-socialist anarchists – Godwin and Stirner especially – but largely to ignore those who were contemporaries of the socialist anarchists (and who, therefore, ought presumably to have known better: there is a parallel here with Marxists' treatment of 'utopian socialists').[1] I shall attempt to rectify this injustice, while still giving due weight to the greater historical influence of the anarchists within the socialist camp.

Despite this initial caution about searching for a comprehensive definition of 'anarchism', we may still be able to point to features which have allowed anarchists of different persuasions to be collected together under a common label. The first and most obvious of these is their hostility to the state: anarchists argue that it should be abolished and replaced by a new form of social organization. To make sense of this claim we need to know what is meant by 'state'. The state is not equivalent to government in general, and indeed some anarchists have made use of this distinction to suggest that their aim is not society without government, but merely society without a state. Looked at in historical perspective, the state is the specific form of government which emerged in post-Renaissance Europe, and has now established itself in every developed society. What are its main characteristics?[2] First, the state is a *sovereign* body, in the sense that it claims complete authority to define the rights of its subjects – it does not, for instance, allow subjects to maintain customary rights which it has neither created nor endorsed. Second, the state is a *compulsory* body, in the sense that everyone born into a given society is forced to recognize obligations to the state that governs that society – one cannot opt out of these obligations except by leaving the society itself. Third, the state is a *monopolistic* body: it claims a monopoly of force in its territorial area, allowing no competitor to exist alongside it. Fourth, the state is a *distinct* body, in the sense that the roles and functions which compose it are separate from social roles and functions generally, and also that the people who compose the state for the most part form a distinct class – the politicians, bureaucrats, armed forces and police.

Anarchists make two charges against the state – they claim that it has no right to exist, and they also claim that it brings a whole series of social evils in its train. To consider these charges in turn, the anarchist in effect first takes the old Augustinian adage, 'Without justice, what are states but bands of robbers?' and removes the qualifying clause. He claims that no state – no institution with the four features listed above – could have come into existence without something akin to an act of piracy on the part of those who would become its rulers. For why would men freely surrender their rights to such a Leviathan? In particular, anarchists have been critical of the social contract theory used by many liberals to justify the existence of the state, whereby

men in a stateless society are said to have agreed to the formation of a
state in order to safeguard their lives, liberty and material goods. In
reply the anarchist may say what Locke first said about Hobbes and
Filmer: 'This is to think that Men are so foolish that they take care to
avoid what Mischiefs may be done them by *Pole-Cats*, or *Foxes*, but
are content, nay think it Safety, to be devoured by *Lions*.'[3] In creating
a state, men create an institution that is far more dangerous to them
than the power of other men taken singly. Furthermore, the anarchist
will continue, even if a generation of men were so foolish as to agree
unanimously to the setting up of a state, how could this agreement
bind their successors who were not party to it? Yet all states claim
authority over the lives of their subjects' children.

But the greater volume of anarchist criticism is aimed at what
states do when they are allowed to exist. This is so wide-ranging that
only the barest summary can be given, and I cannot hope to capture
the flavour of the original. Proudhon's famous denunciation may
provide an example:

> To be GOVERNED is to be at every operation, at every
> transaction, noted, registered, enrolled, taxed, stamped,
> measured, numbered, assessed, licensed, authorized,
> admonished, forbidden, reformed, corrected, punished. It is,
> under pretext of public utility, and in the name of the general
> interest, to be placed under contribution, trained, ransomed,
> exploited, monopolized, extorted, squeezed, mystified,
> robbed; then, at the slightest resistance, the first word of
> complaint, to be repressed, fined, despised, harassed, tracked,
> abused, clubbed, disarmed, choked, imprisoned, judged,
> condemned, shot, deported, sacrificed, sold, betrayed; and, to
> crown all, mocked, ridiculed, outraged, dishonoured. That is
> government; that is its justice; that is its morality.[4]

If we try to unpack this tirade, four main charges are being levelled
against the state (which Proudhon here identifies with government,
contrary to some anarchist usage). First, the state is a *coercive* body,
which reduces people's freedom far beyond the point required by
social co-existence. It enacts restrictive laws and other measures
which are necessary, not for the well-being of society, but for its
own preservation. Thus it censors the press, prohibits harmless but
supposedly immoral activities such as unorthodox sexual behaviour,
and so on. Second, the state is a *punitive* body, which inflicts cruel and

excessive penalties on those who infringe its laws, whether or not those laws are justified in the first place. Anarchists do not necessarily oppose punishment as such, but they certainly oppose the forms and amounts of punishment meted out by the state. Third, the state is an *exploitative* body, which uses its powers of taxation and economic regulation to transfer resources from the producers of wealth to its own coffers, or into the hands of privileged economic groups. Finally, the state is a *destructive* agency which enlists its subjects to fight wars whose only cause is the protection or aggrandizement of the state itself – all anarchists believe that, without the state, there might be small-scale conflicts, but nothing to resemble the horror and devastation of modern warfare.

It would be wrong to conclude that anarchists regard *all* the functions now performed by the state as superfluous. In their view, it would be impossible to account for the state's legitimacy in the eyes of the masses if it did not perform useful tasks as well as socially harmful ones. What tasks are these? Anarchists will not be able to agree on a list, but they are generally to be found in two areas: protection of the person against invasion by others, and co-ordination of the productive work of society. Anarchists admit, in other words, that in these areas some collective (as opposed to individual) action may be necessary; but they refuse to admit that only a state can fit the bill. To see what kind of collective agency anarchists are likely to permit in place of the state, we need to return to the characterization of the state offered above: states were identified as sovereign, compulsory, monopolistic and distinct institutions. Anarchists are likely to find a collective agency more acceptable the further it departs from these four features of the state.

The kind of society envisaged by anarchists is thus not entirely without organization, in the sense of institutions established to achieve collective goals. But these institutions will have characteristics that differentiate them from the state. First, they will not be sovereign, but functionally specific. Each institution will, in other words, have a clearly defined role, and will not be permitted to extend its power beyond that role. Some anarchists, for example, have argued that separate organizations should be established to guide production on the one hand and to maintain social order on the other. In this case neither institution would be 'sovereign' in case of dispute. Second, anarchists will almost certainly insist that the institutions in question should be voluntary rather than compulsory, in the sense that everyone who is to be governed by them should first of all agree to do so of his own accord. This requirement raises questions about anarchists' attitudes towards authority in general, which will be considered in the chapter that follows. Third, some anarchists have been attracted by the idea of different collective agencies co-existing in a particular territory, competing to win the allegiance of the residents. This could be seen as one way of giving people a realistic voluntary choice between agencies. Finally, anarchists often argue that collective institutions are more acceptable to the extent that they are run, not by specialized political functionaries, but by the people *en masse* – either in the form of direct democracy, or through rotation of office, or in some other way.

Of course nothing has been said so far to show that these proposals are realistic. It may be that the anarchist case against the state, formidable in itself, founders on the fact that no workable alternative can be found to replace it under modern social conditions. But it is one thing to say this, and quite another to say that anarchists are essentially negative thinkers, interested only in the destruction of what exists. In fact, anarchists have developed quite elaborate models of the kind of society that they want to see, and these models can teach us a great deal about the possibilities of social organization, even if we are ultimately unpersuaded by them. They also differ very markedly among themselves: no one model of the good society can be singled out as authentically anarchist.

Although the state is the most distinctive object of anarchist attack, it is by no means the only object. Any institution which, like the state, appears to anarchists coercive, punitive, exploitative or destructive is condemned in the same way. Historically, anarchists have discharged almost as much venom towards the church as they have towards the state. This may now appear to us idiosyncratic, but we should recall that many anarchists developed and propagated their ideas in peasant or early industrial societies, where religion was still a potent force, and a major channel of social control. Most anarchists have been atheists, arguing that belief in God is a response to social deprivation in men whose rational faculties are not yet fully developed. But their main enemy is not religion as such, but organized religion – churches which disseminate official creeds whose content is hierarchically controlled. The anarchist critique here has two aspects: first, the authority of priest over believer is often seen as the original of all authority. In other words, once a person has come to accept that in spiritual matters he should defer to the authority of another who is wiser than he, it is easier to induce him to accept authority elsewhere – for instance the authority of a political leader. Second, the church may be used directly to legitimize the state – the priest may use the authority of his position to propagate doctrines of obedience to the political authorities. For this reason Bakunin claimed (with some exaggeration), 'There is not, there cannot be, a State without religion.'[5]

Anarchists have also been severe critics of existing economic systems. Indeed, when reading some anarchist literature, one might be led to think that economic oppression was the primary target, with political oppression taking second place. But here it is especially difficult to generalize about the nature of the critique: the heterogeneity of anarchist thought stands in the way. Take anarchist attitudes to capitalism first. One can safely say that all anarchists have been critical of the state-regulated capitalism which prevails today in the West. But for some this is merely one part of a general critique of capitalism, whereas for others capitalism pure and simple would be acceptable if it were not distorted by the presence of the state. Both camps are likely to see a great deal of collusion between economic and political elites, while being somewhat unclear about which group is the prime mover in the relationship. It is common ground among anarchists, in other words, that the state regularly uses its economic powers to benefit big industrialists and financiers at the expense of the workers, small property-owners, and so forth, but it is less clear whether the state should ultimately be seen as the creature of the *grande bourgeoisie* or the *grande bourgeoisie* as the creature of the state. There is the same ambiguity here as in the case of church and state. Anarchists tend to view society as a giant pyramid, with the great ones – politicians, big capitalists, church leaders, all hand-in-hand – standing at the top and the toiling workers standing at the bottom. The contrast between the ruling class and the exploited mass is clear enough, but the inner dynamics of the former are less so.

To return to capitalism: anarchists will argue that the economic system in western societies today is essentially one of monopoly control by the owners of big business, forcing ordinary men and women to work for a wage that is less than their labour is worth. The system is thus both coercive and exploitative – it places workers in the power of their bosses, and fails to give them a just return for their contribution to production. But anarchists will part company over whether this state of affairs is the inevitable outcome of a capitalist economic system. As we shall see later, some anarchists will claim that private ownership of the means of production leads inescapably to ownership being concentrated in a few hands, allowing this privileged group to use the power of the state to consolidate its position. Others will maintain that, without political intervention, capital will remain relatively widely dispersed, so monopoly is the child of the state rather than its father. This difference of view reflects much wider ideological differences between anarchists in economic matters.

Anarchists have been equally critical of the state socialist systems which have appeared during this century as they have been of capitalism. Indeed they can claim credit for being among the earliest and most perceptive critics of the form of socialism which emerged from the Russian Revolution in 1917. This opposition to state socialism can be traced back to Proudhon, who detected authoritarian elements in the ideas of Marx, and who was also severely critical of the proposals for state-funded workshops advanced by Louis Blanc. It ran through the thought of Bakunin, who grappled with Marx for control of the First International. So when state socialism finally appeared in its fully-fledged form, the anarchists had their critical weapons prepared. Their argument, reduced to its essentials, is that a socialist state is still a type of state, the change in economic system not altering the inner nature of the state itself. Indeed some anarchists would argue that state socialism is simply the fullest and most horrendous expression of that nature, the state now holding all social relations in its grip. Coercion, draconian punishment, exploitation, and destructive warfare all continue. There is still a ruling class controlling the rest of society, even though its composition has changed: there are no longer separately identifiable capitalists, and 'social scientists' have replaced priests. Bakunin, writing in 1872, had a prophetic vision of the result:

> This government will not content itself with administering and governing the masses politically, as all governments do today. It will also administer the masses economically, concentrating in the hands of the State the production and division of wealth, the cultivation of land, the establishment and development of factories, the organization and direction of commerce, and finally the application of capital to production by the only banker – the State. All that will demand an immense knowledge and many heads 'overflowing with brains' in this government. It will be the reign of *scientific intelligence*, the most aristocratic, despotic, arrogant, and elitist of all regimes. There will be a new class, a new hierarchy of real and counter-

feit scientists and scholars, and the world will be divided into a minority ruling in the name of knowledge, and an immense ignorant majority.[6]

Moreover,

> . . . for the proletariat this will, in reality, be nothing but a barracks: a regime, where regimented working men and women will sleep, wake, work, and live to the beat of a drum . . .[7]

What alternative economic system do anarchists favour? Here we find no agreement: quite the reverse. Anarchist proposals range from a free market in which enterprises compete to sell their goods and services to consumers, to a system of common ownership in which goods are produced by independent communes and distributed on the basis of need. All that these proposals have in common is their decentralist nature: anarchists concur in thinking that the economy should be organized from the bottom up, by voluntary association, rather than by central direction. The two versions referred to above – which stand at opposite ends of a spectrum, but which interestingly enough have been developed more fully by anarchists than the intermediate versions – will be discussed in detail in Chapters 3 and 4 below. Here I shall take Proudhon's favoured system as representing some sort of compromise between the extremes, and therefore as an appropriate way of introducing the reader to the constructive side of anarchist economic thought.

Proudhon, who loved to claim of all his proposals that they represented a synthesis of forces whose opposition had hitherto plagued mankind, said that his economic system (sometimes called mutualism) reconciled property and communism. Property by itself meant exploitation, in the form of rent, profit and usury, and unbridled competition. Communism meant slavery: the worker lost his independence and became merely an instrument of the state. Proudhon's proposal was that workers should retain their independence, but be linked by relations of trust and co-operation. (Louis Blanc took a different view: 'To graft brotherhood on to competition is a wretched idea: it is like replacing eunuchs by hermaphrodites.') Specifically, he envisaged three sectors of production: agriculture, where production by individual proprietors would be the norm; artisan production, where people might work individually or in collaboration as they chose; and industry proper, where the benefits of the division of labour meant that large-scale production was necessary for efficiency, and where associations of workers would be formed. Each producer would sell his products to consumers, but instead of prices being set by market competition, they would be pegged to the cost of producing the article in question, measured in hours of labour. In place of money, there would be labour-notes, issued by a People's Bank. Thus the shoemaker who sold a pair of boots that had taken him three hours to make would receive the equivalent in labour-notes which he could later exchange for someone else's product. The People's Bank was also charged with providing interest-free credit to allow producers to purchase their means of production. Ownership would, however, always follow labour: the peasant proprietor would own the land that he worked but he would not be allowed to rent it out to somebody else: similarly with the workers' association. Under this scheme, Proudhon claimed, income would vary only in proportion to labour, and a high degree of equality would prevail.[8]

It is easy to see that, quite apart from any economic difficulties which this scheme may present, it relies a great deal on mutual trust, at two points especially: the consumer must be willing to accept the price asked by the producer as a fair representation of his labour, and everyone must be willing to take the notes issued by the People's Bank. Proudhon's own experiment in this direction did not meet with much success.[9] But this only illustrates a general feature of any anarchist economic system, namely that, with the state removed, the system has no ultimate guarantor – whether to underwrite a bank, enforce contracts, or whatever. The anarchist claim is that no such guarantee is needed; that human beings have sufficient solidarity, or far-sighted selfishness, to make the system work of its own accord. The truth of this claim will be crucial to our final assessment of anarchism as an ideology.

Let me turn finally, in this preliminary sketch of anarchist ideology, to the means of transition to anarchist society. As we shall discover later in the book, anarchists have argued among themselves a great deal about how this transition should be made, and about which element in current society forms the natural point of departure – the liberated individual, the workers' union, the revolutionary mass, and so forth. But they have agreed at least that two commonly advocated routes should be rejected out of hand. The first is the path of parliamentary democracy, the attempt to win an electoral majority for an anarchist programme. Anarchists have quite often been out-and-out abstentionists, refusing even to vote for the party which represents the least of the evils on offer: and when they have abandoned this purist position, they have done so only for short-term tactical reasons. Their unwillingness to follow the parliamentary road stems from two sources. First, they claim that any state, of whatever kind, is limited in the kind of social change that it can bring about. The state is a centralized institution, and its characteristic mode of operation is legislation – the promulgation of general rules which apply indiscriminately to everyone in society. It is therefore simply impossible to will a decentralized society based on a plurality of voluntary associations into existence by statist means – the initiative must come from below, not from above. It follows that the most useful thing which a state can do, from the anarchist perspective, is simply to dissolve itself and let society reorganize spontaneously. But here we meet the second anarchist charge against parliamentarianism. Those elected to represent the people are unable to carry out the programme on which they were elected. Popular control of the legislature is ineffective, and the individuals themselves are co-opted by the ruling class – *homme élu, homme foutu*, as the point is more pithily put. So the idea that an anarchist electoral victory might lead to the immediate dissolution of the state is rejected as plainly naive.

The other transitional route which anarchists repudiate with equal vehemence is the dictatorship of the proletariat, as understood by Marx, and especially by Lenin. This path envisages the forcible destruction of the bourgeois state, and its replacement by a workers' state, in which the revolutionary party plays a leading role. Once capitalism is completely eradicated, and the material foundations of socialism are laid, the state begins, in the classic phrase, to 'wither away'. It will be seen that both of the anarchist objections to the parliamentary route apply with minor modifications to this one too, always assuming of course – the absolutely crucial point – that every state, however it is composed, functions in essentially the same way. (Anarchists have particular criticisms to offer of Leninist parties, which will be discussed below in Chapter 6). Thus even those anarchists who would find little to quarrel with in Marx's description of the Communist utopia are starkly opposed to the methods advocated by Marxists for reaching it.

This reluctance to use conventional political means to bring about the changes that they want to see largely accounts for the popular view that anarchists are simply agents of destruction. To people accustomed to think that every constructive proposal should be put to electoral test, it seems that those who refuse to participate in conventional politics are either trying to establish a minority dictatorship or else are interested only in causing social havoc. It is true, of course, that many anarchist activities have been nothing more than destructive, often culpably destructive. Even allowing for the fact that their goal is a distant one, anarchists have been singularly bad at deciding when an immediately harmful act is justified by its long-term effect in bringing that goal nearer to fruition. But we should not overlook the constructive experiments in which anarchists have engaged – the various attempts to reorganize work, education, and so forth – where means and ends have been more closely aligned. These have not impinged much on the popular view of anarchism, no doubt for the familiar reason that good news is no news, whereas bombs and strikes are headlines.

This helps to dispose of the paradox that anarchists like to think of themselves as constructive thinkers, whereas their popular image is quite the opposite. What of the apparent conflict in anarchist ideology between individual freedom and social solidarity? Here the paradox is more real, and its solution is complicated by the fact that the very terms in which it is posed take on different meanings in different anarchist traditions. So I shall try to disentangle these complexities in the remainder of this part of the book.

The chapter that follows takes up what has often been regarded as the core of anarchism, the attack on the principle of authority, and shows how this attack has been launched from widely differing philosophical positions. Chapters 3 and 4 examine individualist and communist anarchism, two well-defined ideologies which turn out to have little in common beyond their anarchist character itself. Indeed we may eventually find that we wonder less at the paradoxical nature of anarchism than at how such diverse views have come to share a political label at all.

2 Philosophical Anarchism

Behind the anarchist attack on the state and other coercive institutions, there has often stood a fundamental critique of the idea of authority itself. Many anarchists have been attracted by the view that no man can ever rightfully exercise political authority over another, that is have a right to issue directions which the other has an obligation to obey. Since the state, especially, appears to depend on the belief that its directives are to be taken as authoritative by its subjects, it can easily be seen how corrosive is this attack on the principle of authority itself. Of course anarchists do not deny that states are *thought* to possess legitimate authority by many of their subjects; that is a fact about the world which nobody in their senses would try to conceal. The anarchist view is simply that the belief is false, that no state has the right which it claims and which its subjects generally concede. It is an argument about principles, not about facts.

Although this attack on the principle of authority – which I refer to as philosophical anarchism – might seem central to the whole anarchist position (for the reason just given) the point should not be pushed too far. For on the one hand, someone who is simply a philosophical anarchist and nothing else besides may seem a rather bloodless member of the species. Philosophical anarchism entails the view that the state has no right to tell me or anyone else how to behave. One can believe this and respond in a wholly passive way, evading inconvenient or immoral state dictates whenever possible and complying with them when forced to do so, but taking no positive action to get rid of the state and having no constructive view about what might take its place. Men like Thoreau would fit roughly into this category.[1] Although one may recognize their kinship with anarchists of a full-blooded kind, one may want to withhold the label itself. On the other hand, it seems possible to be an anarchist in general without subscribing to philosophical anarchism. Someone may, in other words, attack the state intellectually and wish to overthrow it, but not because he finds the very idea of legitimate authority incoherent. He may put forward rigorous conditions for legitimate authority, so rigorous that no state can hope to meet them, though other forms of political association might – say certain kinds of communal self-government. Or his attack on the state may be couched in terms of the social consequences which flow from its existence rather than in terms of its lack of authority. It therefore seems possible to interpret many anarchists, not as out-and-out opponents of authority, but as opponents of the state who are willing to endorse authority under carefully defined conditions.[2]

It is nonetheless important to examine philosophical anarchism in some detail, for the arguments used to defend it have flowed into the stream of anarchist thinking: every anarchist has been moved by them, even if most have eventually drawn back from their full implications. Philosophical anarchism, it should be stressed, is not a variety of anarchism in the sense in which individualist and communist anarchism are varieties: it does not encapsulate any model of anarchist society, nor any recipe for destroying the state and other coercive institutions. It is rather a philosophical attitude, a way of responding to authority. It can contribute to an anarchist outlook only when combined with a substantive ideology.

Our examination must begin with the idea of authority itself. What does it mean to recognize authority? First of all, it is not the same as recognizing power even though authority and power often go hand-in-hand in practice. If I comply with someone's instructions because of the possible consequences of not complying – say he threatens to have me beaten up or thrown into jail – I am acknowledging his power rather than his authority. Acknowledging authority means recognizing someone's right to direct or command, complying with his will because one believes it is proper to do so. I may acknowledge the power of a lion – say if I change my path to avoid meeting it – but I cannot acknowledge its authority. Anarchists are not so foolish as to fail to recognize the power of states – indeed they draw attention to the potent mechanisms which states have available to enforce compliance with their dictates, ranging from physical force to soft persuasion – but this is a far cry from recognizing their authority.[3]

Next, the moral recognition of authority has to be distinguished from three other ways in which a person may comply with another's commands for moral reasons. First, we are sometimes told to do things which we believe are morally obligatory in any case, so in 'complying' with an order in such a case, we are not recognizing authority but simply acting on our own moral assessment of the situation. So a philosophical anarchist may quite consistently 'keep the law' by refraining from injuring other people, for example, though his reason for doing so is not the legal prohibition of injury. Second, we may find ourselves living among people most of whom do recognize the authority of some institution – a government, say – and, without recognizing its authority ourselves, we may decide that it would be damaging to undermine it by flagrantly violating its commands. Admittedly this is not a line of thought that is likely to appeal much to full-blooded anarchists, though even they may occasionally feel that it is better not to bring down a relatively liberal state, say, if the likely replacement is a more openly repressive one. Third, in a rather similar way, circumstances may require someone to perform a co-ordinating role – say to clear a traffic jam – and everyone will see that they should take their cue from whoever stands up and starts directing the traffic. Here one is not recognizing that person's moral right to issue commands, but merely following his commands as the most efficient way to clear the jam. In all three cases we are acting on our own moral assessment of a state of affairs, but in the second and the third we are taking into account – in a factual way – the existence of an 'authority'. It should be clear enough how this differs from the moral recognition of authority.

Finally, we need to draw a line between recognizing political authority and recognizing the authority of an expert in some field. Anarchists are keen to point out that they have no wish to challenge the authority of the scientist or the skilled craftsman in his own sphere – though even here they are anxious in case such people should try to extend their authority beyond their areas of expertise.[4] To draw this distinction we must contrast authority in matters of belief with authority in matters of conduct. The authority which anarchists are willing to accept is of the former kind. Suppose I want to grow a large crop of wheat. An agriculturalist tells me that I should plant at a certain date, water in a certain manner, etc. I accept these beliefs on authority because I know that the agriculturalist has been scientifically trained, has a record of giving successful advice and so forth. Accepting the authority of the specialist does indeed affect my subsequent conduct, but only because I wanted to grow a large amount of wheat in the first place. Contrast this with a state of affairs where a government official pronounces that on such-and-such a day wheat is to be planted, and I, as an obedient citizen, plant my wheat on that day. Here I am acknowledging authority in a matter of conduct – taking the pronouncement of an official as *in itself* a reason for acting in the way prescribed. This is the kind of authority that anarchists reject.

To sum up so far, philosophical anarchism is the view that no one can ever have legitimate authority over another person, and conversely no one can ever be under an obligation to obey. By implication, the state, which is composed of persons, cannot have such authority. This is not to say that the state has no power (a palpable falsehood), or that, in deciding how to act, one should overlook the fact that a certain authority has been acknowledged by one's fellows; nor finally that one should never defer to expert authority in matters of belief. It is to say that people should always act on their direct moral assessment of any situation, leaving aside as *morally* irrelevant any directives they may have received from others. Such directives will only enter their reasoning as empirical facts, not as moral reasons to act as directed.

It is worth underlining just how subversive a view this is. Although authority is often said to be on the decline in the modern world, this assertion is only true in a limited sense. Our contemporaries are indeed less likely than their ancestors to take authority for granted, because authority no longer seems to be part and parcel of social positions generally, but is instead created for specific purposes – in enterprises, bureaucracies, armies, and so forth.[5] We recognize, therefore, that all relationships of authority need to be justified by the ends that they serve. But in practice we seem perfectly ready to follow the directives of an authority without further question – indeed in some cases alarmingly so.[6] It is this widespread habit of compliance that the philosophical anarchist is trying to subvert.

The subversive campaign has been launched from several different ethical starting-points. I want to look critically at three of these, each conveniently represented by a different thinker: utilitarianism, exemplified by Godwin; egoism, exemplified by Stirner; and radical Kantianism, exemplified by R. P. Wolff. I am interested here only in the arguments that they offer against the principle of authority, and I shall not attempt to give an overall assessment of their views.

William Godwin

In his ethical theory, Godwin was a singularly tough-minded utilitarian. He believed, as all utilitarians do, that the rightness of any action is to be assessed by the total amount of pleasure minus the total amount of pain that it generates; but, unlike most utilitarians, he refused to soften this doctrine in practice to align it more closely with ordinary moral standards. Godwin insisted that the test of utility should be applied directly by each person on every occasion when he or she had to decide how to act. This led to some striking conflicts with the precepts of conventional morality. Godwin argued, for instance, that the distinction we usually make between acts that are obligatory and acts that we may perform if we wish – say between saving a drowning child and buying a friend a present – should be jettisoned, for, 'I hold my person as a trust in behalf of mankind. I am bound to employ my talents, my understanding, my strength and my time, for the production of the greatest quantity of general good.'[7] Likewise we should never be deflected from our duty to promote the general happiness by considerations such as gratitude to particular persons – in deciding whether to confer a benefit on someone, our only thought should be whether such a use of resources would be most productive of future happiness. Godwin also deplored institutions such as promising which encouraged people to act on past undertakings rather than from consideration of future benefit. Finally – and this was the departure from conventional standards which earned him the greatest notoriety – we should never be deflected from our utilitarian duty by personal loyalties to friends or kinsmen: in Godwin's example, if I have to choose whether to save Archbishop Fénelon or his valet (who happens also to be my brother) from a burning house, 'that life ought to be preferred which will be most conducive to the general good'.[8]

But utilitarianism by itself, no matter how tough-minded, does not lead us to anarchist conclusions. Nearly all of those who have adopted it as an ethical theory have gone on to argue that government is necessary to human happiness, so that a utilitarian should offer it at least conditional support, deferring to its authority except in cases where the balance of happiness clearly lies with disobedience. To generate an argument for anarchism, we need a second premise, which Godwin calls the principle of private judgment (the relationship between this and the principle of utility will be discussed shortly). This holds that 'the conviction of a man's individual understanding is the only legitimate principle imposing on him the duty of adopting any species of conduct'.[9] In other words, although we are all duty bound to promote the general happiness, each has the right to decide whether or not to adopt that principle and how to implement it in a particular case. I am never (or almost never) permitted to force you to act in a way that I think is for the best: each of us must be allowed an inviolable sphere of private judgment.

It is easy to see how the two principles – utility and private judgment – together lead to anarchistic conclusions when applied to different forms of government. Take first the case of a benevolent despotism, where the ruler forces his subjects to do what is really in their overall best interests. Godwin's response is that such a government ignores the right of private judgment: each person, instead of being allowed to make his own decisions about how to promote utility, is obliged to act as the ruler thinks fit. On the other hand, consider a government that is established by a social contract involving everyone who will be subject to it. It may seem that no sacrifice of the right of private judgment occurs when such a government demands obedience from its subjects, since they will merely be acting on the provisions of a contract to which they have freely assented. But here Godwin swings back to the principle of utility. No one ought to make agreements which debar him from acting on his own estimates of utility in the future. If ordinary contracts are bad, contracts of government are many times worse, for they involve consenting to numerous laws, some of which have not even been formulated at the time of the contract. Thus a morally upright man would not enter such a contract, and, even if he did so in error, would not regard it as obligatory at a later time.

What, finally, of a system of direct democracy where everyone participates in the making of the laws to which he is then subject? This form of authority might seem the easiest to reconcile with Godwin's premises. But in the chapter of the *Enquiry* headed 'Of National Assemblies' he rejects it almost as categorically as the others. His arguments can be reduced essentially to two. First, if the assembly decides on legislation by majority vote, then those who find themselves in a minority are denied the right of private judgment – they are forced to act according to the majority's will. Second, should the assembly reach a unanimous conclusion, it would still in practice interfere with private judgment. Men, being individuals, can never come independently to share the same beliefs, so unanimity of expressed belief must be 'fictitious'; some people will perhaps have adopted the majority view to keep in with their friends, or because some orator has bludgeoned them into agreeing with him. Godwin is tacitly contrasting this with the genuine unanimity that might result from a private conversation in which two people express their sincere convictions – his own vision of the ideal human relationship. And so he reaches his general conclusion:

> It is earnestly to be desired that each man should be wise enough to govern himself, without the intervention of any

compulsory restraint; and, since government, even in its best state, is an evil, the object principally to be aimed at is that we should have as little of it as the general peace of human society will permit.[10]

This conclusion, while bringing out quite plainly the anarchist tendency of Godwin's argument, also exposes a source of weakness. As can be seen he did not advocate the immediate abolition of government. Until people generally had become sufficiently wise and virtuous – a state of affairs which required a long period of enlightenment – some government was necessary, principally to protect people from the violence of others. In conceding this, he was in effect allowing the right of private judgment to be overridden by the principle of utility. But this immediately raises the question of how Godwin's two principles are to be reconciled. If the universal moral imperative is to maximize pleasure and minimize pain, why give special weight to the principle that other people must be allowed to act on their own judgment? If I can see that Jones is going to cause harm if I allow him to act freely, why, as a utilitarian, should I respect his volition?

Godwin offers two arguments in favour of private judgment which might rebut this challenge.[11] The first refers to human fallibility: since no one can be completely certain that his moral convictions are correct, no one is justified in imposing them on others, which is in effect what a utilitarian does if he forces Jones to act against his private judgment for the sake of utility. But here the utilitarian can make an easy reply. I admit, he may say, that my ethical standard may be a false one and I am willing to listen to arguments (including any that Jones may produce) to that effect. But in the meantime I must act on my fallible beliefs, and if Jones is about to act harmfully, I must stop him, by force if necessary. Godwin's second argument is that a person does not act morally unless he acts from a benevolent motive, so forcing someone to behave well is of no value. This argument is not itself utilitarian (indeed it is anti-utilitarian), but it can be given a utilitarian twist by adding that people only develop benevolent dispositions through free moral activity. The idea here is that, for utilitarian reasons, each person should eventually become a self-propelling moral agent, and to this end he must be given freedom to act, even if he performs some wrong acts meanwhile. So interpreted, Godwin's argument rests on an empirical thesis which is far from self-evidently true. Indeed the converse had often been argued: we become moral by learning to conform our behaviour to certain outward standards – a conformity which may need to be forcibly imposed at first – so that genuine moral dispositions spring from the soil of compulsion and habit.[12]

The irresistible conclusion is that Godwin's belief in the right of private judgment is not genuinely utilitarian: the linking arguments are far too flimsy to convince anyone who did not already hold the belief on other grounds. For Godwin, in fact, a society in which each person acted on his own moral understanding, and in which no one influenced anyone else except by argument and moral reproach, was simply a personal ideal: he described 'the universal exercise of private judgment' as 'unspeakably beautiful'.[13] But in believing this he moved away from utilitarian ethics towards the view that moral autonomy is valuable for its own sake – a view that we shall later examine as developed more explicitly by Wolff, yet one that is also bedevilled by inner contradictions.

Max Stirner

While Godwin argued that a wholly rational man would be perfectly benevolent, Stirner maintained precisely the reverse: thoroughgoing egoism was the only intellectually defensible stance. Yet, paradoxically enough, he reached the same negative conclusions as Godwin about authority in general and the claims of the state in particular. To see how this came about we need to place Stirner's egoism in the context of the left-Hegelian critique of religion that dominated German intellectual life in the 1840s, the time at which Stirner produced his only important work, *The Ego and His Own*.[14]

The radical Hegelians held that religion was a form of alienation: the religious believer abstracted certain of his own essential qualities or aspirations, and projected them upon a transcendent deity. This process diminished him, for he now saw himself as a relatively impotent and worthless creature, whereas the God he had created possessed every desirable attribute. In order to overcome alienation, it was necessary first to recognize the process of projection for what it was, and then to 'reappropriate' the human essence: i.e. to see that the properties attributed to God were really human properties, partially realized in us already, but capable of being fully realized in a transformed society. Thus the critique of religion turned into a demand for social progress.

Stirner extended this form of critique to every other area of human experience in which a similar process of alienation might occur. Wherever men hypostatized some idea, and then saw themselves as owing allegiance to the resulting entity, he swept into the attack. Thus, when humanists such as Feuerbach argued that, instead of worshipping God, we should try to realize the human essence, Stirner retorted that this was simply religious belief in another guise. The human essence was a product of human thought, and so could not serve as an independent standard by which we ought to direct our endeavours. Nothing was real except the human self; all other mental entities were 'spooks', figments of the mind having no objective existence outside their creators' heads.

The proper response to this predicament, Stirner argued, was conscious egoism. One should no longer deceive oneself into thinking that one was serving some objective end – whether religious, moral or political – but recognize instead that the only good reason for acting was one's own choice or fancy. There was no point even in being consistent: it was absurd, for instance, to form an idea of one's own character and then try to act in harmony with that. Instead the egoist should act on momentary caprice. He should also be prepared to use other people completely cynically as means to his own ends – even loved ones should be cherished for his own enjoyment, not for *their* sakes. For Stirner, quite literally nothing was sacred.

It will quickly be seen how philosophical anarchism flows out of this intransigent world-view (which may be called an ethical standpoint in the same way that zero may be called a number – it is a limiting case). Authority is just one of the many fetishes that falls under Stirner's axe. For in recognizing authority, I am recognizing that someone else's command is to be taken as a reason for acting as prescribed. But, according to Stirner, no such outside agency can ever provide a reason for *me*. In acknowledging authority, I take someone else's power – which in itself is merely a matter of fact – and clothe it in sacred garb. The honest egoist will certainly yield to power, if he has to, but he will not pretend that he is doing anything else besides; he will never say that he is acting *rightly*.

The same reasoning is used to destroy all the conventional arguments for obeying the state. Stirner makes mincemeat of the distinctions that liberals and republicans draw between different forms of government. Liberals, for instance, contrast the authority of men with the authority of law. For Stirner, both impinge upon a person's will in an equally objectionable way – indeed legal authority is the more insidious, for one is more likely to be 'enthralled' by it; less

23

likely to recognize that in submitting to it, one is subordinating one's will to another's.[15] Thus the constitutional state beloved of liberals is unacceptable to Stirner. Equally unacceptable is the republican ideal of a state in which every citizen participates in the making of laws. Stirner argues that the laws so made are still despotic from the point of view of the recalcitrant individual. Even if, in the extreme case, a unanimous decision were reached, why should I be bound today by my decision of yesterday?[16] The egoist cannot submit to anything beyond his present experience, not even to his past commitments. Thus, as also with Godwin, even the form of government which appears at first sight most acceptable to the philosophical anarchist – unanimous direct democracy – is finally rejected. Stirner's conclusion is stark:

> Therefore we two, the State and I, are enemies. I, the egoist, have not at heart the welfare of this 'human society', I sacrifice nothing to it, I only utilize it; but to be able to utilize it completely I transform it rather into my property and my creature, – i.e. I annihilate it, and form in its place the *Union of Egoists*.[17]

This last is the name which Stirner gives to the only form of association he is able to accept: an association of egoists which each enters from his own advantage and leaves the moment that he ceases to find it useful. This exercises no authority over its members – it is not, for instance, brought into being by revocable contract – but relies entirely on its members' perception that each may be able to benefit by collaboration. Such associations are not unthinkable – Hume's example of two men rowing a boat together because neither can propel it forward without the other may serve as a paradigm – but they are obviously very unstable. This observation points to a general difficulty with Stirner's position which we must now consider.

It is never made clear whether Stirner's arguments for egoism are intended to apply to everyone, or whether they are intended to apply only to a single person, say to Stirner himself. Both alternatives are fraught with paradox.[18] In the first case, *recommending* that everyone should become a conscious egoist seems to presuppose a moral ground upon which the recommendation can be anchored; one might, say, be a utilitarian and think that everyone would be happier if rid of their spooks. But for Stirner to rely on any such moral ground would be inconsistent with his own argument for egoism. Suppose, then, that we take the second option, and say that the arguments for egoism apply only to the person who expresses them: it is a matter of indifference to him whether others choose to be egoists or not. But then we must add that it cannot really be a matter of indifference. The egoist is somebody who uses others to augment his own powers and possessions. May it not then turn out that it is much to his advantage if others continue to believe in morality, authority and other 'sacred' things?[19] It is easy to see why a union of egoists is likely to break apart: how much better if the egoist can ride on the backs of others who 'religiously' keep their agreements! Or again, if people believe in political authority, may the egoist not wish to profit from this belief by obtaining a post in government himself? All of this raises the question of Stirner's consistency in speaking out loud, rather than keeping his arguments to himself. About this he said:

> But not only not for your sake, not even for truth's sake either do I speak out what I think. No –
>
> > I sing as the bird sings
> > That on the bough alights;
> > The song that from me springs
> > Is pay that well requites.
>
> I sing because – I am a singer. But I *use* you for it because I – need ears.[20]

Yet even birds do not sing when there are predators about. Perhaps Stirner thought, realistically enough, that very few who listened to his arguments would ever be convinced by them, so he could afford the luxury of song.

We can now see the general difficulty in arguing for philosophical anarchism from an egoistic position. Philosophical anarchism involves a universal attack on the principle of authority; it needs therefore to be launched from moral premises. The consistent egoist's aim is to flout authority himself while still encouraging others to recognize it to the extent that their doing so serves his ends. Because his case against authority is part and parcel of a general case against morality, he necessarily lacks the resources to show why other people should ignore authority too.

R. P. Wolff

Having seen that two classical arguments for philosophical anarchism, beginning from utilitarian and egoistic premises respectively, are unsuccessful, let me finally consider a more recent version whose starting-point may be labelled neo-Kantian. The American philosopher R. P. Wolff has tried to show that no recognition of authority is consistent with our overriding obligation to behave as autonomous moral agents.[21] To understand this argument we need to begin with Wolff's idea of moral autonomy.

According to Wolff we are always free to choose how to act, but it does not follow from this that we are always morally autonomous. Much of the time we act on other people's suggestions, or habitually, or out of caprice, but on these occasions we fail to live up to the ideal of moral self-determination. The morally autonomous person decides how to act after weighing up the moral considerations for and against each of the courses of action open to him. Thus before contributing to a charity, for instance, he would balance the good that his contribution might do against the good that would result from the other possible uses of his money, and so forth. Wolff admits that we cannot hope to be fully autonomous all of the time – life is too short – but he claims that we are obliged to be so to the greatest extent possible; we may not wilfully sacrifice our autonomy. This premise is not argued for, but taken for granted – which is why I call the argument neo-Kantian.[22]

It may seem at first that moral autonomy does not exclude the recognition of authority as such, but only the unthinking or uncritical acceptance of authority. Whereas the person who obeys orders without thinking of anything beyond the fact that they are orders has clearly forfeited his autonomy, the conscientious citizen, say, who weighs the commands of the state *against* other considerations, and obeys only when the balance of reasons tips in the right direction, appears to be fully autonomous. But this is not Wolff's view. Such a citizen has given up his autonomy, he claims, merely by allowing the commands of the state to enter his deliberation as commands. To be autonomous it is not enough to act on the balance of reasons as it appears to you: you must only allow certain kinds of reason to count in the first place.

Before examining the cogency of this view, let me draw out its implications. According to Wolff it shows that the idea of a *de jure* or legitimate authority is a contradiction in terms. There are no circumstances in which I should recognize an obligation to obey somebody simply because he has commanded it, because in doing so I would be breaching my primary obligation to be autonomous. By the same token, there cannot be a legitimate state. A legitimate state would be one whose citizens had an obligation to obey its laws merely because they were laws. But no citizens can have such an obligation.

> If all men have a continuing obligation to achieve the highest degree of autonomy possible, then there would appear to be no state whose subjects have a moral obligation to obey its commands. Hence, the concept of a *de jure* legitimate state would appear to be vacuous, and philosophical anarchism would seem to be the only reasonable political belief for an enlightened man.[23]

Oddly enough Wolff goes on to argue that one kind of state does after all meet the conditions of legitimacy, and that is unanimous direct democracy. If everyone agrees to the passage of a law, he suggests, there is no loss of autonomy if later on one of the participants is required to conform to it despite his present inclinations. It is, however, arguable whether this state of affairs necessarily involves the recognition of *authority*. Wolff clearly has in mind the kind of case where Smith decides morally that no one ought to drive a car with more than 80 mg. per 100 ml. of alcohol in his blood, say, but later finds that he wants to drive home when he is over the limit. But here what conflicts with Smith's present desire is not the authority of the law but his own moral judgment.[24] If, on the other hand, Smith's moral views on some matter *change* – so that he finds himself in moral conflict with the unanimously endorsed law – it appears that, as an autonomous agent, he must follow his *present* moral judgment. Why should he take his own past view as authoritative, any more than somebody else's opinion?

Wolff ought, therefore, to have followed Godwin and Stirner in dismissing unanimous direct democracy along with every other form of government as lacking in authority. But now we must ask whether his reasons for rejecting the idea of political authority are any better than theirs. Let us accept for the sake of argument his premise that autonomy is the primary moral desideratum, and simply inquire whether he has drawn the correct conclusions from that premise.

The crucial issue is whether he is justified in maintaining that an autonomous man will only act on certain kinds of reasons. There is obviously a great difference between refraining from assault because of the harm it will cause and refraining from assault because the law commands it, a difference we might mark by saying that the former is a direct reason and the latter an indirect reason for the action. But is it self-evident that autonomy requires us only to take account of direct reasons for acting? It is easy to become mesmerized by the case where Jones is under Davies' sway, so that whatever Davies says ought to be done, Jones does. Here we may indeed want to say that Jones lacks moral autonomy, but we do so because Jones has no reason for acting as he does beyond the bare fact that Davies has commanded it. Compare with this a case in which Jones authorizes Davies to issue instructions by which he agrees to be bound, or in which Jones enters an agreement with several others, the outcome of which is that Davies is given authority over the group. In these cases Jones will later act upon indirect reasons, but the bare reason 'Davies has ordered it' is supported by the reasons for authorizing Davies in the first place. Wolff treats such cases as derogations of autonomy, for which (he concedes) a case can be made.[25] But is this now anything more than a definitional *fiat*? What, for instance, differentiates such engagements from the more straightforward kind of contract where Jones agrees to mow Davies' field on Wednesday in return for Davies' shearing Jones' sheep on Tuesday? In this case, too, Jones' reason for acting on Wednesday will be the engagement he has made. Godwin, we recall, swept all these cases aside by maintaining that a morally autonomous man must be a utilitarian, but Wolff places no such limits on the content of an authentic moral outlook. How, then, can he exclude contractual obligations as reasons for action, and, this being conceded, how can he exclude authoritative commands which originate in contract?

We may press this point further still. A moral agent, unless he embraces a morality of pure intention, must be concerned about the effectiveness of his actions in achieving the goals that he has set himself. Suppose, for instance, that he has decided to make the relief of poverty his first priority. He may well find that only the concerted action of many people will make any impact on the problem, and that concerted action is impossible without an organization in which some people are given positions of authority. Once the organization is established, it becomes not only permissible but obligatory for him to act on authoritative instructions. If he does not then, far from preserving his autonomy, he vitiates it: he fails to act as his principles require of him. Wolff's argument can be turned against itself.

Anarchists, however, will dispute the claim implicit in the last paragraph. They will argue that authority is not in fact necessary to co-ordinate people's behaviour in cases such as that envisaged. But this is an empirical claim about social relationships, not a philosophical claim about moral autonomy. It is one thing to say that authority must be discarded because it necessarily conflicts with our obligation to be autonomous, quite another to say that it should be discarded because we can get on perfectly well without it. This second assertion needs to be backed up by a plausible model of a society without authority relations; I shall explore two such models in the chapters that follow. But here I have been looking critically at philosophical arguments against authority, and have found that none is satisfactory. None of the ethical theories considered gives conclusive reasons for rejecting authority in all its forms.

As noted earlier, anarchists are not in any case bound to embrace full-blown arguments against authority. Their case against the state and other coercive institutions can be made more modestly. They are certainly suspicious of authority, and have welcomed the arguments discussed in this chapter as confirmation of their suspicions (why else, indeed, should they have taken such an unappealing philosophy as Stirner's to heart?). But in the end most anarchists are prepared to accept authority of the right kind and with the appropriate limits. The arguments for philosophical anarchism prove too much: so it is not particularly damaging to anarchism generally that none of them succeeds.

3   Individualist Anarchism

The individualism which forms the subject of this chapter is a well-developed anarchist theory which aims both to indict existing socio-political systems and to offer an alternative model of society. As such, it needs to be distinguished from 'individualism' in a looser sense, the view that people should follow their own inclinations as far as possible, flouting social conventions whenever it suits them to do so. When anarchists are described as individualists, it is sometimes the latter that is meant, often with the further implication that they reject organized anarchist movements and are prepared to use individual acts of terror to achieve their ends. But individualists in this looser sense may have no theoretical basis for their actions at all, whereas the individualism I am concerned with is a relatively coherent body of ideas.

It is no accident that individualist anarchism should have grown and flourished in the U.S.A., for it reflects both the cultural traditions and the economic circumstances of that country. It can usefully be seen as an outgrowth of classical liberalism; indeed these anarchists have liked to describe themselves as 'unterrified Jeffersonian Democrats'.[1] They took the liberal idea of individual sovereignty and extended it until it became incompatible with the idea of the state. Each person was seen as having an inviolable sphere of action within which he reigned supreme, encompassing both his body and the property he had rightfully acquired. Within the privileged sphere he could act just as he pleased, and moreover he was entitled to give away or exchange anything that fell within it. Thus people met as sovereigns in their own territories. The legitimate relations between them were those of exchange, contract and gift. Any interference by one person in another person's private sphere was termed (continuing the international analogy) 'invasion'. Invasion might properly be resisted, by force if necessary, and once it had occurred the injured party was entitled to exact reparation from the invader. Thus a sharp moral distinction was drawn between the use of force by an aggressor and the use of force by a victim of aggression.

The broad implication of this view was that social relations should be modelled on those of the economic marketplace. Each person was expected to exchange his goods or his labour with those of others when it was to his advantage to do so. Alongside the market, and subsidiary to it, lay the realm of private charity, where people might voluntarily contribute to the relief of those in need – say the physically handicapped. Such charity might be praiseworthy, but it was not obligatory, and charitable giving could not be enforced. In contrast to those two legitimate types of social relationships stood various forms of coercion. All political relations were assimilated to this category. Government, it was claimed, is necessarily an invasive body which infringes each person's private sphere without his consent. The rationale for this charge will be examined shortly.

The individualist position appears to consort most easily with a philosophy of natural rights. Each person's private sphere can be marked out in terms of his rights to life, liberty and property. But although this position has tended to predominate in individualist circles,[2] it is not the only possibility. Under the influence of Stirner, several anarcho-individualists – most notably Benjamin Tucker – have embraced egoism.[3] The derivation of individualism from egoism proceeds through the somewhat unlikely assumption that it is in each person's best interest to recognize and leave intact the equal liberty of everyone else; in the long run, robbery and violence don't pay. A third alternative is to rest individualism on a utilitarian basis, to argue that social welfare will be maximized by allowing each person to act freely within his private realm. Arguments of this kind have figured prominently in the works of individualist anarchists, even in those whose philosophy is not formally utilitarian.[4] The fact that similar conclusions can be drawn from such widely differing premises shows, I think, that the crucial ingredient of individualist anarchism is a certain (ideological) vision of man and society, not a philosophical standpoint. If you are convinced that a system of free exchange will work harmoniously to everyone's advantage, you will advocate such a system whether you are a natural rights theorist, an egoist, or a utilitarian.

The attitude of anarcho-individualists towards capitalism has altered significantly with the passing of time. This is indicated immediately by the fact that the earlier individualists, in the nineteenth century, saw themselves in broad terms as part of the socialist movement, whereas their twentieth-century successors are happy to call themselves 'anarcho-capitalists'. It might be thought that this terminological shift merely reflects the fact that in our century the term 'socialist' has acquired more pronounced statist overtones. But the real explanation goes somewhat deeper than this. The economic theory of individualist anarchism has changed in important ways, as we can see by comparing the positions of Josiah Warren, its earliest major exponent, Benjamin Tucker, its main apostle in the late nineteenth century, and Murray Rothbard, a contemporary spokesman.

Warren's view was that 'equitable commerce' – his name for a just economic order – rested on the maxim that all goods should be exchanged for their cost of production. The cost of producing a good was the labour time expended, with due allowance made for the 'repugnance' of the particular type of work involved. Thus it was inadmissible to charge somebody above the cost of a commodity even if he was perfectly willing to pay more. This disposed of profiteering in exchange – say in cases when some good was in short supply on the market – as well as interest on loans and rent on land. Except in cases where a loan represented some real sacrifice to the lender – where he actually needed to use the article or sum of money loaned – it should be made freely. To ensure that a medium of exchange was widely available, Warren proposed replacing conventional money with labour notes: on receiving ten hours' worth of wheat from the farmer, say, the blacksmith would give him a note promising ten hours' worth of blacksmithing (or less if blacksmithing was judged more repugnant than farming) which he could either 'cash' himself for blacksmithing services at a later time, or pass to a third party. An amendment to this scheme which added somewhat to its realism was the provision that all labour notes should be redeemable in a standard commodity such as corn.[5]

An economic system based on these axioms is not in the full sense a market economy. Prices are not set by haggling between buyer and seller, but named by the seller: the buyer's only decision is whether he wants the commodity at the named price. Thus the system assumes that each seller behaves ethically, only asking as much for each commodity as it had cost him in labour to produce, and not increasing the price even if the demand allows him to do so. By the same token, prices cannot in this system serve as signals of demand, so Warren relied on open communication between producers and consumers: in his model of an equitable village, each producer would post up a list of the commodities and services he could supply, and each consumer would list his wants. Armed with this information, and capable of switching easily between different lines of production because the apprenticeship system had been abolished (one of Warren's hobbyhorses), the producer would act on his best estimate of the demand for his products.[6]

It will be seen that Warren's system would work best, if it would work at all, within a small community of farmers and artisans, where demand was relatively stable, costs of production could be estimated accurately, and the population was sufficiently fixed for confidence in the labour-notes to build up. Nonetheless the Warrenites did envisage the application of their ideas to industry, and indeed envisaged something structurally akin to the capitalist firm, with a boss employing subservient workers. The great difference would lie in the distribution of rewards. The industrialist would get the same income as his workers (assuming equal labour-time), since neither he nor anyone else would receive a return on the capital invested in the firm; nor, moreover, would he receive any reward for his special talents and abilities, since on the Warrenite view these natural gifts were irrelevant to justice in exchange.[7] Thus by comparison with orthodox capitalism, Warren's system would be highly egalitarian, and his views fit naturally into the socialist tradition that sees the (present-day) capitalist as exploiting the worker by virtue of the former's monopoly of the means of production.

Turning now to Benjamin Tucker, we find a continuation of certain of Warren's ideas together with some subtle changes of emphasis. Tucker followed Warren in asserting that prices are naturally determined by costs of production, measured in hours of labour. Indeed he used this doctrine as a way of linking together Warren, Proudhon, and Marx as members of an overarching socialist tradition (which, however, divided into two contrary streams when it came to describing the alternative to the existing system).[8] But whereas Warren saw the cost principle as being implemented deliberately by 'equitable' men, Tucker saw it as the by-product of self-interested behaviour under a completely free market. Men would, in other words, always try to sell their commodities for the highest price they could get, but the effect of free exchange was to force all prices towards the point determined by costs of production. A free market was one in which the four major monopolies had been abolished: money, land, tariffs and patents.[9] Tucker gave pride of place to the first of these, arguing that with free banking and issuing of money, rates of interest would fall almost to zero, and any labourer who wished to set up in business would be able to do so. Instead of Warren's scheme of labour notes, he thought it more practical for money to be issued by those with sufficient assets (preferably in the form of land) to guarantee the issue. Concerning the ownership of land, Tucker argued that rent would be eliminated by making the occupier and user of a piece of land in every case its owner (thus tenants would automatically become owners under a system of equal liberty). He was, however, somewhat hazy about how this 'occupancy and use' criterion might be applied in practice.[10]

We see, therefore, that Tucker embraced the orthodox market economy more warmly than did Warren, while still expecting that a really free market would turn out very differently from the capitalism of his day. The capitalist himself was not the villain of the piece – at least not directly: the major villains were the bankers, who held up interest rates, and the landlords, who held up rents. Under Tucker's scheme, employer–worker relations were expected to persist in a large part of industry, but their basis would have changed: it would be a co-operative arrangement for mutual advantage, in which the capitalist would only receive payment for his labour of management. As Tucker put it 'genuine Anarchism is consistent Manchesterism'.[11] Would inequality of rewards also persist? Tucker could see no way of preventing superior skill from obtaining a return (in violation of the cost principle), though at first he believed that nine-tenths of such violations currently resulted from 'artificial, law-made inequalities'.[12] Later he seems to have drifted towards the view that substantial inequalities would remain, and that the anarchist objective was equality of liberty, not equality of outcome.

'If absolute equality is the ideal; if no man must have the slightest advantage over another – then the man who achieves greater results through superiority of muscle or skill or brain must not be allowed to enjoy them. All that he produces in excess of that which the weakest and stupidest produce must be taken from him and distributed among his fellows. The economic rent, not of land only, but of strength and skill and intellect and superiority of every kind, must be confiscated. And a beautiful world it would be when absolute equality had been thus achieved! Who would live in it? Certainly no freeman.'[13]

To sum up: Tucker could claim to be a socialist and to have the welfare of the working class at heart, while still believing in equal liberty and the market system, because of his belief that the current shape of capitalism was powerfully affected by the four monopolies. With these removed a system that was recognizably capitalist would remain, but its coercive and exploitative character would have disappeared.

If we compare Tucker's position with that of present-day libertarians (of whom Rothbard is a representative example), we discover that the latter group embrace capitalism with unqualified enthusiasm.[14] The cost-of-production theory of prices is abandoned in favour of a supply-and-demand theory; and since interest on loans is held to reflect people's time-preferences (the difference in value to them between present consumption and future consumption), it is not presumed that interest rates will fall to a low level under a competitive monetary system. This is not to say that, without the state, the contours of capitalism would remain just as they are now. It is an important part of Rothbard's analysis that government intervention in the economy distorts the market, allowing some producers to reap monopolistic profits.[15] But even without this distortion, there will still be substantial inequalities between capitalists and workers, due to natural differences in ability, differing attitudes towards the present and the future ('the major problem with the lower-class poor is irresponsible present-mindedness', Rothbard remarks)[16] and the effects of inherited wealth, which Rothbard places firmly within the privileged sphere. Indeed the whole thrust of his analysis is towards showing that the productivity engendered by the market makes everyone better off (including the workers) and away from any concern with equality as an end in itself. He defines 'exploitation' and 'coercion' in such a way that it becomes axiomatic that neither can occur within the market, but only as a result of political intervention.[17]

To understand why the economic theory of individualist anarchism has changed in this way, we must look to economic and social developments that have altered the constituency for whom the individualists hope to speak. Warren's ideas belong to the era of 'new worlds' and experimental communities when artisans and small farmers tried to escape from the clutches of money-lenders and merchants. Warren himself was instrumental in establishing a number of these communities, as well as his famous 'time-stores', which will be discussed later in the book. Tucker wrote at a time when agriculture was still the largest source of employment, and when poverty-stricken farmers looked to monetary reform to ease their position: in industry, meanwhile, reform unionism, exemplified by the Knights of Labor, looked to financial and land reform to free the craftsman from subservience to his employer. Both currents of thought plainly flowed into Tucker's anarchism. Rothbard, by contrast, is writing in a period when the capitalist industrial system has become firmly established, and his potential constituents include the small businessmen who resent the favours doled out by government to the large corporations. The ideological core of individualist anarchism has persisted, but its economic content has shifted in line with these social changes.

How do these anarchists conceive of the state? Government is defined as invasion of the individual's private sphere, and the state as a monopoly of government in a particular area.[18] Like all anarchists, the individualists condemn the state for the many ways in which it coerces people directly – by violating their rights of free speech, by conscripting them into the armed forces, and so forth – but they lay special emphasis on the state's interference with the free use of property. Regulation of the market, for instance, even when undertaken for what are seen as reasons of public interest, is condemned for violating the rights of those whose activities are controlled, as well as those of their potential customers. As noted earlier, individualists tend also to argue that such interferences are never really in the public interest. Suppose, for example, that in order to prevent the production of poor quality goods of a certain kind, the state lays down a set of minimum standards and appoints inspectors to check that these standards are met. The likely effects of this, anarcho-individualists will claim, are, first, that the number of firms competing in this field will be reduced, thus tending to push prices up; second, that those able only to afford substandard goods will be prevented from obtaining them legally; and third, that everyone's tax bill will be increased to pay the salaries of the new inspectors. Thus even if a few consumers are saved from their own folly in buying inferior goods, the net effect on social welfare will very probably be negative. A similar analysis is applied to the myriad other forms of intervention currently practised by the state.[19]

What of cases where the state uses its powers of taxation to supply something that every citizen wants – well-lit streets or modern sanitation, for instance? The anarchist reply to this is again likely to have two prongs. First, anarchists will deny that it is ever justifiable to invade someone's private sphere and confiscate his property on the grounds that he will be better off as a result. Paternalistic invasion, in other words, is no more defensible than any other kind. Since taxation is an involuntary process, it stands on all fours with other forms of invasion, no matter for what purposes it is instituted. Second, the anarchist will probably go on to challenge the assumption that everyone is made better off by the tax-funded provision of goods such as street lighting and sanitation. He will point out that people value these goods to different degrees, and under a market regime they would be willing to lay out different sums to have them provided. Thus public provision supplies the goods to some people on the cheap – they pay less in taxes than they would be prepared to pay on the market – whereas others are overcharged. The beauty of the market, it is argued, is that each person can purchase just the quantity of such goods that he is willing to afford, bearing in mind the other possible uses for his money.[20]

Suppose that the state uses tax revenues to support a group of people in need, such as the disabled or unemployed? The anarchist argument is once more two-branched. Charitable giving to those in need is praiseworthy, but it is not obligatory; it therefore cannot be justifiably enforced, either by private persons or by the state. Moreover state provision for the needy tends to be wasteful. Because the tax barrel is more or less bottomless, there is no strong incentive for those administering the relief programme to check that the recipients are genuinely needy cases, as opposed say to malingerers. It is claimed that private charity is more discriminating, and does a better job of getting those able to work back into employment.[21]

This critique of the state applies regardless of the type of state being considered. Anarcho-individualists have little patience with arguments purporting to show that states of a certain kind can avoid their strictures. Take first the contractual theory of the state, which holds that some states are legitimate – and can legitimately interfere with the rights of their subjects – because they are derived from a social contract to which every citizen has been a party. The most blistering assault on this view, as applied to the government of the U.S.A., was launched by the nineteenth-century anarchist Lysander Spooner.[22] Spooner argued that the U.S. Constitution, which was frequently claimed to embody such a contract, could at most have been a contract among the members of the founding generation, with no power to bind their successors. In fact, not even the founding generation had signed it. If it was said that they and their successors had given their assent in some other way, Spooner challenged the contractual theorists to point to the relevant acts. Voting in elections could not count, since voters' motives were many and varied, but virtually never consisted in a wish to affirm support for the Constitution; payment of taxes could not count, because it was compulsory; and so forth. 'It is plain,' Spooner concluded, 'that on general principles of law and reason . . . the Constitution is no contract; that it binds nobody, and never did bind anybody; and that all those who pretend to act by its authority, are really acting without any legitimate authority at all: that, on general principles of law and reason, they are mere usurpers, and that everybody not only has the right, but is morally bound, to treat them as such.'[23] And, we might add, if the U.S. government is not contractually legitimated, what other government is?

A second view that fares equally badly in the hands of these anarchists is the democratic theory of the state. Here it is said that democratic governments can rightfully control the individual and his property because they reflect the views of the majority of their citizens. Anarchists will at once deny that *majorities* have any right to infringe the rights of individuals: invasion is no less invasion because it is carried out *en masse*. But they are also liable to doubt whether rulers in democracies are really responsive to the wishes of their subjects. Rothbard borrows Schumpeter's analysis of party competition in representative democracies to argue that the voters are manipulated by party leaders and their hired persuaders into supporting one or other of the existing contenders for power.[24] Thus opinion flows from the top down rather than from the bottom up. The masses acquiesce passively in whatever their governors decide on their behalf. Even if democracy is some slight improvement on other forms of government, its reality does not match the picture that its defenders paint of it.

If the state as an institution is illegitimate, how have states come into existence and why do they remain in being? The main drift of anarcho-individualist thinking portrays the state as originating in plunder, and persisting because the groups who control and support it believe that they can do better for themselves by forcibly extracting resources than by exchange in the market.[25] The original political class were bandits who extorted tribute from the defenceless population in return for rudimentary protection against other gangs of bandits. When their position was regularized through a system of legislation, the state proper was born. The ruling class was then in a position to co-opt other groups, most notably financiers, landowners, merchants and industrialists, whose support it could win by dispensing economic favours of the appropriate kind; it could also offer public employment to intellectuals willing to speak in its defence. Thus finally the political class consists of the state functionaries proper plus all those who are net beneficiaries of government intervention in the economy. This is still a minority of the population; the exploited majority are kept in check by a combination of brute force and propaganda.

There is, though, a paradox in the individualist position here. A

persistent assumption in individualist ideology is that everyone benefits from free exchange in the market. This view is logically required
by those like Tucker who attempt to derive the principle of equal
liberty from egoistic premises: but, as noted above, it is also prominent in the thought of people like Rothbard who base their argument
upon natural rights and therefore do not strictly require it. But if the
assumption is true, why should some individuals foresake the market
in order to enrich themselves by political means? Is there really a
conflict of interests between the political class and the remainder of
society, or are the ruling group simply mistaken about where their
best interests lie? Could they do better for themselves by abandoning
plunder and returning to honest trade? The resolution of this paradox
will obviously have important implications for anarchist strategy, and
we shall return to it later in the chapter.

Let us look now at what individualist anarchists propose to take
the place of the state. The economic functions which the state now
performs will of course be handed over to individuals in the market.
But what of its protective functions – defence of person and property,
and punishment of criminals? The individualists' radical proposal is
that these functions too can be carried out through the market, by
private firms supplying protection in return for a fee. A sketch of this
idea can be found in Spooner and Tucker, but it has been spelt out in
greater detail by Rothbard and other modern libertarians.[26] In place
of the police and the public courts, the anarchists suggest that each
person should subscribe to the 'protective association' of his choice,
and also possibly to a private court. In the event of an assault on his
person or a violation of his property, he would apply to his protective
association to find the criminal, and, once found, bring a case against
him in his court. The accused person might be defended by *his*
protective association, and he might also wish the case to be heard by
his court (if he subscribes to a different one). If the two courts disagree
in their findings, some sort of voluntary arbitration is envisaged. In
this way, it is claimed, justice can be enforced without a 'sovereign'
body standing at the head of a judicial hierarchy.

Such a proposal clearly faces a number of serious difficulties.
Why, for instance, should people prefer to patronize 'fair' protective
associations and courts rather than agencies which always find in
favour of their customers no matter what the facts of the case? The
answer given is that such agencies will quickly lose any reputation
they might possess for honest dealing, so their verdicts will no longer
be accepted by other associations and courts. But suppose the rogue

agency can back up its decisions by force? The reply here is that conflict between agencies is likely to be very costly (in human life, particularly), so both the agencies themselves and the general public have a strong interest in resolving inter-agency conflicts by arbitration, thereby thwarting the rogue agency. But, then again, may not some people be so keen to win their cases that they are prepared to take the risk of hostilities breaking out by backing the rogue agency to the end? The anarchist model, it seems, would work if people were scrupulously fair-minded, and wanted only to win cases when they were in the right, so that they would only seek out agencies with a reputation for fairness; but the individualists insist that their proposal relies on no such transformation of human nature.

A second issue is whether protective services are not of such a nature that they would naturally gravitate into the hands of a single association in any area. Making this assumption, Robert Nozick has argued that a minimal state might evolve spontaneously from an anarchic social order.[27] The reasoning behind the assumption is that the protective agency which wins most clients is able to offer the most powerful and wide-ranging protection, so there is an incentive for clients of other agencies to switch to it. Of course even if one agency does become dominant in this way in a particular area, it has only a *de facto* monopoly of protective services, and cannot claim a *de jure* monopoly, as states do. (Nozick, however, by means of an involved argument about risk and compensation, suggests that such an agency may be morally entitled to insist that only specified procedures for enforcing justice are used against its clients.) But the difference may not appear very great in practice. How much will this worry the anarchist? He may try to dismiss the problem by saying that if, by purely voluntary means, we get back to something that looks very like a state, he is as happy with this outcome as with any other. But the awkward question then is why we should go through the disruption and upheaval that is likely to surround the initial destruction of the state. The challenge cannot be evaded so lightly.

The third issue that I want to raise concerns the rules of justice that the voluntary agencies will enforce. State sponsored courts, as everybody knows, broadly speaking enforce rules laid down for them by legislatures. Under anarchy there is no legislative activity as such: the rules are 'discovered' by the various courts that apply them. What if there should be a dispute about which rule to apply? Individualists assume, of course, that everyone will acknowledge the fundamental axiom of a free society: the inviolability of person and property. But this still leaves a very great deal open to debate: consider, for instance, the many controversies that surround the issue of property acquisition. Now the picture that individualist anarchists paint is of an area of dispute that steadily narrows as precedents are established through decisions reached in particular cases. But one may well doubt whether the best way to obtain a consistent and fair body of law is through a series of contested individual suits.[28]

The problem of supplying protection through the market also illustrates a wider difficulty for individualist anarchism. Protection against invasion has in part the quality of being a public good. A public good can, for present purposes, be defined as a benefit which cannot be supplied to any one member of a given 'public' without being supplied to all members; clean air is a familiar example. Protection has this character because, although one person can arrange to have his property defended and trespassers sued privately, the benefits tend to spill over on to others. To the extent that protective associations deter would-be criminals and incarcerate actual ones, every law-abiding citizen is benefited, whether or not he subscribes to an association himself (subscribers still receive *better* protection, which is why the good is not purely public). As is well known, public goods tend not to be supplied through the market, because with private subscription it pays everyone to hold back in the hope that others will subscribe first and supply the good, thus saving the non-subscriber his fee. If everyone except me pays dues to a protective agency, then I can obtain virtually as much general protection as I could if I paid up, while saving myself the actual cost. The result is that nobody will subscribe, and the good will not be provided. The solution usually recommended is that public goods should be supplied by a compulsory levy on all the beneficiaries; in other words by a political authority with the power to demand payment.

Since anarchists are bound to reject this solution, they must find another way of avoiding the public goods problem. Protection is only one, and not the most serious, instance of this problem. Other examples are defence against external aggression, public amenities (roads and parks) and environmental conservation. Some anarchists would try to circumvent the difficulty by appealing to man's moral nature: if I, along with everyone else, benefit from a good, isn't it simply fair that I should pay my share of its cost? But the individualists, whether they are explicitly egoists or not, tend to avoid such appeals, and look instead for ways in which it can be made in people's interest to pay for these goods. The most obvious way is to make the public good into a private good by finding a way of supplying it only to subscribers. In the case of a park, for instance, it would not normally be difficult for its owner to fence it off and to charge an entrance fee sufficient to cover the costs of maintaining it. Other cases, such as streets and roads, present more problems, and anarchists have needed to exercise their ingenuity in thinking up schemes whereby travellers could be charged for using highways by their owners.[29] Defence against foreign invasion is an even more intractable case, for no amount of technological sophistication is likely to alter the fact that I cannot be defended without my neighbours being defended too, so here there seems no feasible way of making the public good private. An alternative solution, in cases such as this, is for an entrepreneur to offer to supply a benefit (such as defence) to a community *provided* everybody in the community contracts to pay his dues – so would-be defaulters are made to realize that anyone choosing to opt out undermines the whole scheme. The difficulty with this solution is that no community of any size is likely to be wholly unanimous about the provision of public goods; in the case of defence, for instance, there will be a few convinced pacifists for whom military protection against invasion is not seen as a benefit. The entrepreneur needs to exclude such people from the scope of his contract (otherwise they will simply refuse to sign), but by doing so he creates an incentive for others to *pretend* not to value the good in question in order to avoid payment.[30] So neither of the non-compulsory solutions to the public goods problem can be guaranteed to work.

In the face of this conclusion, individualist anarchists have opted for one or more of three 'fall-back' positions. The first involves standing fast on the principle of individual sovereignty (which may, as we have seen, be expressed in the language of natural rights), and saying that it is better for public goods not to be provided than for individuals to be compelled to pay for them: in effect, *fiat justitia, ruat caelum*. The second involves pointing out that, if the state is entrusted with the task of providing public goods financed by compulsory taxation, state officials have neither the knowledge nor the incentive to decide when such provision really is beneficial; so that, along with a few genuine public goods we will have a large number of bogus 'goods', and certainly an increase in the size of the bureaucracy.[31] The third fall-back position is to argue that the state, once established, is unlikely to confine itself to the provision of public goods however widely defined, so the dangers involved in establishing a state far outweigh the possible benefits. This is a prudential argument which draws upon general anarchist scepticism about the possibility of limited or constitutional government.

The final aspect of individualist anarchism that we must examine is the proposed means of transition from existing state-controlled capitalist systems to stateless societies. In particular, what are the forces that might be mobilized to bring about such a transition? Individualists place greater reliance than most other anarchists on people who have been converted to the anarchist point of view by rational argument alone. In principle, more or less anybody might fit this bill – we saw earlier that there was a strong tendency among individualists to say that a perfectly free market would serve everyone's interests best in the long run. Practically, however, the direct beneficiaries of state action are placed beyond the pale, since it is very much against their short-term interests, at least, to act to destroy the state. How widely should this circle be drawn? Earlier individualists like Tucker saw the whole of the capitalist class as benefiting from state-created monopolies, so their hopes lay mainly with the working class and the self-employed. Recent contributors to the tradition such as Rothbard draw finer distinctions between capitalists in the monopoly sector and capitalists in the competitive sector, and argue that the latter group stand to gain considerably from the deregulation of the economy. Thus a broad coalition embracing businessmen, workers, students, media people, and ethnic minorities can be formed.[32] In neither case is a revolutionary movement of the type favoured by the left (including collectivist and communist anarchists) envisaged. Individualists have both instrumental and moral objections to revolution by force. Instead, some combination of three possible methods is advocated. The first is voting into power candidates with libertarian sympathies – though all writers in this tradition express grave doubts about such a strategy, and some, such as Tucker, reject it out of hand. The second is passive resistance, particularly in the form of a refusal to pay taxes. It is claimed that large-scale resistance of this kind might be an effective way of crippling the state. The third is the sponsorship of alternative institutions, outside of but in competition with the state, such as mutual banks or voluntary arbitration courts.

Since no individualist movement has ever grown to a point where these strategies might be tested as a serious way of challenging the state, we cannot say how realistic they are. On the other hand it is at least clear that they are consistent with individualist premises. An ideology that starts with the idea of individual sovereignty ought to end with a programme of change that places the rational individual, far-sightedly pursuing his interests, in the driving seat. The ideology itself may be thought one-sided, blind to important elements of human nature, and narrow in its understanding of socio-economic processes; we shall shortly see how starkly it contrasts with the assumptions made by other versions of anarchism. But its inner coherence may help to explain the doggedness with which its proponents, so far relatively few in number, have held to their views.

4 Communist Anarchism

If the central idea of individualist anarchism is that of individual sovereignty, the kernel of communist anarchism may be said to be social solidarity. Anarcho-communists maintain that the natural and proper relationship between people is one of sympathy and affection, expressed in acts of mutual aid and co-operation. In existing societies, however, solidarity is displaced (though not extinguished) by antagonism and competition. People see themselves as isolated and self-sufficient, and other people as their rivals at best and their enemies at worst. But this is a distorted view of the world. Everyone would be better off, in both material and human terms, if social harmony could be established in place of the present system. So the idea that individuals should be sovereign in their private spheres is, from an anarcho-communist point of view, an illusion thrown up by bourgeois society. Individualists and communists would no doubt agree that their fundamental aim was personal freedom: but whereas individualists would define this negatively, as the absence of interference or coercion, communists would define it positively, as the opportunity to satisfy needs and wants, and claim that, far from one person's freedom being limited by the freedom of others, no one could be really free except in a solidaristic community where each person worked to promote the well-being of the rest. Thus Malatesta: 'The freedom we want, for ourselves and for others, is not an absolute metaphysical, abstract freedom which in practice is inevitably translated into the oppression of the weak; but it is real freedom, possible freedom, which is the conscious community of interests, voluntary solidarity.'[1]

I shall return to some further contrasts between the two schools of anarchism later in the chapter. Now I need to say something about the identity of the communist school. Anarcho-communism took shape on the far left of the European socialist movement in the late nineteenth century. The major line of division within the revolutionary wing of that movement lay between the Marxists and the anarchists, and indeed we can date the origins of anarchism as an organized political force to the split between Marx and Bakunin inside the First International in the years around 1870. Because the Marxists at this time described themselves as 'communists', the anarchists chose to call themselves 'collectivists' in order to emphasize that the form of production under socialism would be chosen freely by the producers themselves and not imposed by a 'workers' state'. (The disagreement between anarchists and Marxists, which will be analysed much more fully in Chapter 6, centred on the contrast between economic and political methods of achieving socialism.)[2] Bakunin himself appears to have envisaged that, under anarchy, the instruments of production would become the collective property of groups of workers who would reward each member according to his labour, while not excluding the possibility that such a system might evolve voluntarily towards communism.[3] By the end of the next decade, however, increasing numbers of anarchists – prominent among them Kropotkin, Malatesta and Elisée Reclus – were beginning to argue that communism was the only reasonable mode of economic organization for an anarchist society, and, moreover, that this mode of organization would be adopted spontaneously by the workers as soon as existing property relations were destroyed. There was clearly a difference of emphasis between collectivists and communists, therefore, but one should not harden this into a rigid opposition. The collectivists admitted that developments in the direction of communism might occur; and the communists insisted that communism must never be imposed, but would emerge by voluntary means from the experience of the workers themselves. Anarcho-communism can thus be seen as the purest expression of an anarchist ideology of which collectivism (and also, I believe, the later anarcho-syndicalist position) are less extreme expressions.[4] Here I shall concentrate on the pure form, as set out in the writings of the founding generation, and also by later anarchists such as Alexander Berkman, Emma Goldman, Nicolas Walter and Murray Bookchin.

Much anarcho-communist writing starts with an attack on capitalist society not readily distinguishable from that found in Marxist literature. A vivid assault is launched upon the exploitative relationship between capitalist and worker, resulting in poverty, drudgery and the constant threat of unemployment for the latter, and idle luxury for the former. Closer analysis reveals, however, that exploitation in this narrow sense is less central to the anarchist critique of capitalism than it is to the Marxist critique.[5] The heart of the anarchist critique consists in two claims. First, capitalism constricts the development of society's productive powers, depriving the great majority of its members of the necessities of life which would otherwise be freely available to them. It does so because it is a system of production for profit, not production for need. Thus goods will only be produced where the demand for them is backed by money, and production cutbacks, with resulting unemployment, will occur even where people are crying out for the goods in question.[6] Second, capitalism confers individual titles to things which are really the collective products of society. The great mass of machinery, technical skill and scientific know-how which the capitalist uses to make 'his' products are the outcome of centuries of collective human endeavour. In this respect, of course, capitalism is no different from any other system of private property. But the anarchist charge is that capitalism, by making producers increasingly interdependent, removes the last shreds of justice from the claim that each person has a right to his private acquired wealth.[7]

Of course anarcho-communists contend not only that wealth is privately owned under capitalism, but that it is very unevenly distributed. The appropriation of the worker's product by his capitalist boss is a major aspect of the system. But exploitation of this type is only symptomatic of the exploitation that occurs throughout the system. The worker is bled by the tax-collector as well as by his employer. The peasant is exploited by his landlord and by the middleman who buys his produce. Even the small businessman is not safe from the extortions of the monopolist or the financier. Social relationships generally are dominated by a struggle for existence in which the powerful few win and keep most of the spoils.[8]

Anarchists have added other charges to this list at various times. Some have drawn attention to the dehumanizing work routines which capitalism imposes.[9] Others have pointed to the imperial ventures in which capitalists engage when domestic demand is insufficient to absorb their products, and the wars between states that result.[10] More recently, capitalism has been attacked for its destructive effect on the natural environment.[11] All of these charges are, of course, common property in the socialist tradition, and in that sense there is nothing distinctively anarchist about them. In so far as anarchists bring anything fresh to this particular ideological barricade, it consists in the two ideas emphasized above: the idea that mankind has at its disposal an immense productive capacity which the capitalist system is shackling, and the idea that this capacity is itself the outcome of centuries of human co-operation – thus an unconscious expression of the law of solidarity.

What sets anarcho-communists apart from the main body of

socialists is their insistence that the state itself is as much an enemy of human well-being as is capitalism. Capitalism is attacked first only because it can be made to appear more directly oppressive to the worker. But the state, besides acting as a necessary support to capitalism, is an engine of oppression in its own right. The interrelation between these two malevolent deities in anarcho-communist ideology is a subject that requires careful examination.

On the one hand, the state serves the interests of the capitalist class. The poverty and injustice generated by capitalism could not be sustained without a body prepared to use force to protect the property rights of the owning class, and willing also to provide a legal framework that conceals these ills under a cloak of 'equality before the law'. The point is generalized by Kropotkin:

> When we observe the basic features of human societies, abstracting from secondary and temporary appearances, we find that the *political* regime to which they are subject is always the expression of the *economic* regime which stands at the heart of society.[12]

It therefore appears as though anarcho-communists are offering a class theory of the state, very similar to that presented by Marxists, according to which the state is the instrument of the economically dominant class at any time, and *a fortiori* of the capitalist class under capitalism. But on the other hand, the state is also seen as a body with its own essential nature and internal dynamics. This nature is summed up in the following passage by Malatesta:

> The basic function of government everywhere in all times, whatever title it adopts and whatever its origin and organization may be, is always that of oppressing and exploiting the masses, of defending the oppressors and the exploiters; and its principal, characteristic and indispensable, instruments are the police agent and the tax-collector, the soldier and the gaoler – to whom must be invariably added the trader in lies, be he priest or schoolmaster, remunerated or protected by the government to enslave minds and make them docilely accept the yoke.[13]

From this it might properly be inferred that the state is an independent body whose main aim is to exploit the masses, and which will enlist the economically dominant class in the service of that aim.

Although there is an obvious tension between these two views of the state, they are not wholly irreconcilable. The general attitude of the anarcho-communists is somewhat as follows. There are two independent sources of power over others: direct force, giving rise to political power, and deprivation of the means of subsistence, giving rise to economic power.[14] These two forms of power might be combined in a single set of hands, as they were in the case of feudal barons for instance, in which case there will be a unified ruling class which can be described indifferently as economically or politically dominant. Alternatively they may be divided between two separate classes. In the latter case the political class and the owning class will enjoy a relationship involving both conflict and mutual dependence. The owning class needs the political class to safeguard property and impose a legal order; the political class needs the owning class to organize production and provide it with a secure source of revenue. At the same time each will try to subject the other to its will: the owning class will attempt to control the government, directly or indirectly, while the political class will try to enrich itself at the expense of the owning class.

Some flesh can be put on these rather abstract bones by considering Kropotkin's theory of the state, the most elaborate account so far offered from an anarcho-communist perspective.[15] Kropotkin argued that political relationships first arose from the breakdown of the primitive village community. New leaders emerged who combined the military power needed for defence with the judicial power that sprang from a specialist knowledge of customary law. These men proceeded to exploit the remainder of the population economically through the institution of serfdom (so here economic power grew out of political power). The consolidation of the feudal ruling class into a state proper was at first resisted by the communes that formed in the cities of medieval Europe.[16] But when these were destroyed, as a result partly of internal decay and partly of the military might of the barons, the state itself – centralized, unitary and authoritarian – took their place. It proceeded to expand the scope of its authority and to destroy all independent social organizations. Eventually it was captured by the growing bourgeoisic, but not before a fierce struggle in which the rights and liberties that characterize the modern bourgeois state were wrested from the political class. So runs Kropotkin's account. It bears out the view that the political regime and the economic regime tend always to come into alignment, but not the further claim that the economic regime is always the dominant partner in the relationship.

To summarize the anarcho-communist view of the modern state: it combines the exploitative and oppressive features of all political regimes with the further fact of being largely controlled by the capitalist class, who are exploiters in their own right. It is the first and greatest enemy of human welfare and freedom. This indictment is not altered by the form of the state – whether liberal or illiberal, monarchical, republican or democratic. Civil liberties, the anarchists argue, are certainly of some value to their possessors, but they must be seen as a reflection of the balance of power between the state and its subjects, not as the willing gift of the authorities. They were won by struggle, and are preserved by the threat of struggle.[17] Nor does popular representation, even when it takes the extreme form of universal suffrage, alter the essential character of the state. The bourgeois class allowed the suffrage to be extended only when it was confident that it could exercise sufficient ideological control over the working class to forestall the election of candidates who might seriously threaten the system. Moreover, even if a few revolutionary candidates were elected, they would quickly be frustrated by the operation of the parliamentary system, and eventually co-opted by the ruling class.[18] The anarchist interpretation of the workings of a parliamentary regime is a subject I shall return to in Chapter 6.

So much, then, for the communist anarchists' critique of capitalism and the modern state. The remedy that is proposed for these evils is radical indeed: nothing less than a complete reshaping of social and political life so that it comes to embody the principle of social solidarity. It would be wrong, however, to say that such anarchists are proposing to create a completely new set of social institutions with no roots in existing societies. They would interpret their proposals (how accurately we shall discuss later) as an amplification and extension of institutions which have always been present in human societies, though often submerged by the opposing set of institutions, those embodying domination and exploitation. This self-interpretation is particularly evident in the case of Kropotkin, who ransacked human history (and even the animal realm) in search of practices of 'mutual aid' – his generic term for voluntary institutions set up to satisfy the needs of each person participating in them.[19] Other anarchists were less historically minded, but they shared Kropotkin's general attitude. As Malatesta, for example, wrote, 'in order to understand how a society can live without government, one has only to observe in depth existing society, and one will see how in fact the greater part, the important part, of social life is discharged even today outside government intervention, and that government only interferes in order to exploit the masses, to defend the privileged minority, and moreover it finds itself sanctioning, quite ineffectually, all that has been done without its intervention, and often in spite of and even against it.'[20] Thus, appearances notwithstanding, anarcho-communists would deny that the model of society they envisage represents a total break with the existing social system.

In appearance it certainly does. The capitalist economy is to be replaced by common ownership of the means of production and distribution of goods and services according to need. The state is to be destroyed, and its place taken by voluntary associations, either territorially or functionally based. No one will be compelled to work, and no one punished for criminal behaviour. How might such a society be organized?

Economically, capitalism will be destroyed by the workers' directly taking over the means of production (how such a seizure might come about will be discussed below in Part II). Simultaneously, the local community will take over the available means of consumption – food, clothing and so forth. Some anarcho-communists would insist that full communism should be implemented immediately, without any transitional stage; others would say that evolution in the direction of communism would be gradual, as other economic arrangements were tried and rejected.[21] All would agree, however, that there should be no intermediate regime of centrally directed 'state socialism'; whatever arrangement emerges, it must be freely chosen by the workers in each locality. The essential faith of these anarchists is that the workers will, more or less rapidly, opt for a communist system.

Communism involves the abolition of the wages system, and indeed of exchange relations generally; money would disappear since it would no longer have any function to perform. In an ideal state, goods would be available in sufficient abundance that everyone could take what he needed from the communal stock. But the anarcho-communists, particularly those who envisage an immediate transition to communism after the seizure of the means of production, are aware that such ideal conditions cannot be taken for granted. How, then, would goods be distributed? 'In a word, the system is this: no stint or limit to what the community possesses in abundance, but equal sharing and dividing of those commodities which are scarce or apt to

51

run short.'[22] But 'equal sharing and dividing' should not be interpreted too literally. It is clearly envisaged that people should receive different amounts of goods according to their different needs; 'if this or that article of consumption runs short, and has to be doled out, to those who have most need most should be given'.[23] This presupposes both some means of identifying needs, and a mechanism for allocating goods in the appropriate way. Anarcho-communists have taken a rather cavalier line on both issues. Differences in need are obvious – at least to ordinary people who have not been corrupted by bourgeois prejudices. No special allocative machinery is required, because the people, having taken over the available goods in each locality, will quite spontaneously see to it that they are shared out on the basis of need. Food will be rationed out, with larger amounts going to the sick, the elderly and the children. Housing will be reallocated so that each family has adequate living space, and so forth.[24]

Consumption is, however, only one side of the economic problem. Production must also be arranged in a way compatible with communism. Here we need always to bear in mind the anarchist perception that human productive capacity is much greater than it appears under capitalism. The revolution will liberate this potential, so that many more goods can be produced, even with a shorter working day than at present.[25] The organization of production must as far as possible be decentralized. The workers in each factory and the peasants on each farm must take over their own places of work, and decide what to produce and how to produce it. There is to be no central direction, and no external compulsion of any kind. Since they are bitterly opposed to the bureaucratic organization which seems to be the inevitable accompaniment of large-scale industry, anarchists need to show that industries can be broken down into small components without loss of efficiency. To this end, radical changes in technology are often envisaged.[26] In the case of industries which have necessarily to be organized at national or international level, such as communications and transport, the principle of federation will be applied: workers in each locality will enter into voluntary agreements with those in other places to co-ordinate their activities.[27]

We have still to discover how producers will identify the needs of consumers in the absence of an economic market. How can thousands of autonomous productive units, factories, farms and so forth, dovetail their output with the requirements of almost as many units of consumption, namely local communities? The anarcho-communists envisage, first of all, that production will be localized to a much greater extent than is now the case. Each district will be more or less self-sufficient, producing its own food and most of its manufactured items. (Here again, the anarchist case depends heavily on the possibilities of technological change.) The local commune might then serve as a means of transmitting the needs of the consumers to the producers. Yet two awkward problems remain. The first is the construction of a schedule of needs, and the second is the allocation of tasks between different productive units (what if both beans and potatoes are needed, but everyone prefers growing beans?). The anarchist literature is distressingly vague about both issues. Kropotkin, who made the fullest attempt to depict an anarchist society in operation, assumed that people's time would be divided between a few hours of necessary labour to meet needs that were common to everyone, and time spent satisfying idiosyncratic personal needs such as those for art, music and science, where each person could supply his own resources or combine with others of similar tastes. He also suggested that technology could be used to make everyone's necessary labour agreeable to him.[28] But this still leaves the problems of drawing the line between common and individual needs and of allocating people to different kinds of 'agreeable' work. The anarchist case relies heavily here on 'the good sense of the people'.

It must be understood that, for the anarcho-communists, the economic question is not to be answered wholly or even mainly in terms of economic efficiency. No doubt they believed that a communist system would produce more goods and distribute them more effectively than a capitalist or a state socialist system. But the crucial point is that the economic system must be in harmony with social relationships generally in the new order. As we have seen, these are to be relationships of solidarity among equals; each person will be bound by ties of sympathy to the rest, and will express that sympathy in acts of mutual aid. Clearly, free communism is consonant with that ideal, whereas a system of exchange would reintroduce competitive relationships and a planned economy would create a new hierarchy between controllers and controlled. This connection between the anarcho-communists' economic proposals and their general ideals can be seen quite plainly in their response to collectivism, with its suggestion that workers should continue to be remunerated according to the amount and type of labour they had contributed, even after the means of production had passed into social ownership. The communists replied to this, first, that individual contributions to collective products could not, in practice, be distinguished; but secondly, and more crucially, that the spirit of this suggestion was quite at odds with the solidarity which the revolution itself expressed. As Kropotkin put it, 'collectivists begin by proclaiming a revolutionary principle – the abolition of private property – and then they deny it, no sooner than proclaimed, by upholding an organization of production and consumption which originated in private property . . . well, for us it is evident that a society cannot be based on two absolutely opposed principles. . . .'[29] Malatesta summed up the communist view in simple terms:

> Men must love each other and look on each other as members of one family, if things are to go well with them. Property ought to be common . . . it is needful to establish perfect solidarity between the men of the whole world. Therefore, instead of running the risk of making a confusion in trying to distinguish what you and I each do, let us all work and put everything in common. In this way each will give to society all that his strength permits until enough is produced for every one; and each will take all that he needs, limiting his needs only in those things of which there is not yet plenty for every one.[30]

Let me turn now to the kind of organization which the anarcho-communists would like to see in place of the state. Of course, in view of their thesis that the state serves mainly as an instrument of exploitation, the answer to this, over a large range of activities, is nothing. But there remain certain useful functions which the state now performs, chiefly in the area of social control, and we have seen that in addition an institution to co-ordinate economic activities will be needed. Anarcho-communist thought on this issue turns on two ideas: free association and federation. The first implies that, wherever a common need is perceived, men will spontaneously form associations to meet it; but the shape these will take cannot be laid down in advance, and moreover participation must always be voluntary, so dissenting individuals cannot be forced to co-operate. In practice, it is envisaged that the basic unit of association will be the local commune, a natural unit whose precursors include the village council and the commune of the medieval city. These communes in turn will associate in a federal structure. This means that a higher-level council will be formed, to which each commune will send delegates carrying the ideas of its members. If, at this higher level, agreement can be reached on some joint programme of action, the various associated communes will carry it out. But no federal decision is to bind the constituent associations against their will, and any association is free to leave the federation at any time. These provisions clearly separate the anarchist idea of federation from the more conventional liberal idea, which sees the federal institution as having some degree of authority over its constituents.[31] It is clear, too, that the form of organization proposed does not amount to a recreation of the state.

Besides these territorial associations, which perform the basic functions of social control and economic co-ordination, anarchists are keen to predict that associations for more specific purposes will arise and flourish. Some of these will simply be formed for the edification of their members, such as learned societies, but others will be altruistically motivated: Kropotkin and Malatesta both picked out the Red Cross and the Lifeboat Association as examples of institutions which throve even amid the egoism of capitalist society, and suggested that many more such bodies would spring up once the dead hand of government was removed.[32] In so far as we can speak of an anarcho-communist solution to the public goods problem, therefore, we must find it here. Given the communist assumption that a society based on solidarity will release the natural altruism of its members, there will be no difficulty in motivating individuals to contribute to projects whose benefits are enjoyed by everyone.[33]

Returning now to the local communes, it may be asked in what sense they can serve as instruments of social control. For they are free associations: no one is obliged to join them, and no one has an obligation to abide by their decisions. How, then, can they cope with anti-social behaviour, whether this is a matter of crime in the ordinary sense, or a refusal to contribute to production? These are familiar questions to anarchists. In reply they point out that the main agency of social control is always society itself. People quite spontaneously follow rules of behaviour which they have learnt from those around them, and which are enforced, if necessary, by public opinion. This will not change under anarchy; indeed, it is said, social bonds will be strengthened. Moreover, in so far as crimes occur in present-day societies, they are largely attributable to the conditions of life facing the criminal. Theft and violence are born of the confrontation between poverty and the conspicuous wealth of the rich. In communist society, where most goods are available freely, there will be no motive to commit crimes of this kind. Personal crimes, such as *crimes passionels*, may still occur. But these, it is claimed, can be dealt with directly – say by restraining the aggressor until his emotions have subsided – without the need for any formal machinery of punishment. Anarchists deny, moreover, that present methods of punishment are effective in keeping down the overall volume of crime.[34] Finally, if all else fails, any social group is entitled to expel a malefactor from within its midst. This is not a solution which anarchists relish, but provided the outcast is given some means of subsistence, they are willing to accept it as a last resort.

The problem of the work-shy or unco-operative person is handled in the same way. In circumstances where nobody is able to live idly on the profits created by others, there will be a moral consensus that everyone should contribute his share to production, so the would-be parasite will have to brave public opinion. But in any case, laziness is not a natural human quality: on the contrary, almost everyone wants to be usefully employed, provided that the work is agreeable and suits his capacities. Berkman puts the point bluntly: 'there really is no such thing as laziness. What we call a lazy man is generally a square man in a round hole.'[35] Under capitalism, people are restricted in their choice of occupation by such factors as inherited status, and there is no incentive for the capitalist to make conditions of work attractive so long as there is a surplus pool of labour waiting to be employed. Moreover much slacking and shoddy workmanship is born of resentment at the employer's profits. Under anarchist communism, everyone will be working for the community, people will be able to choose their work freely, and the work environment, even in factories, can be made salubrious. For the tiny minority who resist such blandishments, the ultimate sanction of exclusion remains. The recalcitrants will have to fend for themselves, or find some other group willing to take them in.[36]

By these means – changed social conditions, pressure of public opinion, and the final threat of exclusion – anarcho-communists claim that they can solve the problem of anti-social behaviour. Without asking at this point whether their solution is adequate, I want to relate it to a more general issue, namely whether the social order envisaged has really dispensed with a system of authority.[37] We saw in Chapter 2 that anarchists have often been attracted by comprehensive arguments against authority, but also that these arguments attempted to prove more than was really necessary to make the anarchist case against the state. How should we assess anarchist communism from this point of view? It is clear, first of all, that no compulsory authority is envisaged, in the sense that adhesion to any association, whether territorial or functional, is regarded as voluntary. It is also made clear that no coercion shall be exercised against people who dissent from an association's decisions. On the other hand, it is apparent that such dissenters face sanctions if they carry their dissent into action. Public opinion will be turned against them, and under anarchy this will be a more potent force than it is now. Ultimately they risk expulsion from the association, with the material and spiritual costs that this may involve. Such sanctions would remain hypothetical if associations only made decisions when they had reached unanimity. But although anarcho-communists clearly regard unanimity as the ideal, and are eager to point out that people will naturally concur on such matters as a list of basic human needs, they are realistic enough to concede that, where a decision is imperative, the majority will must prevail.

> For if it is unjust that the majority should oppress the minority, the contrary would be quite as unjust; and if the minority has a right to rebel, the majority has a right to defend itself . . . it is true that this solution is not completely satis-factory. The individuals put out of the association would be deprived of many social advantages, which an isolated person or group must do without, because they can only be procured by the co-operation of a great number of human beings. But what would you have? These malcontents cannot fairly demand that the wishes of many others should be sacrificed for their sakes.[38]

Nor is it enough to say that everyone will sooner or later find a group that suits his inclinations, as some anarchists have done. This ignores the costs involved in uprooting oneself from one locality and settling elsewhere, costs that anarchists would be quick to point out if a similar solution were proposed, say, to the problem of regional unemployment under capitalism.

We must conclude that the social order anarcho-communists favour does encompass a form of authority, though unlike the authority of the state it is non-compulsory, non-coercive, functionally specific, and exercised collectively by everyone who lives in a particular locality or shares a particular interest. But even such a circumscribed form of authority may alarm anarchists who are not communists. I want to end this chapter by asking how the anarchists at the other end of the economic spectrum – the individualists – would regard the communist solution, and how in turn the communists might reply to an individualist critique.

An individualist's primary question is likely to be whether the social arrangements proposed by the communists respect or violate the sovereignty of the individual. The communists demand that the means of production should be seized from the ruling class and put under the collective control of the workers in each locality, who will then move more or less rapidly towards communism in production and distribution. What of the person who declines to take part in this collective endeavour, and prefers to live and work independently? When pressed, anarcho-communists have generally conceded that such a person should be given access to land and the other means of life; but they have drawn the line at allowing him to engage in exchange or employment relationships with others. This, for the individualists, amounts to a crucial violation of individual rights. How can a person be free if he is not permitted to exchange his products for those of other people, offer his labour for sale, or buy the labour of another?[39] Since the communists intend to outlaw these activities by force, the social organization they propose is nothing more than a variant of the state. Despite their claims, they are not genuine anarchists.[40]

From the communists' point of view, the arrangements advocated by individualists are equally defective. Two main charges are laid. First, the idea of a free market in which each person receives the product of his own labour is hopelessly anachronistic. We have already seen how, in their critique of collectivism, the communists claim that the complexity of modern industry makes it impossible to separate individual contributions to joint products; by the same token, it would be impossible to draw up a series of contracts whereby each participant in a collective enterprise would receive a fair return for his labour. Second, any market system will revert by degrees to a capitalist system, and the defence associations advocated by the individualists to protect property rights will take on the character of states, organs serving to perpetuate the exploitation of the workers by the capitalists.[41]

It will be seen that the two camps largely argue past each other, because of their different views about how matters will work out in practice under the two regimes being considered. The communists assume that, because of natural human solidarity, very few persons will wish to be independent of the collective organization of production, and so communist arrangements need not be enforced. The individualists assume, on the contrary, that people have a natural propensity to truck, barter and exchange, so communist production runs right against the grain and can only be preserved by compulsion. There is a similar divergence with respect to the individualists' market regime. We must therefore face up to the radical ideological cleavage between the two schools. The individualists' ideology revolves around the notions of personal sovereignty, private property, economic exchange, freedom as the absence of constraint, and justice as the reward of desert. Communist thinking, on the other hand, centres on the notions of social solidarity, common ownership, mutual aid, freedom as access to the means of happiness, and justice as distribution according to need. The ideological matrices in question are not hard to identify. Individualist anarchism is plainly an extreme version of classical liberalism – extreme because it takes certain liberal attitudes (the belief in free competition, in the minimal state, and so forth) and pushes them to the limit. Communist anarchism is just as plainly a version of communitarian socialism: its basic ideological commitments are little removed from those of the young Marx, for instance. Given this fundamental cleavage, it is inevitable that the two schools should disagree about the merits of each other's proposals, and, indeed, about whether these proposals deserve the label 'anarchist'.[42]

Seeing this should make us aware that anarchism cannot easily be placed on any simple left–right political spectrum, and should also make us cautious about accepting critical claims beginning 'anarchism fails because . . .' and going on to say something about human nature, economic mechanisms or whatever. Perhaps few such criticisms will apply to all versions of anarchism. Our critical faculties need not be anaesthetized, however. Indeed each school provides ammunition with which to attack the other. Have the communists really shown that individuals will remain free under the arrangements they envisage, and that the workers' councils and the communes do not amount to a new form of the state? Have the individualists said anything coherent about how a free market can be preserved, and have they sold the pass by permitting defence associations to enforce property rights? These are questions that we must return to later. One of the joys of anarchism is that it provides not only a critique of every other political ideology, but of itself as well.

Part II Anarchism as a Revolutionary Ideology

5 Human Nature and Historical Progress

In the first part of this book, we have been examining the fundamental ideas of anarchism: the critiques various anarchists have offered of the economic and political institutions of contemporary society, and their proposals for a new social order. The intention in the second part is to look at how anarchists have attempted to bring about the transformation that they desire. This will require us to investigate both what they have said and what they have done – theory and practice have not always corresponded in anarchist circles. The present chapter serves as a bridge between the two parts of the book, for it raises two (connected) theoretical issues which have a crucial bearing on any proposed anarchist practice. The first issue is the anarchist view of human nature and its possible mutations; the second is the extent to which anarchist ideas are embedded in a theory of historical progress. Let me begin by explaining the connection between these issues and their relevance to anarchist practice.

I have called this part of the book 'anarchism as a revolutionary ideology', a phrase whose meaning must be properly understood. Not all anarchists have been revolutionaries in the sense of advocating a sudden and violent overturning of existing social institutions; some, as we shall see, have argued for a slow, gradual and peaceful process of change. But in another sense anarchism is necessarily a revolutionary ideology. The goal common to all anarchists – a stateless society – represents a qualitative break with anything that we are familiar with, at least in modern industrial societies. We cannot escape the fact that, in these societies especially, the state exerts an immense influence on social relationships generally. The anarchists ask us to envisage a social order with this influence removed, and in some cases with other major transformations as well – for instance the disappearance of the economic market. Taking revolution in its sociological sense of a complete remaking of social relationships, and without now distinguishing between sudden and gradual transformations, we can see that all anarchists must be classed as revolutionaries.[1]

As such, they face a problem shared by all revolutionaries of whatever ilk. They must explain how the new order is possible in the light of what is known about human nature. In the anarchist case, for instance, they must explain how violence can be contained without recourse to a system of authority that would properly be called a state. But, at the same time, they cannot make assumptions about human nature that would make what is already known to have happened in human history impossible. No doubt, if you take a rosy enough view of what human nature is really like – if you assume that people are always by nature peaceful, co-operative and altruistic – you can make anarchy seem a plausible and attractive ideal. But then you have to explain why it has not arrived already – why, if human beings are really like that, they have so far engaged mainly in violence, oppression and exploitation. So it seems that revolutionary ideologies are caught in a trap: the assumptions that they need to make their ideals plausible at the same time make it impossible to understand what has happened already and what is now happening.

What is needed, obviously, to escape from this trap is some account of how the same human raw material can produce one kind of behaviour at a certain moment and another kind at a different moment. It is here that a theory of historical progress may be brought in to provide the account. Human beings will behave differently at t2 than at t1 because between t1 and t2 events have occurred that have changed their make-up. The theories of this kind so far advanced have tended to fall into three major categories, although mixed versions are also possible. First, there have been enlightenment theories, which have maintained that human reason moves steadily from error to truth, so that later generations understand their world better than earlier ones. Human desires do not necessarily change, but people come to act on their desires in a more enlightened and therefore successful way. Next, there have been idealist theories, which have held that human consciousness moves historically through a series of stages, each stage representing a resolution of the contradictions and inadequacies of the one preceding it, and therefore an advance. In these theories, desires and beliefs are often said to change together. Finally, there have been materialist theories, which have found the source of transformation in the changing physical circumstances of men's lives – in new technologies, in forms of production and consumption, and so forth. Again these factors may be held to influence beliefs, or desires, or both together.

It should be clear how a theory of progress of one of these three kinds lends itself to a revolutionary ideology. Previously, it is claimed, human beings have been mired in ignorance, or victims of false consciousness, or slaves of a hostile physical environment. Now, for the first time, they are able to give full expression to an essential nature which has so far remained latent. The social changes advocated correspond to this full flowering of the human essence. Such claims have an obvious attraction. But they carry with them a hidden danger for the revolutionary. If there is indeed a regular pattern to historical progress – if humanity moves from lower to higher stages in a law-governed way – what place is left for conscious intervention on the part of the revolutionary himself? How can he push history in the direction that he wants: either it is travelling that way already, in which case his intervention is redundant, or it is not, in which case his efforts will be fruitless? As Weber once said of the third theory of progress, 'the materialist interpretation of history is no cab to be taken at will; it does not stop short of the promoters of revolutions'.[2] It may appear that, by using a doctrine of historical progress, the ideologue has purchased theoretical coherence at the expense of a rationale for his own revolutionary activity.

There are various means of countering this charge, which it would not be profitable to pursue here in general terms. I want instead to look at the way in which anarchists have handled the problem, examining, first, their views of human nature, now and in the future social order; second, their ideas about how human nature can be transformed, if indeed such a transformation is posited; third, the extent to which they rely on a theory of historical progress in giving this account; and fourth, what difficulties such a theory, if it is used, poses for their understanding of revolutionary practice. There is no single anarchist position on any of these questions, so it will be necessary to look briefly at a number of alternative views, chosen – I hope fairly – to represent the range of anarchist thinking. At the end we shall see how far it is possible to reach general conclusions.

I shall begin with views which fall broadly under the rubric of enlightenment theories, in so far as they see the transition to anarchy as occurring through some general process of mental illumination. The quintessential account here is Godwin's, another aspect of which has been discussed above in Chapter 2. In this chapter I shall focus on his view of human nature.

The first point to make is that Godwin sees human nature as highly malleable, and in that sense can be said to have no fixed view of human nature at all. He argues at length that human beings are made what they are by the environment in which they are educated, education being interpreted broadly to include the experiences we receive by no conscious design and the prevailing climate of opinion (which Godwin attributes to the form of government under which we live) as well as formal teaching. These influences together form the character of human beings, and there is no 'innate' set of ideas or instincts which might resist them.[3] Godwin avoids succumbing to a fatalistic form of determinism, according to which it is impossible for men to modify their characters or situation by conscious choice, only because he believes that men are endowed with the capacity to reason, a capacity which they may use to improve their motives and behaviour to an indefinite extent. (Quite how Godwin's environmentalism and his rationalism are to be reconciled remains obscure to me, as it does in the case of a number of other enlightenment thinkers.) This belief in human perfectibility – a term that Godwin is happy to use – rests on two theses: first that our conduct can be entirely governed by reason, and second that reason prescribes a unique line of conduct, namely universal benevolence.[4] So a fully rational man will always act so as to promote the greatest happiness of everyone else.

Godwin's view of human nature thus has a dual aspect. On the one hand, men are now formed by an inauspicious environment (especially by forms of government of varying degrees of badness) and are predictably selfish in their behaviour and unenlightened in their beliefs. On the other hand, each has the capacity to reform himself by the use of his reason and so is capable of limitless improvement. As Godwin sums up the argument:

> Sound reasoning and truth, when adequately communicated, must always be victorious over error: Sound reasoning and truth are capable of being so communicated: Truth is omnipotent: The vices and moral weakness of man are not invincible: Man is perfectible, or in other words susceptible of perpetual improvement.[5]

At the same time, Godwin does not expect the process of enlightenment to be especially rapid. Each generation has the chance to improve on its predecessor, but the final dissolution of government is spoken of as occurring far into the future. Thus there is to be no sudden shift from selfishness to benevolence in human conduct, but rather a gradual increase in the power of reason, accompanied by progressive changes in behaviour and corresponding changes in social institutions.

We may still wonder why reason should begin its salutory work now, rather than at some other historical moment. Godwin cannot in the end avoid tackling the issue of historical progress, though he is visibly uneasy about it. He argues first, contrary to the view that human nature is much the same in all times and places, that men have taken vast intellectual strides away from their primitive condition, advances which appear especially in the invention of speech and writing.[6] On the other hand, he rejects the Panglossian view that everything which has happened is for the best, pointing to the enormous disfigurements that men have inflicted on each other. 'The whole history of the human species, taken in one point of view, appears a vast abortion.'[7] He is also aware that such progress as has occurred has not been steady, but intermittent, as the decline of civilization after the classical era shows.[8] But finally he seems to believe that intellectual progress has more or less been guaranteed since the invention of printing enabled knowledge to be preserved and diffused throughout society. His closing remarks are optimistic. 'The general diffusion of truth will be productive of general improvement; and men will daily approximate towards those views according to which every object will be appreciated at its true value . . . Each man will find his sentiments of justice and rectitude echoed by the sentiments of his neighbours.'[9]

Thus Godwin relies on what I have called an enlightenment theory of history to support his view of human nature. But has he done so at the expense of his own potential role as a revolutionary? We must recall, first of all, that Godwin rejects conventional revolutionary methods along with other forms of political action as a way of moving towards his ideal. This follows directly from his belief that social improvement can only flow from intellectual improvement, while intellectual improvement itself can only come about through discussion and reflection. Attempts by the enlightened few to impose more advanced institutions upon the backward masses are doomed to failure.[10] The practice of revolution is especially severely condemned. Revolutions divide societies into hostile camps and provoke irrational passions on both sides. These passions, once aroused, are fatal to liberty of thought and speech, and thus 'suspend the wholesome advancement of science, and confound the process of nature and reason'.[11] Godwin is scarcely more charitable to conventional party politics. Parties, he argues, rather than promoting calm intellectual inquiry, encourage conformity to the party creed, emotional harangues, pandering to mass prejudices to win office, and political sensationalism.[12] However, the fundamental defect of all political activity as conventionally understood is that it places the cart before the horse; 'the only method according to which social improvements can be carried on, with sufficient prospect of an auspicious event, is when the improvement of our institutions advances in a just proportion to the illumination of the public understanding'.[13]

Is an anarchist of Godwin's persuasion then condemned to political quiescence? He may of course, and indeed should, participate in the public communication of truth, but he can only do so as one individual among many. Godwin admits that some men are more enlightened that others, but the *illuminati* can do little more than wait patiently for the remainder to catch up. Besides this he condones certain forms of collective activity, such as participating in groups which form to remove some pressing evil and then dissolve.[14] This rather uninspiring programme is all that Godwin's view of human nature and historical progress permits.

A very different view of human nature, but a rather similar reliance on intellectual enlightenment, can be detected in the writings of individualist anarchists. The individualists' account of human nature differs from Godwin's in two respects: it does not presuppose that human nature will change in any significant way when government is replaced by anarchy and it assumes that human beings are, to a greater or lesser extent, selfish in their behaviour. There is some divergence on the second point. We have seen already that a number of nineteenth-century anarcho-individualists were converted to Stirnerism. This amounts to the belief that men always behave egoistically, though they may pursue their interests with a greater or lesser degree of intelligence and success. Moralizing is both fruitless and unnecessary, on this view. Social harmony can be achieved by getting people to follow their interests in a clear-sighted way. Other individualists have taken a different line; self-interest is and should be circumscribed by respect for the rights of others, and there is room for a small and subordinate sphere of charity. Lysander Spooner spoke of the immutable laws of justice which everyone must obey and contrasted them with the moral (i.e. voluntary and unenforceable) duties of care owed to our fellows.[15] These views are echoed among present-day anarchists by Murray Rothbard, who, while denying that he subscribes to any fixed theory of human nature, clearly expects that most people will provide for themselves by self-interested activity within the bounds set by natural rights, while a few may depend on the charity of the rest.[16]

The choice, therefore, as far as the individualists are concerned, lies between egoism pure and simple and circumscribed egoism. In neither case does the argument for anarchy rest on a belief that human nature can be changed. As Rothbard puts the point:

> The anarchist view holds that, given the 'nature of man', given the degree of goodness or badness at any point of time, anarchism will maximize the opportunities for the good and minimize the channels for the bad. The rest depends on the values held by the individual members of society.[17]

But this view, while it disposes effectively of the idea that all anarchists are moral reformers, leads us directly to our original question in slightly different dress: if human nature is not to change, how are anarchy and the present statist order both possible? The individualists all rely here on the enlightenment of self-interest. Anarchy is possible because human beings can be made to see that their interests are best served by having it. The present order is upheld by a minority group who believed (mistakenly perhaps) that they would do better for themselves by exploitation than by peaceful competition, and who have succeeded in indoctrinating the majority with statist ideas. But this indoctrination can be broken down by evidence and argument. Anyone is potentially persuadable, though efforts at persuasion are best directed at those who have most to gain immediately from the abolition of the state.

Here, then, an enlightenment theory is brought in not to explain a change in human nature but to show how an unchanged human nature can sustain a new social order. The individualists rely very little on a theory of historical progress: their account of the origins of the state is crude and timeless. In so far as they have tried to explain why their ideas should begin to prevail now, after centuries of state domination, they have pointed in two directions. They have turned first to the Enlightenment, and its intellectual product, classical liberalism. Anarcho-individualism, they claim, represents the logical working-out of traditional liberal ideas. Andrews, for instance, argued that the whole modern era had been devoted to the freeing of the individual from institutional bondage, that Protestantism and democracy were the expression of this idea in the religious and political spheres respectively, and that what remained was to free the individual in the social sphere.[18] Similar claims to liberal parentage can be found in Tucker and Rothbard. Beside this stands a more down-to-earth claim. State oppression is becoming daily more intolerable, so the potential for resistance is increasing. Writing in the 1970s, Rothbard argued that 'not only has a crisis of statism arrived in the United States, but it has fortuitously struck across the board of society, in many different spheres of life at about the same time. Hence, these breakdowns of statism have had a synergistic effect, reinforcing each other in their cumulative impact . . . All we need are libertarians to point the way.'[19]

But even if political developments may be thought to provide the opportunity for anarchists to act, the basic task for the individualists remains one of enlightenment. Quite consistently, they have rejected methods of social change which suppose otherwise – acts of violence, revolutions, parliamentary politics. Their objective has always been to persuade a sufficiently large number of people of the truth of their ideas. In that respect, and despite their contrasting view of human nature, they stand alongside Godwin and apart from the revolutionary anarchists whose activities have furnished the dominant view of anarchism in practice.

Turning to these more familiar figures, I shall begin by taking Proudhon and Bakunin together, despite the hazards involved in doing so. Neither is a particularly consistent thinker, and there are important differences between them. For present purposes, nonetheless, we can usefully extract some common elements from their thinking about human nature and history. Both had some appreciation of the complexity of human motivation, and both maintained that the human essence as it now existed was a historical product. They shared, too, a conviction that moral ideas were of paramount importance in fostering a revolutionary spirit. Although neither would have welcomed the description, their theories of history are predominantly idealist in character, in the sense indicated above.

Proudhon was the more pessimistic about human nature. Like Rousseau, he believed that the primitive ingredients of the human character were egoism and sympathy, with egoism by far the stronger impulse. Society originated in a series of accommodations between egoistic creatures, each of whom was forced to recognize the claims of the rest. Once social relationships had developed, however, men began to form ideal conceptions of those relationships, which Proudhon calls ideas of justice.[20] The development of society proceeds through a series of confrontations between the ideal and the actual. On the basis of the ideas held at any moment, a social order emerges, complete with rules and institutions for enforcing those rules. But ideas of justice continually develop, while the social order remains rigid, so its inhabitants become disillusioned. Rather than trying to change their society, they give way to despair, which according to Proudhon can express itself in a number of ways. One of these is a rebirth of narrow egoism. The social order is preserved, not by genuine moral conviction, but by the combined force and persuasion of state and church. This, for Proudhon, is a period of decadence, and the history of humanity shows many such periods.[21] If there has been progress, it has taken the shape of a tilted spiral rather than a steady gradient. Upward movement occurs when the rift between ideal and actual becomes too great, precipitating a revolution.

Bakunin was less anxious than Proudhon about the pervasiveness of egoism, and less impressed by the idea of decadence, but his image of the primitive human being was somewhat similar. '[Man] was born a ferocious beast and a slave, and has gradually humanized and emancipated himself only in society.'[22] Like Proudhon he stressed that morality was a product of social life, and that moral ideas developed historically. At any time, however, the mass of men would simply receive and transmit a body of ideas from the past. 'This servility, this routine, this perennial absence of the will to revolt and this lack of initiative and independence of thought are the principal causes for the slow, desolate historical development of humanity.'[23] Fortunately a small number of individuals are able to break free from their social conditioning and develop more advanced moral ideas. When the poverty of the masses has brought them to the depths of despair, these ideas will coalesce with their own submerged revolutionary instincts. 'It is necessary that the populace have a general idea of their rights and a deep, passionate, one might even say religious, belief in these rights. When this idea and this popular faith are joined to the kind of misery that leads to desperation, then the social revolution is near and inevitable, and no force on earth will be able to resist it.'[24] Like Proudhon, Bakunin did not regard revolution as a singular event leading to some final condition of justice, but as a recurrent phenomenon which would propel society forward in a series of leaps.

Neither man can be called an idealist in the sense in which Hegel was one.[25] They would have repudiated with some vehemence the notion that history was the expression of a transcendent spirit, and they would have found the idea of a progressive series of historical epochs too cut-and-dried and too deterministic in its implications; both were aware of retrogression in history, and neither thought in terms of a definitive resolution of the contradictions which have hitherto provoked historical change (Proudhon claimed that the fundamental flaw in Hegel's philosophy was his belief that the first two terms in the dialectic, the thesis and the antithesis, could be resolved into the third, the synthesis; in Proudhon's view, only a balance between opposing forces was possible – and an unstable balance at that).[26] Yet in another sense the label is appropriate. Both held that history is a process whereby men emerge from their brutish condition and become, through the influence of social relationships, moral beings. Both believed that only in the present era had men reached a point at which they could live without the state and the other agencies of repression ('the State is an evil, but a historically necessary evil, as necessary in the past as its complete extinction will sooner or later be, as necessary as primitive bestiality and men's theological ramblings have been', Bakunin wrote).[27] And finally both held that a necessary though not sufficient condition of revolutionary change was the diffusion of ideas of justice that condemned existing social relationships.

The very looseness of this interpretation of history saved the two anarchists from the deterministic implications that have sometimes flowed from both idealist and materialist philosophies of history. But it exposes them to another challenge: why believe that any revolution which might presently occur will take you to the destination that you favour? Even if each revolution is progressive, in the sense that it lifts society on to a higher moral plateau, what reason is there to think that the next occurrence will result in anarchy? Proudhon, who took a sombre view of revolution, admitted that the future could not be charted with any clarity; revolution was unavoidable, but he could not say how many episodes might be needed to take us beyond the reach of government. His hope was that the revolutionary process might be conducted in as bloodless a way as possible.[28] Bakunin, on the other hand, was temperamentally attracted to revolution. He saw it as a moment when the human spirit was freed from the deadening routine of everyday life, and in that sense as a therapeutic experience. But he, also, was unclear about how and when the stateless society would arrive. Both men placed their faith in the legacy of the French Revolution. Seeing anarchism as the logical consequence of ideas which first took hold of the masses at that time, they believed that the revolutionary process would not stop short of the full realization of these ideas.[29]

For a more systematic account of human nature and historical development, we must turn to the evolutionary theories which were espoused by a number of late nineteenth-century anarchists, in particular by Kropotkin and Elisée Reclus. Both of these men had been trained in the natural sciences (by coincidence both were professional geographers), and they tried to link anarchism to the new scientific outlook of their period.[30] In particular this meant coming to terms with Darwin and Darwinism. Against the view that Darwin's idea of evolution through a competitive struggle for survival provided a justification for the capitalist system, they argued that evolutionary theory properly understood pointed us towards anarchy. To reach this conclusion they needed to offer an alternative account of human nature and the history of the species to that found in the writings of the social Darwinists.[31]

The key notions for both anarchists were those of solidarity and mutual aid. Men, it was claimed, were naturally sociable and co-operative, and were capable of identifying their interests with those of their fellows. From this instinctual source sprang moral ideas and, more concretely, a variety of practices aimed at satisfying the needs of each participant, and maintained by voluntary means, which they termed practices of mutual aid. Mutual aid was the means whereby the species coped with a hostile natural environment, and as such was the major factor in human evolution. In place of the social Darwinist idea of a struggle between individuals leading to the survival of the fittest, the anarchists offered the view that the unit of competition was the species as a whole, and that those species which had achieved the greatest degree of co-operation between their members were most likely to prosper. As Reclus put it:

> But whether it is a question of small or large groups of the human species, it is always through solidarity, through the association of spontaneous, co-ordinated forces that all progress is made . . . The historian, the judge who evokes the centuries and who makes them march before us in an infinite procession, shows us how the law of the blind and brutal struggle for existence, so extolled by the adorers of success, is subordinated to a second law, that of the grouping of weak individualities into organisms more and more developed, learning to defend themselves against the enemy forces, to recognize the resources of their environment, even to create new ones. We know that, if our descendants are to reach their high destiny of science and liberty, they will owe it to their coming together more and more intimately, to the incessant collaboration, to this mutual aid from which brotherhood grows little by little.[32]

Yet if human evolution obeyed this law, ought not the history of the species to reveal a steady march towards 'science and liberty'? Kropotkin and Reclus were aware that it did not, and so they were obliged to admit a second human instinct alongside the instinct of solidarity, an instinct of self-assertion which could take the form of a will to dominate and exploit one's fellows. This will expressed itself in authoritarian institutions which won popular support by taking over and perverting practices of mutual aid. Thus Kropotkin argued that legal systems were formed by incorporating customary rules which served to hold society together alongside other rules whose only function was to protect the material interests of the ruling minority.[33] The pattern of history, therefore, ran somewhat as follows. In any social group, institutions of mutual aid would naturally develop to ensure the group's survival. At some point an assertive minority would succeed in moulding these institutions to its own purposes and create a regime of authority. This in turn would eventually provoke a reaction among the dispossessed majority. In the ensuing upheaval, some would attempt to destroy authority and recreate genuine practices of mutual aid, whereas others would try to use the occasion to establish themselves in power.[34] Evolution, therefore, was not a matter of steady progress. Kropotkin, for instance, saw the replacement of the medieval commune by the modern state as a retrograde step – though on this issue Reclus took a different view. Yet underneath the vicissitudes of history a stream ran constantly towards mutual aid; wherever authoritarian institutions left a space, institutions of this kind would appear spontaneously and flourish. Even under capitalism, a system which fostered the most selfish aspects of human nature, many striking examples of mutual aid could be observed.[35]

In what sense does this amount to a theory of historical progress? Both anarchists appear to waver between the essentially ahistorical view that there is a constant struggle between the libertarian and authoritarian tendencies in human life, of which the present conflict between the ruling class and the masses is merely one instance, and the more progressive view that there is an underlying advance towards more sophisticated and extensive forms of mutual aid. What do they say in favour of the latter view, which is clearly that needed to support a belief in the eventual triumph of anarchy? Both subscribed to a belief in moral progress: the primitive instinct of solidarity had expressed itself in moral ideas which became steadily more refined and comprehensive over time (Kropotkin wrote a history of ethics to bear this out). In addition, Kropotkin argued that technological changes had made people increasingly dependent upon each other – for instance modern methods of production required an advanced division of labour – so individualist ideas were becoming steadily less plausible, and communist ideas steadily more so.[36] Writing in this 'progressive' vein, he argued that,

> the two most prominent, though often unconscious, tendencies throughout our history have been: first, a tendency towards integrating labour for the production of all riches in common, so as finally to render it impossible to discriminate the part of the common production due to the separate individual; and second, a tendency towards the fullest freedom of the individual in the prosecution of all aims, beneficial both for himself and for society at large. The ideal of the anarchist is thus a mere summing-up of what he considers to be the next phase of evolution.[37]

Such a view of history had a somewhat ambivalent effect on these anarchists' understanding of revolution. On the one hand, it was a source of optimism. Revolution was not a breach of evolutionary laws, but their natural expression. Reclus wrote a pamphlet explaining that revolutions were merely the abrupt phases of long-term evolutionary changes in ideas and patterns of life.[38] Moreover the fact that evolution was an historical law meant that the present stage of bourgeois domination was certain to end sooner or later. Finally, the human instinct of solidarity and its natural expression in mutual aid meant that there was nothing to fear from the process of revolution itself: where the state abdicated its power, new institutions would spontaneously emerge to fill the vacuum. On the other hand, this same optimism could turn into fatalism. If evolutionary laws meant that bourgeois society would inevitably be swept away to be replaced by a higher form of social organization, what place was left for active intervention by anarchists? This is precisely the revolutionary's dilemma that we identified above.[39] During the time when they were most actively involved in the anarchist movement – in the Jura Federation in the late 1870s – Reclus and Kropotkin escaped from it by maintaining, first, that revolutionary change could not occur unless the masses were consciously pursuing the new social ideal and, second, that such a consciousness could be stirred up in a relatively short time by anarchist practice (we shall examine the forms of practice they advocated in subsequent chapters). But later on both took a more pessimistic view of the revolutionary potential of the proletariat, and slipped slowly into a kind of fatalistic gradualism, according to which the revolution must indeed inevitably come, but it was no use trying to make it happen before the masses had reached a sufficient level of enlightenment.[40]

The danger of such a slide into fatalism has made other anarchists wary of embracing such evolutionary theories of history. Malatesta, who was a life-long activist, criticized Kropotkin both for his attempt to ground anarchism in natural science and for his view that ordinary people were 'naturally' moral. The first, he claimed, led to fatalism, which in turn encouraged anarchists to withdraw from active struggle; the second led to excessive optimism, which prevented them from thinking realistically about the problems of revolution and its aftermath.[41] Malatesta therefore stressed the co-existence throughout history of both solidaristic and exploitative instincts in man, without suggesting that evolutionary laws favoured the former.[42] A similar view has been expressed more recently by Nicolas Walter, who argues that the anarchist view of history is not linear but dualistic: 'the principles of authority and liberty, of government and rebellion, of state and society, are in perpetual opposition. This tension is never resolved; the movement of mankind is now in one direction, now in another.'[43]

If we now try to make a general survey of anarchist beliefs about human nature, historical progress, and revolution, I believe that Malatesta's and Walter's views will turn out to be more representative than Kropotkin's or Reclus's. Although it is superficially attractive to encase anarchism in an evolutionary theory, the cocoon quickly becomes an embarrassment. History visibly fails to display an evolutionary pattern of the appropriate sort, and the implications for revolutionary practice are disheartening. Anarchists are better served by a view of the following kind: first, that throughout history we can observe contradictory tendencies in human society, with authoritarian and libertarian patterns of organization predominating in different periods; second, that the present period, whether for spiritual or material reasons or a combination of both, offers a unique opportunity for the libertarian tendencies to triumph; and third, that the condition of such a victory is a mass revolution guided by a social ideal, and inspired by anarchist propaganda.

Such a view is not a theory of history, although historical evidence may be used to support it. I have commented at various points in this chapter on the flimsiness of anarchist accounts of history, and now we are able to see that this flimsiness is not really a weakness. Anarchism is not, in its essence, an historical ideology. It is a moral protest against existing economic and political institutions, and it relies upon moral indignation to initiate revolutionary change. The value of historical researches such as those of Kropotkin and Reclus, from an anarchist point of view, is not that they reveal a pattern of history with anarchy as its outcome, but that they bring to light modes of social life which show that the present mode is not eternal. In particular they reveal people's capacity for co-operative living (other researches might reveal less appealing capacities).

What does this imply for the anarchist perspective on revolution? We have seen that anarchists can broadly be divided into two camps. First, there are those who see the arrival of anarchy as the consequence of popular mental enlightenment, and who consequently eschew revolution in the narrow sense in favour of education and the gradual dissemination of truth. About them there is little more to be said in this part of the book, since they have not participated in the revolutionary activities whose rationale I shall attempt to discuss. Second, there are those who believe that anarchy can only be created by a mass revolution, in which the subterranean instincts of the proletariat coalesce with explicit ideas propagated by anarchists. Proudhon, Bakunin, Kropotkin, Reclus, Malatesta, Walter and many others share this general understanding, despite differences of detail. For all these anarchists, although there may be characteristics of modern society which explain why it is especially ripe for anarchy, there are no rigid laws which dictate when the transformation will occur. There is nothing in anarchism which corresponds, for example, to the 'iron laws of capitalist development' which some Marxists have claimed to discern, as we shall see in the following chapter. Revolution, for the anarchists, is fundamentally a matter of instinct, will, and moral ideals, and anarchist activity is to play a vital part in bringing it about.

A final word must be said here about anarchist views of human nature. I hope that the evidence presented in this chapter has dispelled two common errors: one, that all anarchists hold the same beliefs about human nature; the other, that these beliefs are excessively optimistic, in the sense that they present human beings in far too favourable a light. We have seen that anarchists can be as unflattering as anyone else about the motives and characteristics that men actually display – indeed a riposte they frequently make to defenders of the state is that no one is good enough to be trusted with the reins of power. There is, however, a different question that may be asked of anarchists: namely, what capacities must people have if an anarchic social order is to be feasible? I have not tried to answer this other and more contentious question.

6 Anarchism and Marxism

Having investigated the basic assumptions lying behind the anarchist approach to revolutionary practice, we are now in a position to compare anarchism with the other major tradition of revolutionary thought in the West, Marxism. The point of doing so is not merely to discover some interesting contrasts. Anarchist revolutionary ideas cannot be properly understood unless we see that they took shape in direct opposition to the principles propagated by Marx, Engels and their followers. As noted earlier, anarchism and Marxism as revolutionary *movements* both sprang from the same source, the cleavage in the First International from the mid-1860s until its collapse in 1872. Before that time working-class movements in the various European countries had been, to a greater or lesser degree, socialist in orientation, but their socialism was of a diffuse kind. The debates in the International, which centred on the issue of whether economic or political means should be used to bring about the emancipation of the working class, created two distinct positions, which thereafter led independent (although often intertwined) lives. The Marxist movement was generally the stronger (although not always in the Latin countries), and eventually had a successful revolution to its credit, but the anarchist movement continued to play the role of a disreputable younger brother, always prepared to ask awkward questions at the wrong moment.

The relationship between these two ideologies is indeed a curious one.[1] In their general perspective they had a great deal in common. Both were severely critical of the capitalist economy, of bourgeois society, and of the liberal (and later the liberal-democratic) state. In these areas anarchists and Marxists were willing and able to borrow from one another, anarchists absorbing the Marxian critique of capitalism, and Marxists the anarchist exposure of liberal politics. Both had similar visions of the society that they wanted to create – a society of liberty and equality, with social ownership of the means of production, and no political apparatus. Finally both looked to the working-class movement as the agency which would bring these visions to fruition, and each tried to win the movement to its way of thinking.

The revolutionary heritage of the nineteenth century, beginning with the first Revolution in France, and continuing through to the Paris Commune and beyond, was held in common.

Yet despite these close resemblances, anarchism and Marxism came to diverge in important respects, and eventually appealed to different constituencies. It would be quite wrong to suppose that the disagreement over revolutionary methods referred to above was all that divided them. This disagreement was an inevitable outcome of differences at a more fundamental level. In exploring these differences I shall try to look at the anarchist view of Marxism and the Marxist view of anarchism in as even-handed a way as possible – which is not how the subject is usually treated.[2]

The most fundamental difference concerns the materialist conception of history, often regarded by Marxists as the crowning glory of their system, but looked on with less favour by anarchists. We saw in the last chapter that anarchists have tended to eschew rigorous theories of history, and in so far as they have appealed to loose philosophies of history to support their views of human nature and revolution, these have predominantly idealist in character. Thus anarchists have raised two major objections to historical materialism. One is that the notion of a series of historical stages through which every society passes – the position that Marx advances in his Preface to the *Critique of Political Economy*, for example[3] – is too inflexible, and by implication too deterministic about the revolutionary possibilities presented by different societies. This was linked – by both Bakunin and Kropotkin, for example – to the 'metaphysical' character of Marx's dialectical method. No empirical study of history would, they argued, reveal such a fixed pattern; instead we would find that, measured in terms of our ideals of liberty and justice, societies took large backward as well as forward steps; and moreover that societies at a similar level of economic development were far from equally ready to realize these ideals.[4] The second objection to historical materialism is that it underestimates the role of ideas in historical change, and thus the importance of a 'revolutionary spirit' to any future revolution. This in turn encourages a quiescent attitude, a posture of sitting and waiting for the laws of history to create the revolution by themselves – a posture which was anathema to the anarchists, with their activist outlook.

This attack on historical materialism has been linked to another, more directly political, attack on Marxism by several anarchists. It is claimed that the Marxian aspiration to create a 'scientific' form of socialism – which finds its culmination in historical materialism – leads inevitably to elitism. Once scientific truth has been discovered, it becomes the preserve of the few, who then try to impart it to the masses, and are intolerant of any criticism. One can find this line of attack foreshadowed in a letter written by Proudhon to Marx, on one of the few occasions when the French anarchist addressed himself explicitly to Marxian ideas:

> By all means let us work together to discover the laws of society, the ways in which these laws are realized and the process by which we are able to discover them. But, for God's sake, when we have demolished all *a priori* dogmas, do not let us think of indoctrinating the people in our turn. . . . Let us not set ourselves up as the apostles of a new religion, even if it be the religion of logic or of reason. Let us welcome and encourage all protests, let us get rid of all exclusiveness and all mysticism.[5]

Bakunin took up the theme when protesting against what he saw as Marx's attempts to foist an official ideology on to the First International:

> As soon as an *official truth* is pronounced – having been scientifically discovered by this great brainy head labouring all alone – a truth proclaimed and imposed on the whole world from the summit of the Marxist Sinai, why discuss anything?[6]

Bakunin was not, however, particularly clear about the role which social science *should* play in the revolutionary movement, claiming both that it was indispensable to the proletariat and that it was one-sided because it could only deal with generalizations and not with 'real' individuals.[7] A better argument was offered by Kropotkin when he pointed out that authentic scientific laws were always conditional in nature – they took the form 'If A occurs, then B will follow' – so that it was impossible to show scientifically that any particular event must happen. Rather than revealing the laws of history, therefore, science could only teach us how best to achieve whatever ends we had chosen to pursue.[8] From this it followed that the social scientist had no claim to direct the revolutionary movement, but could only serve as its handmaiden.

Such scepticism about 'scientific socialism' later found a particularly warm response among anarchists in Russia, where the arguments of Bakunin and Kropotkin coalesced with a mistrust of intellectuals that was indigenous to the political culture of that country. In particular Jan Waclaw Machajski developed the view that Marxism was the ideology of the new professional intelligentsia who were trying to establish themselves as a ruling class in place of the capitalists. According to Machajski the idea that the revolution must wait until the economic contradictions of capitalism had matured served the interests of this class, who would then, by virtue of their technical expertise and monopoly of knowledge, be strong enough to assume control.[9] Although the Bolsheviks were later to show no such respect for the laws of history, this did nothing to allay the fears of the anarchists, as we shall see shortly.

The Marxist response to these attacks on historical materialism and its political uses ran as follows. First, the anarchists were consistently accused of being idealists in a derogatory sense. Their vision of a society of liberty and justice, Marx and his followers argued, was held up as an eternal verity, with no understanding of the historical conditions which had produced it, or of those which might make it feasible. This accusation ran throughout Marx's lengthy critique of Proudhon in *The Poverty of Philosophy* and was repeated in his more fragmentary attacks on Bakunin.[10] It has since become Marxist–Leninist orthodoxy.[11]

Second, to the charge that their theory of history was too rigidly patterned, the Marxists replied that the anarchists were blind to the differences between the various economic modes of production found in the history of human society, and therefore divorced the socialist revolution from the economic development of capitalist society. From this ahistorical perspective, revolution became entirely a matter of voluntary initiative, without economic preconditions. Marx's comments on Bakunin are typical:

> Since all the economic forms, developed or undeveloped, that have existed till now included the enslavement of the worker (whether in the shape of the wage-worker or the peasant, etc.) he presumes that a *radical revolution* is equally possible in all of them. What is more, he wants the European social revolution, which is based on the economic foundation of capitalist production, to be carried out on the level of the Russian or Slav agricultural or pastoral nations, and not to overstep this level . . . The basis of Bakunin's social revolution is the *will*, and not the economic conditions.[12]

Finally, the Marxists responded to the anarchist critique of 'scientific socialism' by arguing that the anarchists were offering nothing more than a 'cult of ignorance', that they were trying to whip up the emotions of the working class with ultra-revolutionary phrases and fantastic visions of the utopia ahead, with no real understanding of how such a transformation might come about. This response has been crystallized in orthodox Marxism–Leninism:

> Marx and Engels countered the declarative and speculative anarchist propositions and their dogmatism and idealism with a concrete analysis of reality and the experience of the working-class movement . . . and showed the dialectical laws of the mass revolutionary struggle. They countered the revolutionary rhetoric with a scientific solution of the fundamental problems in the revolutionary transformation of the world.[13]

It can be seen that the differences between anarchism and Marxism are real enough – but that neither side can avoid caricaturing the views of the other. We shall find ample confirmation of this proposition as we examine some more specific contrasts between the two ideologies.

The second such contrast concerns the relationship between the economy and the state. From an anarchist perspective, Marxists are guilty of a form of reductionism which portrays the state as nothing more than a tool in the hands of the economically dominant class. They fail to see that political systems have their own dynamics which allow them to escape from the control of any economic class, however powerful. Above all, Marxists are blind to the fact that states have certain properties *just because they are states*. States enshrine a hierarchical mode of organization, they use repressive measures to control their subjects, and they engage in aggressive acts against other states, for instance. All of this, of course, bears very directly on the Marxist advocacy of a 'proletarian dictatorship' as the means of overthrowing capitalism. As we shall see shortly, this became one of the major tactical differences between the two movements. But it is important to observe that the anarchist challenge to this proposal flowed directly from a general critique of the Marxist theory of the state. In their belief that a proletarian state would not be objectionable because the workers would now be the ruling class, the Marxists overlooked the fact that what they were proposing was precisely the creation of a *state*.

These ideas were first expressed by Bakunin in the course of his confrontation with Marx. Marx, he argued, 'holds that the political condition of each country is always the product and the faithful expression of its economic situation; to change the former it is necessary only to transform the latter. . . . He takes no account of other factors in history, such as the ever-present reaction of political, juridical and religious institutions on the economic situation.'[14] Marx believed that the economic development of Europe had been accompanied by a strengthening and enlargement of the state, so he willingly envisaged that the workers' state would exercise still greater powers (this ascription was accompanied by some unflattering comparisons between Marx and Bismarck). But he failed to see what this implied: foreign conquest, state education and censorship, a police force, minority rule, and suppression of the individual.[15] As Bakunin summed up the challenge, '. . . mankind has for too long submitted to being governed . . . the cause of its troubles does not lie in any particular form of government but in the fundamental principles and the very existence of government, whatever form it may take.'[16]

We shall look later at the specific reasons anarchists have given for expecting a proletarian dictatorship to reproduce all of these obnoxious features of the state. Now we must consider the Marxist counterattack on the general issue of the relationship between economy and state. This amounts to the charge that the anarchists have a purely abstract view of the state. They see a certain form of organization appearing in various times and places, and analyse it quite unhistorically and unsociologically. They ignore the fact that its real significance depends on the social forces which use it to promote their interests. Thus rather than a general theory of the state, the Marxists contend, there should be separate theories of the feudal state, the capitalist state, and so forth. It follows that practices such as elections cannot be assessed without reference to their social context – elections under socialism will take on a quite different character, for example.[17]

Connected with this charge of abstraction was the claim that anarchists saw economic relations as entirely a resultant of political relations. Engels put the point with characteristic simplicity: '. . . Bakunin maintains that it is the *state* which has created capital, that the capitalist has his capital *only by the grace of the state*. As, therefore, the state is the chief evil, it is above all the state which must be done away with and then capitalism will go to blazes of itself.'[18]

Neither of these characterizations was accurate, of course. Marx, especially, had quite a subtle view of the relationship between capitalism and the various state-forms that were compatible with it, and the anarchists, far from seeing capitalism as merely the offshoot of the state, were quite undecided about which of these demons was the more potent.[19] The Marxists indeed tended to emphasize the dependence of the state on the economic system, and the anarchists to emphasize the autonomy of the state, but these tendencies were exaggerated to the point of travesty by each camp in its interpretation of the other.

The same can be said about the third matter over which anarchists and Marxists disagreed: the identity of the agents of revolutionary change. Although both aligned themselves with the nascent working-class movement, this common identification concealed an important difference: the anarchists had much the broader notion of the working class. Not seeing the socialist revolution as tied (as the Marxists did) to the development of the capitalist mode of production, they used terms like 'proletariat' to refer indiscriminately to factory workers, artisans, peasants, down-and-outs and so forth – anyone not included in the ruling stratum of capitalists and state functionaries. (Some anarchists, such as Emma Goldman, also recognized the existence of a 'middle class' between these two blocs.) The Marxists, by contrast, distinguished rigorously between the proletariat proper, the peasantry, the petty bourgeoisie and the lumpenproletariat, and assigned the leading role in the revolution firmly to the proletariat – i.e. to the urbanized factory workers.

The anarchists objected to this on two counts. First, they were doubtful whether the factory workers really had the highest revolutionary potential. They pointed to the existence of an 'aristocracy of labour' – a comparatively well-off stratum of skilled manual workers – which was particularly evident in countries such as England and Germany, the countries which the Marxists regarded as most ripe for revolution. 'By virtue of its relative well-being and semibourgeois position, this upper layer of workers is unfortunately only too deeply saturated with all the political and social prejudices and all the narrow aspirations and pretensions of the bourgeoisie,' Bakunin wrote.[20] Instead the anarchists looked to 'that great mass, those millions of the uncultivated, the disinherited, the miserable, the illiterates' – in other words to landless peasants, to impoverished artisans, to the unemployed and down-and-outs in the cities – to lead the revolution, carrying the 'respectable' working class in its wake. This followed from the anarchist belief that revolutions were born of poverty and elemental passions; the urban working class, in their view, were too well-cushioned materially and too well-drilled intellectually to make good revolutionary material.

The second objection to the Marxist faith in the proletariat was that, even if the urban working class were able to carry through a revolution, they might do so at the expense of the peasants and the other dispossessed classes. Bakunin raised the spectre of the proletariat becoming the 'fourth governing class', immediately going on to explain, however, that real power would quickly pass into the hands of a small elite ruling in the name of the proletariat.[21]

Not all anarchists went as far as Bakunin in his mistrust of the urban workers and his faith in 'the great rabble of the people'; on the other hand, none went as far as Marx in deifying the organized factory worker. Men like Kropotkin and Malatesta, born in countries with predominantly peasant populations, tended always to think of rural uprisings when looking for models of the future revolution. Those anarchists who became syndicalists could not of course deny the revolutionary potential of the urban working class, but even here – in the case of Goldman and Berkman, for example – we can find suspicions of the aristocracy of labour[22] and pleas for the integration of urban and rural workers.[23] A recent critique of Marxism by the American anarchist Murray Bookchin goes right back to Bakunin in its insistence that the anarchist revolution must be a mass revolution cutting across conventional class lines. In Bookchin's view, the traditional class conflict between capitalist and worker merely serves to stabilize capitalism by improving the worker's material circumstances, and the worker's mode of life makes him conformist rather than revolutionary. 'The worker begins to become a revolutionary when he undoes his "workerness", when he comes to detest his class status here and now, when he begins to shed exactly those features which the Marxists most prize in him – his work ethic, his character-structure derived from industrial discipline, his respect for hierarchy, his obedience to leaders, his consumerism, his vestiges of puritanism.'[24] According to Bookchin, revolutionaries are those who have broken with the dominant culture and begun to live subversive life-styles – no matter from what economic class they are drawn.

To this charge that they are infected by 'workeritis', Marxists have responded by accepting their identification with the urban working class and then challenging the revolutionary credentials of the classes to whom the anarchists look instead. The Marxist contention – which applies equally to the petty-bourgeoisie, the peasantry and the lumpenproletariat – is that these classes are subject to abrupt shifts of political consciousness, at one moment holding ultra-revolutionary attitudes, at the next reactionary views. (Anarchism is said to correspond to the ultra-revolutionary phase of consciousness.) Both the petty-bourgeoisie and the peasantry are, from a Marxist perspective, doomed to be swept away by the historical development of capitalist society: the artisan or the shopkeeper will be driven into the ranks of the proletariat proper as small property is absorbed by large capitalist property, while the small-holding or tenant farmer will be converted into a rural wage-labourer. Faced thus with extinction, members of both classes will seek to arrest the course of history – either by searching for some radical utopia in which (for instance) everyone is a small property-owner or a landed peasant, or by attempting to retreat to a golden age before the onset of capitalism. This second, reactionary, phase of consciousness was illustrated, in Marx's view, by the French peasants' support for Louis Bonaparte – 'historical tradition gave rise to the belief of the French peasants in the miracle that a man named Napoleon would bring all the glory back to them'.[25] As for the lumpenproletariat – a class delightfully itemized by Marx as consisting of 'vagabonds, discharged soldiers, discharged jailbirds, escaped galley-slaves, swindlers, mountebanks, *lazzaroni*, pickpockets, tricksters, gamblers, *maquereaus*, brothel-keepers, porters, *literati*, organ-grinders, rag-pickers, knife-grinders, tinkers, beggars . . .'[26] – they were politically unreliable. They might take to the streets in a riot against the government, but they might equally be conscripted by the authorities, to serve as *agents-provocateurs* or as police spies. Thus the same Bonaparte was able to form these elements into the Society of December 10 as a kind of private army.[27]

In contrast to these groups, the Marxists regarded the factory workers as having interests in line with the historical transition from capitalism to socialism. Their conditions of work made them interdependent, thus preparing them for the fully socialized production of the future, while their economic struggle with their employers gave them an immediate interest in expropriating private capital. While peasants and petty-bourgeois might play an auxiliary role in the revolution, therefore, they must do so under the tutelage of the urban proletariat.[28]

In retrospect, it is difficult not to concede that both anarchists and Marxists had a point. The Marxists were right in thinking that, of all social groups, the urban workers would be most consistently attracted to socialist ideas and programmes. The anarchists, however, were right to suspect that more often than not this would amount to a reformist and statist version of socialism. They were right, too, in believing that if revolutions was going to occur, they would do so among the peasantry, the artisans, and the 'immature' urban working class, which had not yet been drilled into the routines of industrial life. The Marxists, though, were right to doubt whether revolutions under those circumstances could really lead to a viable form of socialism – even if many of them were later willing to set aside this doubt, in Russia and elsewhere.

The fourth contrast between anarchists and Marxists concerns the appropriate means for bringing about the revolutionary transformation of society. The Marxists advocated the use of political methods, involving the formation of a socialist party which would take power, either legally or illegally, and then proceed to use the machinery of the state to socialize the system of production. The anarchists preached abstention from any form of politics, and insisted that the revolution should involve the immediate seizure of the means of production by the workers and peasants, with no 'transition period' and no 'workers' state' to follow. Their division on this issue, which polarized the two camps in the First International and afterwards, flowed inevitably from the differences we have already traced.

In the case of the anarchist critique of Marxist revolutionary methods, I shall look first at their general reasons for thinking that political means could not be used to create egalitarian socialism. I shall then turn to their more specific attacks on the two paths which Marxists have chosen to follow in different times and places: the parliamentary path, requiring an electoral victory by socialist party candidates and then the use of existing state machinery to introduce socialism; and the revolutionary path, involving the destruction of the existing state and the creation of a new regime – the dictatorship of the proletariat – to bring about the transition to socialism. The first path is best illustrated by the case of Germany, where the Social Democratic Party, broadly Marxist in orientation from its foundation in 1869, set its sights on winning a majority in the Reichstag. The second is epitomized by the career of the Bolshevik party in Russia, established after the break with the less radical Mensheviks in 1903, culminating in the October Revolution and the Soviet regime that followed. Anarchists have had a good deal to say about both examples.

Two general considerations lead anarchists to dismiss the political road to socialism. First, if revolutionaries attempt to use the state – whether the pre-existing state or a replacement – to achieve their ends, they unavoidably reproduce all the features of that institution. Every state is an agency whereby a ruling minority exploits and oppresses a majority. Even if the new rulers are drawn from the ranks of the previously oppressed majority, and even if they are made formally responsible to that majority by democratic elections, they will escape from effective control and form themselves into a new privileged class. They will then use the immense powers of the state to protect their own newly acquired interests, not the general interests of society. The cause of this degeneration does not lie in the innate maleficence of men, but in the corrupting effects of power. As Bakunin once wrote:

> Nothing is as dangerous for man's personal morality as the habit of commanding. The best of men, the most intelligent, unselfish, generous, and pure, will always and inevitably be corrupted in this pursuit. Two feelings inherent in the exercise of power never fail to produce this demoralization: *contempt for the masses, and, for the man in power, an exaggerated sense of his own worth.*[29]

Consequently,

> . . . if there should be established tomorrow a government or a legislative council, a Parliament made up exclusively of workers, those very workers who are now staunch democrats and Socialists, will become determined aristocrats, bold or timid worshippers of the principle of authority, and will also become oppressors and exploiters.[30]

The second reason has to do with the nature of the constructive task facing a socialist government. The anarchists, as we know, had a definite vision of the society that a socialist revolution should produce – it must be communist and decentralist, with decision-making in the hands of producer groups and local communes, and so forth. In itself this vision did not differ materially from the 'higher stage of communism' envisaged by Marx as the final goal of the proletarian revolution. But the anarchists categorically denied that statist methods could take humanity to this goal. The state was constrained by its own nature to behave in certain ways. Its principle of organization was hierarchy, and its mode of action was legislation. Thus a socialist state would attempt to incorporate all local groupings into a single, centralized authority structure, and it would attempt to lay down uniform regulations for every district and region. In doing so it would stifle the initiative of the masses and their immediate organs of self-government – factory committees, local communes, etc. This would not only be disastrous from a revolutionary point of view, but also hopelessly inefficient. The central authorities could have no real understanding of the specific needs of each locality. The people best able to carry out the constructive tasks of the revolution – the people on the spot, with direct knowledge of the problems and the resources available to solve them – would be stymied by the bureaucratic machinery of the state.

These ideas were expressed by many anarchist critics of state socialism – by Bakunin, Malatesta and Berkman, for example.[31] But it was perhaps Kropotkin, with his profound sense of the 'organic' quality of the social life which the revolution must release from the grip of the state, who expressed them most forcefully. As he wrote in 1880, 'to allow any government to be established, a strong and recognized power, is to paralyse the work of the revolution at once'. For:

> The economic change which will result from the social revolution will be so immense and so profound, it must so change all the relations based today on property and exchange, that it is impossible for one or any individual to elaborate the different social forms which must spring up in the society of the future. This elaboration of new social forms can only be made by the collective work of the masses. To satisfy the immense variety of conditions and needs which will spring up as soon as private property shall be abolished, it is necessary to have the collective suppleness of mind of the whole people. Any authority external to it will only be an obstacle, and beside that a source of discord and hatred.[32]

This prediction was amply borne out, in Kropotkin's eyes, by his later experience of the Bolshevik regime in Russia.[33] We shall return to this shortly.

Anarchists, then, have levelled two general charges against the use of statist means for achieving socialism: those who find themselves in positions of authority are inevitably transformed into a new ruling class, and in any case statist methods are antipathetic to the constructive tasks of the revolution. To these they have added more specific critiques of the parliamentary road to socialism, and its alternative, revolutionary dictatorship.

From an anarchist point of view, the story of parliamentary socialism is always one of a gradual slide into collaboration with the bourgeoisie. The very act of setting up a party to contest elections signals a willingness to play the game of parliamentary politics, and attracts ambitious members of the bourgeoisie into the party. Thus Bakunin thought that the German S.P.D., from its inception, stood for a compromise between socialism and bourgeois democracy, and implicitly for class collaboration.[34] Once the party is formed, it has to engage in electoral politics. This means that it has to adjust its platform to reflect the current views of its working-class supporters, views which bear the imprint of the dominant capitalist ideology. 'The proletariat', Bakunin wrote, 'wants one thing, but clever people, profiting by its ignorance, make it do quite another thing . . .'[35] The socialist party, as a result, has to jettison its most radical demands and present a more moderate face to the electorate.[36] It also becomes involved in what Kropotkin called 'the sad comedy of elections' – false promises, bribery, patronage and so forth – activities which debase its own candidates.[37]

Even if a few sincere socialists are elected to parliament, however, they are still liable to be co-opted by the ruling class. They are likely to find themselves in a small minority in a body whose main purpose is to conduct the day-to-day business of the bourgeoisie. What should they do? If they stand up and deliver revolutionary speeches, they will quickly become objects of derision, and anyway these speeches will achieve nothing. So they become involved in the practical details of legislation. The socialist, Berkman argued, 'comes to feel that he must find some way to take a serious part in the work, express sound opinions in the discussions and become a real factor in the proceedings'.[38] But he then finds himself in the impossible position of having to legislate on thousands of matters of which he has no direct knowledge, so he is forced to rely on the guidance of his leaders. Against his will, he is turned into a party hack.[39]

The development of the S.P.D. (Social Democratic Party) in Germany appeared to the anarchists to confirm this prognostication fully. Johann Most and several others who had criticized the party for its parliamentarianism were expelled in 1880 and joined the anarchist movement. The party's later role in supporting the First World War and suppressing the German revolution of 1918–19 came as no surprise to them.[40]

None of these strictures, however, appear to apply to those revolutionary Marxists who advocated smashing the existing state machinery and replacing it with a new apparatus manned entirely by proletarians – the view of Lenin, for instance, in *The State and Revolution*. Some anarchists did, indeed, believe that Lenin and the Bolsheviks had moved close to an anarchist position by the summer of

1917, their official Marxism notwithstanding. But events later in that year and in the year following quickly disabused them of that belief.

The general terms of the anarchist critique of Bolshevism had been set beforehand by Bakunin, when he spoke of a new class of scientific intellectuals ruling in the name of the proletariat, and by Kropotkin, when he contrasted the spontaneous creativity of the masses with the dead hand of party dictatorship.[41] The anarchists believed, indeed, that the real revolution in Russia took place not because of the Bolsheviks but in spite of them, and not in October 1917, when the Bolsheviks seized power, but in the months before, when the masses destroyed the Provisional Government by retreating from the war, by taking over the land, and by controlling the factories. The people proceeded to create their own organs of revolutionary self-government – the factory committees, the peasant communes, the co-operatives, serving as links between town and country, and the soviets.[42] The Bolsheviks paid lip-service to these organs, the anarchists claimed, and in this way managed to win a good deal of popular support. When strong enough to do so, they carried through their insurrection. The effect of this was not to advance the revolution but merely to formalize what had already been done. Immediately, however, the Bolsheviks began to bring the popular organs under their control in order to secure their rule. As Goldman later saw it, 'all the succeeding acts of the Bolsheviki, all their following policies, changes of policies, their compromises and retreats, their methods of suppression and persecution, their terrorism and extermination of all other political views – all were but the *means to an end*, the retaining of the State power in the hands of the Communist Party'.[43] As a result the popular institutions began to wither and die, as Bolshevik agents forced them into line with centrally decided policy.[44] Kropotkin, although for a long time silent about the defects of the regime, eventually wrote to Lenin that '*what is needed is local construction by local forces* . . . The influx and bossism of party men, predominantly fledgeling Communists . . . have already destroyed the influence and creative strength of these much-vaunted institutions, the soviets.'[45]

Other anarchists had joined the attack sooner. As early as December 1917 Maximov described the Bolsheviks as 'a force of stagnation' and called for a 'third revolution' to destroy the new organs of power which the soviets had become.[46] In September of the following year he labelled the new regime 'State capitalist' – a term of little theoretical value, but clear emotive force: 'The people are being transformed into servants over whom there has risen a new class of

...inistrators – a new class born mainly from the womb of the ...called intelligentsia. Isn't this merely a new class system looming ... the revolutionary horizon?'[47] Both the long-standing fears of the anarchists had materialized: the popular revolution had been subverted by the centralized party, and the party itself had turned into a ruling class. Whether the Bolsheviks were interested merely in acquiring power, or whether they genuinely wished to promote their ideals, was irrelevant. Once they had come to identify the safety of the revolution with their own tenure of power, the revolution was lost.

Even so, under the circumstances of civil war and foreign intervention which followed the Revolution, some anarchists were willing to offer qualified practical support to the Bolsheviks. This continued until the Bolsheviks suppressed virtually the entire anarchist movement in 1921.[48]

This concludes my discussion of the anarchist critique of Marxist revolutionary strategy. Let me now, very briefly, consider the Marxist attitude to anarchist revolutionary methods (here, as elsewhere, I omit from consideration what either camp might say in self-defence when challenged by the other). This was far from complimentary: 'a pageant of futility and decadence' as one of them put it. Marxists argue that anarchists have no real understanding of the nature of revolution, and merely offer high-sounding phrases with no practical value. Their talk about 'abolishing authority' ignores the fact that revolutions are contests of force. As Engels put the point, 'a revolution is certainly the most authoritarian thing there is; it is the act whereby one part of the population imposes its will upon the other part by means of rifles, bayonets and cannon – authoritarian means, if such there be at all; and if the victorious party does not want to have fought in vain, it must maintain this rule by means of the terror which its arms inspire in the reactionaries'.[49] In this vein Marx and Engels mocked the ineffectiveness of Bakunin's attempt to decree the abolition of the state during an uprising in Lyons and his later participation in an abortive insurrection in Bologna.[50] But Marxists have also detected a different element in anarchist strategy, one that relies on acts of terror and appeals to social outcasts and criminals. Marx and Engels seized upon Bakunin's association with Nechaev to claim that the inner secret of anarchism was terrorism. 'There anarchy means universal, pan destruction; the revolution, a series of assassinations, first individual and then *en masse*; the sole rule of action, the Jesuit morality intensified; the revolutionary type, the brigand.'[51] The danger of this was not that the programme might actually be carried out in full, but that isolated incidents would give the bourgeoisie the opportunity to take repressive measures, to the detriment of the socialist movement generally. This view was loudly echoed by Plekhanov in the 1890s;[52] and Lenin, although not accepting Plekhanov's identification of anarchists with brigands, held that 'the anarchists always do help the bourgeoise *in practice*' because of the divisive effect their 'abstract revolutionism' had on the working-class movement.[53] Finally Engels and later Lenin were to observe that anarchist abstention from politics was liable to turn suddenly into collaboration with bourgeois parties, as it had in Andalusia during the insurrection of 1873, for instance.[54] In summary, then, anarchism was an ideology of the radical petty-bourgeoisie, but its political effects were helpful mainly to the bourgeoisie itself.

The single most striking theme that runs through this controversy between anarchists and Marxists over revolutionary strategy is the congruence (or lack of it) between means and ends. Sharing the same ultimate goal, the Marxists advocated reaching it by methods – especially the proletarian dictatorship – whose character is diametrically opposed to that of the goal itself. They did so because of their faith in the working class and its historical destiny. As Marx made clear, a worker remains a worker (with all that that implies) even when serving on a political body.[55] The anarchists were not inclined to idealize the proletariat in this way (believing that their class interests were not necessarily identical with those of the oppressed generally); they had a stronger sense of the imperfections of human nature, especially the recurrence of domineering and exploitative instincts; and they were more conscious of the inner dynamics that governed every political institution, whatever its name or formal structure. They demanded, therefore, that the stateless society must be prefigured in the revolutionary strategy used to attain it: means and ends must be congruent. Of course it was one thing to demand this, and quite another to find a strategy that actually worked, as we shall see in the following chapters.

7 Revolutionary Organization and Strategy

Through their confrontation with, and rejection of, the Marxian idea of political revolution, the anarchists arrived at their own distinctive view of the revolutionary process. We are now in a position to understand its main elements. First of all, the revolution had to be a mass affair, not a matter of a few politicians legislating the new society into existence, nor indeed of any particular class 'leading' the remainder into socialism. Second, the masses must in the course of the revolution acquire moral ideas that would guide them in their constructive task of creating the institutions of the future. Third, existing institutions which embodied the principle of hierarchical authority – the machinery of the state, the judicial system, capitalist property and so forth – must be completely destroyed, not taken over and used, *per impossibile*, for new purposes. Fourth, the new society must not reinstate the authoritarian principle, whether in the form of a 'workers' state', a 'dictatorship of the proletariat' or whatever; free association must be the pattern of organization from the first day of the revolution onward.

This was the anarchist position: I have suggested that its central idea was the congruence of means and ends. But it was still necessary to find a form of organization and a strategy for revolution that was both consistent with these principles and practically effective. Indeed anarchists have often found themselves impaled on this very fork. Either they have stuck rigidly to their principles, and found themselves the helpless spectators of events whose outcome they could not influence; or they have tried to be politically effective, and become involved in a series of compromises with other groups which has meant jettisoning sacred principles such as political abstention. But before we conclude that this dilemma is inescapable, we must examine anarchist revolutionary strategy in greater detail. This chapter looks at the insurrectionary strategy adopted by the mainstream of the anarchist movement. The two that follow it examine specific strategies which anarchists have pursued on occasion, not always with the approval of the movement as a whole: first, the resort to terror, and second, the use of trade unions as a revolutionary weapon.

94

The basic ingredients of the problem are easily described. On the one hand there are the masses, oppressed and exploited, and (in the anarchists' view) instinctively prepared to revolt against their oppressors, but not consciously anarchist in outlook. On the other hand there are a small number of conscious anarchists. How should these anarchists organize themselves, consistently with their principles? And what should their relationship to the masses be? How is it possible to guide them in an anarchist direction without contravening the spontaneity which, according to the anarchists, is vital to the revolution?

Some critics have accused the anarchists of the same elitism for which they have condemned others.[1] In so far as this accusation has any substance, it derives it from the case of Bakunin, who at times both spoke and acted in a way that justified Marx's description of him as 'Jesuitical'. Bakunin had a recurrent weakness for conspiracies and secret societies. During his career as an anarchist he attempted to form a number of the latter, drawing up elaborate constitutions and programmes for organizations which often barely existed outside of his imagination.[2] His intention appears to have been to create an international organization of professional revolutionaries ready to direct the course of a future European revolution. He maintained that a small number of men in each country – perhaps as few as a couple of hundred – would be able to do this directing provided they were well organized and sufficiently dedicated to the cause.[3] Bakunin did not of course believe that such a body could make a revolution by itself, but it could prepare the ground by disseminating socialist ideas, and then, when the moment of action came, exercise moral hegemony (so to speak) over the masses. It should be, he wrote, 'a sort of revolutionary general staff, composed of dedicated, energetic, intelligent individuals . . . capable of serving as intermediaries between the revolutionary idea and the instincts of the people';[4] or again (varying the metaphor), 'we must be the invisible pilots guiding the Revolution, not by any kind of overt power but by the collective dictatorship of all our allies . . .'[5]

The elitism which infects these passages is apparent, though on Bakunin's behalf it should be said that he was opposed to the anarchist vanguard establishing any formal structure of power after the revolution, or even holding public offices of any kind.[6] Later anarchists were to reject Bakunin's ideas about revolutionary organization, while still allowing that minority groups had an important role to play in creating a revolutionary consciousness. Kropotkin, for example, whose faith in the revolutionary potential of the common people was unbounded, still conceded that conscious anarchists were likely to remain in a small minority up to the moment of the revolution. His conviction was that, in the course of social upheavals, minority ideas which corresponded to the hidden aspirations of the masses would always come to the fore.[7] Emma Goldman argued even more forcefully that new ideas and movements were always created by small minorities, and that the masses were at most times a reactionary force, since they were imbued with the conservative ideas of the ruling class.[8] Neither Kropotkin nor Goldman, however, envisaged the conscious minority continuing to play a role *after* the revolution; nor did they believe in organizing it beforehand into a clandestine 'international brotherhood' directed from the centre.

How, then, should it be organized? To these later anarchists it was essential that their organization should embody the principles of the future social order. This meant, in essence, free association and federalism. Local groups of anarchists would form and try to agree upon a common programme of action. If agreement were reached, action could proceed, but if not no one could be ordered to act against his will, or disciplined for failing to obey a majority decision. Groups formed in this way could federate into regional, national and finally international alliances, but once again the federation must be voluntary, and decisions made by congresses at the higher level were not to be mandatory for the federated groups. This might sound like a recipe for disorganization rather than organization, and indeed it effectively prevented the anarchists from forming themselves into anything resembling a conventional party, but we shall see that it had certain strengths as well as weaknesses.

Some anarchists have been positively in favour of organizational fluidity. A French anarchist from the 1880s wrote:

> We do not believe . . . in long-term associations, federations, etc. In our view, a group . . . should only be established at a precise point, for an immediate action; once the action is accomplished, the group reshapes itself along new lines, whether with the same members or with new ones . . .[9]

An obvious merit of this proposal, anarchistically speaking, is that it would prevent any growth of bureaucracy in the movement. A more practical consideration is that it would (and did) make it very difficult for the police to penetrate the movement effectively. A police agent could easily join an anarchist cell, but he would find it very hard to obtain an overview of the movement as a whole. In contrast, when anarchists opted for more durable forms of association, their plans were frequently revealed to the police in time for the latter to take preventative action, as we shall see shortly in the case of the Italian anarchists.

The drawbacks of this disaggregated form of organization can be appreciated by looking at the attempt to create a 'libertarian' International after the effective collapse of the First International in 1872. The new International did, indeed, come into being inasmuch as congresses were held annually between then and 1877 (except in 1875). But at the second of these, in Geneva in 1873, it was agreed that congress decisions should not be binding on any federation or section which dissented from them. The effect of this was that quite basic questions of strategy – such as the attitude to be taken towards the general strike, and towards political participation – could be debated repeatedly, without the constituent groupings becoming united around a single policy.[10] The International was really nothing more than a talking shop. Even an attempt to set up an international information bureau came to nothing. It collapsed when its most active component – the Jura Federation – decided that its congresses were no longer worth attending.

Even if, *mirabile dictu*, a European-wide social revolution had broken out, the International would plainly have been in no position to direct its course. The same can be said of the anarchist movements within each country. This is well illustrated by the case of Russia, where the anarchists gathered a good deal of popular support during the summer of 1917 through their participation in the movement for workers' control and the peasant communes. When the moment arrived for insurrection, however, the Bolsheviks had a well-disciplined party machine, while the anarchists could not even boast of a single national organization.[11] They were ineffective then, and equally ineffective later in their attempts to resist the growing power of the Bolsheviks – hampered especially by the internal division between anarcho-syndicalists and anarcho-communists. Goldman later reflected sadly that:

> Most of the Russian Anarchists themselves were unfortunately still in the meshes of limited group activities and of individualistic endeavour as against the more important social and collective efforts . . . their work would have been of infinitely

greater practical value had they been better organized and
equipped to guide the released energies of the people toward
the re-organization of life on a libertarian foundation.[12]

She did not stop to ask whether these failures were not implicit in
the anarchists' attitude to organization itself.

I shall have something more to say later about a particular aspect of
this question – namely anarchist military organization – but I want
now to turn to the question of revolutionary strategy. In approaching
this question it is important to bear two points constantly in mind.
The first is that the anarchists did not conceive of themselves as
making a revolution in the ordinary sense, but as helping to create a
state of mind in which the masses would make the revolution by
themselves. The second is that they were perennially over-optimistic
about the readiness of the masses to participate. Especially in the
heyday of the anarchist movement, Europe appeared to them as a vast
gunpowder keg, needing only the right spark to set it off. Kropotkin,
for instance, believed in the 1870s that the European revolution would
arrive in a matter of years rather than decades. The issue was only
where and how to apply the spark.

At first the anarchists confined themselves to verbal propaganda.
Their aim was to convey anarchist ideas to the masses by discussion,
by speech-making and through books and pamphlets. Indeed this has
always been their predominant mode of activity, taking the movement
as a whole. But it quickly became clear, to the impatient anarchists of
the 1870s, that converting the masses by these means would take far
too long. Bakunin set the tone for the future when he declared, in
1873:

> I am now convinced that the time for grand theoretical dis-
> courses, written or spoken, is over. During the last nine years
> more than enough ideas for the salvation of the world have
> been developed in the International . . . This is the time not
> for ideas but for action, for deeds.[13]

So there emerged the idea of propaganda by the deed, an idea
which has since acquired infamous associations. Many critics of
anarchism have simply equated it with a strategy of terror. But at first
this was not so. Propaganda by the deed denoted a wider conception of
revolutionary strategy, which admittedly did not exclude acts of
violence, but on the other hand did not reduce to them. When, later

on, it came to refer simply to individual acts of terror – bombings and assassinations, for instance – anarchists like Kropotkin who had been influential in developing the original idea of propaganda by the deed turned against it. This later development will be discussed in the following chapter. Here I want to look at the original, broader idea.

The thought lying behind propaganda by the deed is that the masses are generally impervious to ordinary forms of written and verbal propaganda but can be aroused by forms of direct action against the state and against capitalist property that take place before their eyes. Brousse and Kropotkin, in a famous article defending this strategy,[14] pointed out that peasants and workers who were labouring for eleven or twelve hours a day had no inclination to spend their evenings reading socialist literature. What was needed was an act which both excited attention and conveyed a message. The Paris Commune was a good illustration. Beforehand almost no one had grasped the idea of communal autonomy, despite Proudhon's magnificent books. But once the idea had taken living form, everyone was forced to respond to it, positively or negatively. Brousse and Kropotkin concluded that anarchists should try to seize a commune and carry through the anarcho-communist programme (collectivizing property and so forth). Even if they were ultimately defeated by outside forces,

> The idea will be broadcast, not on paper, not in a journal, not in a picture, it will no longer be sculpted in marble, nor carved in stone, nor cast in bronze: it will march, in flesh and blood, living, before the people.
> The people will salute it as it passes.[15]

These views were later to be adopted by the Jura Federation as a whole. Their original authorship, however, lay not with Brousse and Kropotkin but with the Italian anarchists (especially Cafiero and Malatesta) who had developed them in response to what were seen as the particular social conditions of that country. Their strategy involved an armed band of anarchists moving from commune to commune and displaying 'socialism in action' to the inhabitants of each.[16] An abortive attempt had already been made to put this strategy into effect, at Bologna in 1874. During a period of popular unrest over high food prices and low wages, the anarchists tried to stage an insurrection which would spark off a series of uprisings throughout Italy. An armed band gathered outside Bologna, but reinforcements from neighbouring towns were intercepted by the police, and the insurgents judged themselves too weak to carry through their attack. They disbanded, but their leaders were captured by the police. (Bakunin, who had travelled to Bologna to lead the insurrection, spent the night hidden in his room and later escaped disguised as a priest.)[17]

A city of Bologna's size was certainly too tough a proposition for an anarchist contingent which turned out on the night to be much smaller than its leaders expected. Three years later, a similar attempt at San Lupo was more successful because more modest in its initial targets. This was to provide the classic model of 'propaganda by the deed' and helped to inspire the panegyric by Brousse and Kropotkin cited above. It was carried out among small villages in a mountainous area of Italy, thus enabling the anarchists to escape, for a while, the attentions of the police. The aim was for an armed band to 'move about in the countryside as long as possible, preaching war, exciting to social brigandage, occupying the small communes and then leaving them after having performed those revolutionary acts that were possible and advancing to those localities where our presence would be manifested most usefully'.[18] In the event only twenty-six anarchists could be mustered at San Lupo, but these marched to the village of Letino, where they declared the revolution and burnt the municipal archives. According to the participants' later reports, these actions were applauded by the peasants of the village, and even the local priest spoke in support of the revolutionaries. Weapons found in the village hall were distributed to the peasants, and they were left to carry on the social revolution while the anarchists moved on to the neighbouring village of Gallo. Here the same actions were repeated, while in addition the tax collector's receipts were distributed and the counting mechanisms on the grain mills broken. But the local peasantry declined to offer the anarchists their active support, and the band was obliged to move on to evade a military cordon that was being thrown around the area. Two days later, after a vain attempt to escape across a mountain, they were captured in a state of exhaustion by troops. They were tried in Benevento, after which the insurrection is often named.[19]

Was the insurrection, then, a dismal failure? As David Stafford has pointed out, the advocates of propaganda by the deed were able to rely on a perfect intellectual safety-net. If an insurrection should succeed, so much the better; if it should be suppressed, it would still serve as a 'living idea' to arouse the consciousness of the people.[20]

Thus in the aftermath of the Benevento affair, anarchists both in Italy and elsewhere were able to hail it as an act of pure propaganda. By burning the archives, distributing tax receipts and so forth, they had taught the people contempt for property and the state (in reality, however, the peasants' delight at seeing their civic obligations go up in smoke can hardly be said to express disdain for *property*!). But this easy gloss on the affair failed to address a crucial difficulty for the strategy of propaganda by the deed if it was to amount to more than just consciousness-raising (and this seems certainly to have been the intention of Malatesta and others before the event): how would a small number of isolated communes avoid being picked off one at a time by the police or the army? Both at Bologna and San Lupo, the police were alerted to the anarchists' plans well before the event, and were easily able to muster sufficient forces to defeat and capture the insurgents. Communications between groups of anarchists in different locations were poor, and so the rebellion was crushed before it had really begun. Moreover the arrest of the leading spirits threatened to destroy the movement as a whole – though in the Benevento case Malatesta and the others were fortunate to be acquitted at their trial after sixteen months of custodial imprisonment.

The lesson to be drawn here, I believe, is that the insurrectional strategy only had a chance of success when the civil authorities were disabled by some external cause from suppressing the rising. The clearest cases would be foreign invasion or civil war, and we shall come to some instances of these shortly. Where the authorities were at full strength, the insurrection was too easy to put down, and the action too costly for the participants. Propaganda by the deed, in its original connotation, had to be a public act of resistance to the state, so that the 'living idea' could appear in the full light of day, and there was no way for the perpetrators to avoid recognition. After experiences such as those I have described, the attractions of clandestine operations become apparent: they can be carried out by very small numbers of people – even by single individuals – and the participants can hope to escape detection. Whether they can have the same propaganda value as open insurrections is a matter to be discussed in the following chapter. It is no surprise, then, that the conference of the Jura Federation in 1880 which advocated 'total destruction of existing institutions by force' and 'propagation of the revolutionary idea and the spirit of revolt by deeds' should also have recommended its constituent groups to study 'the technical and chemical sciences' which had 'already rendered services to the revolutionary cause' – in plainer words, to learn how to make bombs.[21] This was to set the tone for the 1880s and 1890s.

For further evidence of the strengths and weaknesses of the insurrectional strategy, we need to move forward some forty years in time to the Russian Civil War and the Ukrainian insurrection led by the guerrilla fighter Nestor Makhno. The peasants of that region had already gained some experience of communal self-management in 1905 and again in 1917, so Makhno's ground was better prepared than that of Malatesta and his comrades. Makhno himself came of a peasant family, and was a man of action rather than an intellectual, but nonetheless a committed anarchist. He was active in the peasant uprisings in the Ukraine during the summer of 1917, but his main chance came in the following spring, when the Brest-Litovsk treaty handed the region over to the Germans and the Austrians. Makhno formed a band of partisans to resist the foreign invaders and the forces of their puppet ruler, the Hetman Skoropadsky. Using classic guerrilla tactics – rapid movement, lightning attacks and withdrawals, merging with the peasantry when cornered – the *Makhnovshchina* wore down their opponents and grew steadily in strength.[22] The Germans and Austrians withdrew towards the end of 1918, and the Hetman fell from power. Makhno then turned his forces – by now numbering as many as 20,000 – against the Petliurists, Ukrainian nationalists who took control of most of the region in the aftermath of the Hetman. After a decisive engagement in mid-December 1918, the *Makhnovshchina* found themselves in control of a large area of Southern Ukraine. They lost no time in encouraging the peasants and workers to form communes and soviets, and a number of such institutions did indeed appear (I shall consider their effectiveness later). Regional congresses were held in January and February 1919, and the second of these established a Revolutionary Military Soviet to act as its executive. The proceedings of these bodies were dominated by the military needs of the moment, with the region being threatened both by the Bolsheviks and by the white army of Denikin. A 'voluntary and egalitarian mobilization' was declared, meaning that each village was to supply a stated number of soldiers for Makhno's army (the degree of voluntariness of this arrangement remains in dispute).

Between the spring of 1919 and the summer of 1921 (when they were finally suppressed), the *Makhnovshchina* were fighting in turns against Denikin's Cossacks alongside the Bolsheviks, and then against their erstwhile allies, who attacked the partisans whenever they felt strong enough to do so. Thus the territory the partisans gained was never held securely – towns would pass back and forth between them and the White forces. Makhno was trying to foment a social revolution in the small space left to him between two powerful enemies. His achievements prompt two questions in particular: how far was Makhno's military organization consistent with anarchist principles? And, how successful was he in encouraging the workers and peasants to form organs of self-government?

As to the first, there is no doubting that Makhno's army was a people's army. It was composed of peasants and workers, commanded by peasants and workers, and it relied at all times on the support of the local population for shelter, food and horses (in that respect it can be regarded as the prototype of many later guerrilla armies). Its declared principles of organization were voluntary enlistment, the election of officers, and self-discipline according to the rules adopted by each unit.[23] I have already observed that the practical meaning of the first principle remains in some doubt. The second was not adhered to consistently. Makhno nominated his leading officers and retained the right to annul other elections. At the same time officers disliked by the units they commanded were usually transferred.[24] The overriding factor was Makhno's personal popularity with the men he commanded, which allowed him to control a large fighting force without as rigid a system of authority as armies usually require. If this was not self-government, it was certainly government by consent.

A more serious weakness (from an anarchist perspective) was the revolutionary movement's failure to establish civilian control of the army. The Revolutionary Military Soviet, a representative body which was supposed to exercise such control on behalf of the workers' and peasants' congresses, never did so effectively. This was partly due to Makhno's own growing unwillingness to listen to advice. As an anarchist group which broke with him in 1920 commented, 'Bat'ka Makhno, as leader of the *Makhnovshchina*, while possessing many valuable revolutionary qualities, belongs, unfortunately, to that class of person who cannot always subordinate their personal caprices to the good of the movement.'[25] Even apart from Makhno's personality, however, it would have been impossible for the soviet to direct guerrilla warfare of the kind that the insurgent army fought. This was characterized by rapid movement across the region, on-the-spot tactical decisions, and opportunist deals with other forces in the area. Thus, paradoxically, the form of warfare which kept the insurgents closest to the peasants as a whole also demanded the greatest discretion for the commander on the ground, whether Makhno or one of his subordinates.

Looking now at the second question, commentators sympathetic to the *Makhnovshchina* stress their very limited opportunities for engaging in social reconstruction. The general pattern was for the army to arrive in a town or village, remain long enough to issue a few general pronouncements, and then move on from military necessity. The liberated community might enjoy a few weeks or a few months of autonomy before it was retaken by hostile forces. The insurgents, although encouraging the formation of communes and soviets along the lines indicated by anarchist theory, did not impose any particular form of organization, and indeed proclaimed complete freedom of speech, subject only to the qualification that party committees were not to be formed (they had the Bolsheviks especially in mind). How did the local population respond? It appears that the peasantry were generally willing to form communes to dispose of the land appropriated from the *pomeshchiks*, although in most cases this meant handing it over to private cultivation. Only in a few places, mainly around the Mecca of the *Makhnovshchina*, Gulyai-Polye, was common ownership put into practice. But at least the peasantry formed their own institutions and were able to send delegates to the regional congresses. In the cities the response was much poorer. Makhno's attempts to organize soviets among the industrial workers of Aleksandrovsk and Ekaterinoslav (held for short periods late in 1919) were largely unsuccessful. This seems to have been partly a result of the workers' unfamiliarity with the ideas propagated by the insurgents, and partly a matter of the much greater difficulty of organizing industrial production than peasant agriculture. How, in particular, were workers in particular industries to be remunerated? The *Makhnovshchina* never began to grapple with questions such as this.[26]

Three strategic lessons may therefore be drawn from this episode. First, the power vacuum created by a civil war may indeed give anarchists the chance to control a sizeable amount of territory and so avoid the problem of isolation which scuppered the insurrectionary attempts of the Italian anarchists. Second, the vacuum will however be filled by a military body which is difficult if not impossible to organize along anarchist lines, even if it is led by committed anarchists. Third, there is no guarantee that the population at large will be intellectually or morally prepared for the constructive tasks facing it – since the destruction of established institutions will have been carried out not by a local insurrection but by military means, and for reasons that are partly external to the locality in question.

It is useful here to compare Makhno's experience with those of the anarchists in the Spanish Civil War – though the organizational principles and constructive achievements of Spanish anarchism will be discussed more fully in Chapters 9 and 11. Before the outbreak of the war, Spain had already witnessed a number of attempts at anarchist insurrection, reaching back as far as 1892 when an army of peasants marched into Jerez wielding scythes and shouting, 'we cannot wait another day – we must be the first to begin the Revolution – long live Anarchy!'[27] There were several more such episodes in the years before 1936. In January 1933, for example, the anarchists launched an uprising in a number of Catalonian towns and cities. In one of these, Ripollet, 'the red and black flag was hoisted. The real estate archives were burned in the public square in front of groups of curious onlookers. An edict or proclamation was made public, declaring money, private property and the exploitation of man by man abolished.'[28] But the police and the army were prepared for the assault, and suppressed it rapidly. It was the Benevento story all over again, albeit on a much larger scale. So long as the authorities could count on the loyalty of the troops, the anarchists had no real chance.

In July 1936, when Franco launched his revolt, most of the army followed him, so the Republican government was forced to rely for its support on the spontaneously formed workers' militias. The disappearance of state power in a number of areas naturally created a revolutionary opportunity for whichever group was strongest in a particular place. The anarchists seized upon this chance, especially in the cities of Catalonia and the countryside of Andalusia, traditionally their areas of greatest strength. In many Andalusian villages, the inhabitants imprisoned or killed the Civil Guard, burnt the archives, expropriated the landowners' estates, and set up communes. These attempts at *comunismo libertario* were on the whole short-lived, as Franco's army soon overran the region. In Catalonia, by contrast, there was no immediate military threat to the anarchists' revolutionary gains, but here it proved more difficult to carry the revolution from the industrial cities – where the soil had long been prepared, as we shall see in Chapter 9 – to the surrounding countryside, and beyond to other regions where Republican forces were in control.

Whereas the peasants of Andalusia were overwhelmingly landless labourers, those of Catalonia, Aragon and Castile were often smallholders or tenant farmers, who were not necessarily in favour of collectivizing the land. As the anarchist militias advanced, they drove off or killed the landowners and invited the villagers to form communes and decide on the issue of collectivization. In many places collectivization of land occurred, though in some cases private owners who worked their own land were allowed to continue doing so. The extent to which these decisions were voluntary is a matter of some dispute. The official anarchist line was that collectivization should be introduced by persuasion and example, but eye-witness accounts do not always support this. Borkenau, for instance, found a marked contrast between two neighbouring villages in Aragon. In one 'the agrarian revolution had not been the result of passionate struggle by the peasants themselves, but an almost automatic consequence of the executions [carried out by an anarchist militia] . . . Now most of the peasants were bewildered by the new situation.'[29] In the second, however, 'the local committee under anarchist guidance had abolished rents and expropriated four large estates with the agricultural machinery belonging to them . . . the peasants had not just stood bewildered before the achievements of the revolution, they had utilized them.'[30] Some anarchist sources at the time conceded that forcible expropriations had alienated a substantial part of the peasantry from the militias.[31]

The successes and failures of the collectivization programme will be discussed below in Chapter 11, but now I want to turn to the anarchist militias themselves. (It is an important fact about the Spanish Civil War that each political group organized its own military units.) The militias were organized along federal lines; each group of ten men elected a delegate, ten such groups formed a century (again choosing a delegate), and the centuries united into columns, each headed by an elective committee of war. Professional soldiers were sometimes attached to these columns as advisers, but authority remained firmly in the hands of the elected bodies – indeed in many cases in the hands of the constituent groups, since none could be commanded to take action against its wishes. The elected men were not distinguished in any way (by uniform or pay, for instance), and contemporary reports speak of the complete social equality that existed between the ordinary militiamen and their elected commanders.

So far so good (from an anarchist point of view): but were the militias militarily effective? An early problem that exercised the volunteer army (and caused some heart-searching among its anarchist members) was discipline. In October 1936 the anarchist Defence Committee of Madrid was obliged to introduce a harsh set of regulations to deal with cases of disobedience and desertion.[32] Clearly the much-vaunted ideal of spontaneity was proving a liability in a military context. To keep things in perspective, however, one should note Orwell's observation that 'a newly raised draft of militia was an undisciplined mob not because the officers called the privates 'Comrade' but because raw troops are *always* an undisciplined mob . . .' In Orwell's view the militias held together far better than a conscript army would have done under similar circumstances.[33]

A more important problem than individual discipline was co-ordinating the groups and the columns in the way that the war demanded. The Spanish War, it is important to realize, was not a guerrilla war (here the contrast with Makhno's partisans is clear) but a war between entrenched armies defending areas of land. The militias were crippled by the fact that every operation had to be agreed on unanimously by those who would take part in it. Where swift action was needed, there would be long and sometimes inconclusive debates between the section commanders. Militias with different political affiliations would compete with one another, and there was great reluctance to hand over arms or supplies even where there was a clear military case for doing so.[34] Eventually the anarchists themselves had to concede that the militia system was defective. According to a report from the *Federación Anarquista Ibérica*:

> Our militias, unpractised in firing, without military training, disordered, who held plenums and assemblies before under-taking operations, who discussed all the orders and who many times refused to obey them, could not oppose the formidable apparatus which Germany and Italy made available to the rebels . . .[35]

The militias were incorporated into the regular army of the Republic between September 1936 and March 1937.[36]

Spanish experience thus confirms the conclusions that were reached at the end of my discussion of the *Makhnovshchina*. Isolated insurrections, even with local support, can easily be suppressed and fail to spark off a general conflagration. Only the collapse of state power gives anarchist insurgents the chance to start a revolution. But civil war imposes a military logic which makes it hard for the com-batants to stick to their anarchist principles of organization, and may even oblige them, as it did in Spain, to merge their forces into an army with a regular structure. Moreover a revolution carried through in this way has to cope with a population who are at best unprepared for, and at worst actively hostile to, anarchist ideas of self-government and free communism. In short, with anarchists only forming a small minority of the people, the insurrectionary strategy could never succeed as its originators had hoped. It remains to be seen whether other anarchist strategies had any greater chance of success.

8 Anarchism, Violence and Terror

The association of anarchism with heinous acts of violence has, as I have already observed, become well established in the popular mind. From an historian's point of view this may appear quite unwarranted. Only a small proportion of anarchists have advocated terrorist methods – and only an even smaller proportion have tried to practise them – and moreover anarchist terrorism has been very largely confined to two decades, the 1890s and the 1970s. Looking at the picture in another way, acts of terror have been performed by republicans, by nationalists, by revolutionary socialists and by fascists, and if one tried to quantify the anarchist contribution to this catalogue of horror, it would turn out to be relatively small. So some anarchists, and some commentators on anarchism, have tried to dismiss the topic of this chapter as an irrelevance. Why a discussion of anarchism and violence any more than a discussion of anarchism and beer-drinking, since some anarchists have drunk beer? I believe that this reaction is as blind to one aspect of anarchism as the popular image is to another. We need to see that anarchist ideology is capable both of justifying violence and of condemning it; every anarchist must decide for himself which of these impulses is the stronger.

A word must be said first about the distinction between violence and terror. I take 'violence' to be the broader term, covering all illegal acts that involve damage (or the threat of damage) to person or property. Acts of terror, on the other hand, are clandestine acts of violence carried out to create a climate of fear which will lead to political changes (new policies or a new regime). The point of the distinction can be seen if we consider a public demonstration which involves a confrontation with the police; even if violence breaks out and policemen are injured, this does not in my view amount to a terrorist act, because the actions in question are public and there is no intention of creating a general atmosphere of terror. Political assassinations and bombings, on the other hand, carried out by small groups of individuals who try to escape detection (even though the organizations they belong to may 'claim responsibility') are prime examples of terrorism.

This distinction is important, because many anarchists who would accept certain acts of violence as part of an insurrectionary strategy of the kind outlined in the previous chapter would nonetheless strongly oppose terrorism. It is not always easy to draw in practice, however. To take a couple of historical examples, there occurred in Chicago in 1886 a confrontation between a large crowd of demonstrators and the police which has gone down in anarchist chronicles as the Haymarket affair. The demonstration was part of the agitation for an eight-hour day being conducted by the American unions. As the meeting neared its end, the police moved in to disperse the crowd and at this point a bomb was thrown (by an unknown hand), killing a policeman and wounding others. The police opened fire, and in the ensuing exchanges more policemen and a number of demonstrators were killed.[1] Supposing that the bomb was indeed thrown by an anarchist (in fact the evidence for this is only circumstantial), should it be regarded as an act of terror? On the one hand the act occurred in the course of a wide-ranging political movement which had already brought workers and police into open conflict; on the other hand it seems difficult to regard this particular act as an unavoidable part of that confrontation (as one might, for instance, regard the later exchange of fire as necessary self-defence by the workers). So the bomb-throwing seems to fall somewhere between pure terror and the kind of violence which commonly if regrettably accompanies direct action. Again, in the course of the military campaigns during the Spanish Civil War referred to in the last chapter, anarchist militias carried out a number of executions of landowners, priests and others thought to be sympathetic to the fascist cause. It is once more difficult to tell whether these should be regarded as acts undertaken for reasons of military security (and therefore as 'violence') or as acts designed to inspire fear among the population generally (and therefore as 'terror'). Perhaps the truth again lies somewhere between these two interpretations.

Despite these caveats the distinction between violence and terror will be clear enough in many cases. The bulk of this chapter will be concerned with the narrower issue of terror. I shall first give a brief historical survey of anarchist terrorism and then look at the arguments which anarchists have offered both for and against this strategy. Finally I shall raise the broader question of violence and see whether a cogent case can be made out, on anarchist grounds, for a strategy which completely rejects violence.

As mentioned earlier, the history of anarchist terrorism falls largely into two discrete sections: the closing years of the nineteenth century, and the very recent past. In both periods the incidence of terror spread widely throughout continental Europe, and touched the U.K. and the U.S.A.; although in the earlier period the centres of terrorist activity were France and Spain, whereas in the 1970s the main foci were Germany and Italy – countries, it may be noted, where a tradition of political violence had been preserved through the period of fascism. Two background factors are common to both episodes. First, the acts of terror occurred during a time when terrorism gener-ally – of different political complexions – was prevalent on the inter-national scene. In the nineteenth century the anarchists followed in the wake of the Russian populists who among other things had assassinated the Tsar in 1881, the Italian republicans, and individuals on the fringes of the S.P.D. in Germany, two of whom had tried to kill the Kaiser in 1878.[2] The recent spate of terror was again part of a wider phenomenon which embraced groups such as the Palestinian guerrillas, the Provisional I.R.A. and (in Italy specifically) the neo-fascists. Second, the anarchists themselves had already been involved in confrontations with the authorities which on occasion took a violent form, so that terrorist methods could be presented as merely a further step in an upward spiral of violence. In the earlier period this usually meant economically motivated clashes between workers and the police, at a time when in several countries the union movement was beginning to flex its muscles. In the later period the background was more specifically the student movement of the 1960s and the opposi-tion to the American war in Vietnam. These background factors are not offered as a complete explanation of the resort to terror – that would be tantamount to denying any ideological connection between anarchism and terrorism, a view I have already rejected by implica-tion[3] – but provide a context in which that resort can be made more intelligible.

The main source of anarchist terrorism during the 1890s was unquestionably France. Between 1892 and 1894 there occurred a series of incidents which did indeed create something of a climate of terror, in Paris especially, and which can plausibly be said to have inspired several anarchist attempts elsewhere in the world.[4] These incidents were not planned by any organization, but were rather the work of solitary individuals whose only connection was one of example. The first of these was the legendary Ravachol, who placed bombs in the houses of two French judges – in revenge, he later claimed, for their part in sentencing workers involved in the May Day

111

demonstration of 1891. Although condemned only to forced labour for these offences (since neither bomb caused any deaths) he was later executed for previous crimes, including three murders. Meanwhile a second anarchist, Meunier, had bombed a barracks, and later the restaurant where Ravachol had been betrayed to the police, killing the proprietor and a customer. Next Emile Henry placed a bomb outside the offices of a mining company, which exploded after it had been removed to the local police station, causing five deaths. Shortly afterwards a young shoemaker called Léauthier decided to follow Ravachol's example by plunging his knife into the first bourgeois that he met – the unlucky victim was the Serbian Minister to France, who survived his injuries. The next incident was more dramatic still: Vaillant hurled a bomb into the Chamber of Deputies, though miraculously it failed to kill anyone. He was, nonetheless, condemned to death.

The following year, 1894, saw a number of similar acts of terror, of which two are particularly noteworthy, though for opposite reasons. Henry struck again in February, this time throwing a bomb into a busy cafe, killing one customer and injuring twenty others. This was the least discriminate of the anarchist attempts in France; the most discriminate (if the expression is permissible) was the killing of President Carnot by an Italian anarchist in June, an attempt which, however, gave the authorities an ample excuse for a general round-up of anarchists, and effectively brought the era of terror to an end.

Elsewhere the mixture of blunders and atrocities continued. This was particularly true of Spain, where the level of terrorism was little below that in France. A particularly unpleasant act was the bombing of a Barcelona theatre in 1893, which resulted in twenty deaths. In the U.S.A. Alexander Berkman, later to become one of the best-known exponents of anarcho-communism, tried in 1892 to assassinate Henry Frick, a wealthy industrialist who had locked the workers out of his steel plant at Homestead, Pennsylvania.[5] There was even an incident in England during this period, though its nature has never been properly cleared up.[6] A man named Bourdin, who had connections with anarchists in London, blew himself up carrying a bomb across Greenwich Park. The intended destination of the bomb was never discovered, but the incident, which occurred only three days after Henry's cafe bombing in Paris, created an atmosphere of public alarm which the press duly fostered. This was indeed symptomatic of public attitudes generally during the period. Although the total number of anarchist outrages was actually quite small, and although they were carried out by isolated and often somewhat unbalanced individuals, it was widely believed that there existed an international conspiracy to overthrow the regimes of Western Europe by violence. The result was a general feeling of revulsion against anyone who could be labelled an anarchist. In such a hostile climate of opinion the police were able to arrest anarchists even where there was nothing to link them directly with terrorist acts. Leading anarchist intellectuals also came to realize that their propaganda efforts were being harmed rather than helped by the campaign of terror, and began to pronounce more critically on the various incidents. These two factors, together with the growth in several countries of a militant trade union movement in which anarchists could hope to participate (see below, Chapter 9) sharply decreased the volume of anarchist terrorism from the mid-1890s onwards, although isolated incidents, such as the assassination of Empress Elizabeth of Austria in 1898, of King Umberto of Italy in 1900, and of President McKinley of the U.S.A. in 1901, helped to keep the popular image of anarchism alive.[7]

The second phase of terror grew out of the New Left movement of the 1960s, which radicalized a sizeable proportion of young people in the advanced capitalist countries. There is some question whether the terrorist groups (which emerged as the movement as a whole went into decline) can properly be described as anarchist. Certainly the best-known among them – such as the Baader-Meinhof group in Germany and the Brigate Rosse in Italy[8] – rejected the label and preferred to call themselves revolutionary communists. However there are two reasons for including them in this analysis. First, other groups involved in the same campaign of anti-state terror, such as the 2nd June Movement in Germany, the Angry Brigade in Britain, and the various 'autonomist' groups in Italy, were quite explicitly anarchist in their orientation; since there was some overlap of membership between the 'anarchist' and the 'communist' groups (this can clearly be seen in the German case, for instance), it would be wrong to think of the alternative labels as representing a significant tactical or political division. Second, this is confirmed when we look at the ideological stance of the 'communist' groups. They interpreted themselves as forming the spearhead of an armed struggle by the proletariat against an imperialist and/or fascist state. In so characterizing the target of their struggle, they obliterated the traditional Marxist distinction between capital and state and created a composite monster of the kind that is familiar in anarchist thought. No doubt they were also influenced by Maoist ideas about guerrilla warfare against imperialism, but by domesticating these ideas and making the state apparatus the main object of their attack, they placed themselves squarely in the anarchist tradition. From this point of view the main difference between 'communist' and 'anarchist' groups is that the former were willing to accept a greater degree of discipline and central co-ordination and were correspondingly more successful in carrying out their terrorist campaigns (this was also how the participants tended to interpret their differences). I shall confine the discussion to the campaigns in Germany, Italy and Britain.

In Germany the campaign started in 1968 when a Frankfurt department store was set on fire following a number of violent confrontations between police and student demonstrators protesting against the Vietnam war. Two of those involved, Andreas Baader and Gudrun Ensslin, helped to found the Red Army Fraction (more popularly known as the Baader-Meinhof group) in 1970. The group's activities continued until 1977 when three of its leading members died in their prison cells – whether these were killings or suicides remains a hotly disputed question. They had begun with a series of bank robberies to raise the money for weapons, cars and so forth. The year 1972 saw a series of bombings – of the U.S. Army headquarters in Frankfurt, of the police headquarters in Ausburg, of the Axel Springer building in Hamburg and a number of other such places. Several people were killed in these incidents and many more wounded. Most of the original group were subsequently arrested, tried and imprisoned. But this in turn provoked counter-measures by survivors and new recruits, including an armed invasion of the German embassy in Stockholm in 1975, and the killing of the industrialist Hans-Martin Schleyer later that year, in both cases with the aim of securing the release of the imprisoned R.A.F. leaders. Meanwhile the 2nd June Movement, formed in 1971, had carried out several bombings (mainly in Berlin), had assassinated the president of the German Supreme Court, and had kidnapped the leader of the Christian Democrats in Berlin, Peter Lorenz (who was later released unharmed). Again the movement was eventually crushed by police arrests.[9]

The Italian terrorist movement has been larger in scale than the German, though somewhat less spectacular in its main incidents. The Brigate Rosse, formed like the R.A.F. in 1970, began with a series of arson attacks on the property of top industrial managers and of known neo-fascists. They also kidnapped a number of such men and subjected them to 'proletarian trials', afterwards releasing them. From about 1974, however, their operations and those of associated groups became more lethal, involving an intensification of the arson campaign, and attacks on state officials, including the chief magistrate of Geneva, Francesco Cotta, and the president of the Christian Democrats, Aldo Moro. The number of incidents rose to a new height in 1978, with 2,395 terrorist attacks recorded by the Ministry of the Interior (this figure of course includes actions undertaken by neofascists and others, as well as by members of the left groups). The Italian police appear to have been less successful than their German counterparts in apprehending those responsible – whether this is due to the inefficiency of the police or the greater skill of the terrorists in concealing their traces remains open to debate.[10]

In Britain, by contrast, anarchist terrorism was confined to the very beginning of the 1970s. A series of incidents occurred during 1970 and 1971, almost all involving the planting of bombs. Public figures whose houses were attacked included Peter Rawlinson, Robert Carr and John Davies, all sometime Ministers in the Conservative government. In addition there was a machine-gun attack on the Spanish embassy, an attempt to blow up the B.B.C. van broadcasting the Miss World contest, and bomb attacks on the Biba boutique in Kensington High Street and the police computer in Tintagel House on the Embankment. Responsibility for these acts was claimed by the Angry Brigade, though it remains uncertain who precisely carried out which attacks. At their subsequent trial the eight accused persons – the Angry Brigade or the Stoke Newington Eight, according to your point of view – maintained their innocence of the bombing charges. The evidence on which four of them were convicted was indirect. On the other hand it seems indisputable that some of the bombings *were* the work of a loosely organized anarchist group, whether or not of these particular members.[11]

If we now look back over the whole range of anarchist actions that fall under the category of terrorism, we can divide them into four broad classes. First there have been attacks on agents of the state – dignitaries, politicians, policemen, judges and lawyers. These range from, at one extreme, functionaries who are identified as having carried out particular actions, or as supporting particular policies – for instance, judges who have passed sentence on workers or political activists – to, at the other extreme, people whose political position is purely symbolic; an example here would be the Empress Elizabeth, assassinated in 1898, who at that time played no role at all in Austrian politics. Second, there have been attacks on the owners and managers of industry: again I should wish to distinguish between those selected because of particular things they had done (like Henry Frick) and those selected as symbolic representatives of a class (like Hans-Martin Schleyer). Third, a number of acts of violence have not been directed at anyone in particular, but at places and persons supposedly representative of the whole social order the anarchist aims to destroy – I should include here Henry's bombing of the Cafe Terminus, the arson committed by Baader and others at the store in Frankfurt, and the attacks in Britain on the Biba boutique and the Miss World contest. Fourth, some terrorist acts are merely instrumental to others – for instance robberies undertaken to raise money, or kidnappings whose objective is to secure the release of comrades in jail. These raise no special questions of justification, in the sense that they will be seen as justified if and only if the whole campaign of terror of which they form a part is justified.

Leaving aside the fourth category, anarchists have offered three general defences of acts of violence of this kind. The first portrays the acts in question as acts of revenge or retribution. It is significant here that the incidents tend to occur in clusters, with later events being interpreted in the light of earlier ones. Thus Ravachol directed his attacks against judges whom he held responsible for imposing severe sentences on two workers; then Meunier threw his bomb in order to avenge Ravachol; and so forth. Moving forward in time, the terrorist movement in Germany was clearly inspired in part by the death of Benno Ohnesborg on 2 June 1967 (he was shot by a policeman while taking part in a demonstration) – witness the naming of the 2nd June Movement. However this justification appears to lose whatever plausibility it may otherwise have when the individuals chosen for retribution have no direct connection with the actions to be avenged. Here the anarchist case shifts to a doctrine of collective responsibility: violence is being exercised by the state against its subjects and by the capitalist class against the workers, so anyone who acts as a state functionary or a servant of capital bears some measure of responsibility for the damage suffered by the victims. In this way, anarchists – or some of them – would include all the deeds in the first two classes under the rubric of revenge (others would concede that, from a propaganda point of view at least, it is wise to make the distinction made above between those bearing direct responsibility for certain acts or policies and those lacking such responsibility).

But can the argument of revenge possibly be stretched to cover the anonymous victims of cafe or store bombings? Emile Henry did

indeed try to do so in the defence that he offered at his trial.[12] He
argued first that Vaillant's bomb had sparked off an indiscriminate set
of repressive measures against anarchists generally. Since the bourgeoisie had not distinguished among the anarchists, why should the
anarchists distinguish among the bourgeoisie? In the latter class
should be included not only politicians, judges and the police, but also
'those good bourgeois who hold no office but who reap their dividends
and live idly on the profits of the workers' toil' and even 'all those who
are satisfied with the existing order, who applaud the acts of the
government and so become its accomplices, those clerks earning three
or five hundred pounds a month . . . in other words, the daily
clientele of Terminus and the other great cafes'.[13] Finally, if it should
be said that bombs such as his endangered the lives of women and
children, Henry's reply was that the bourgeoisie had not thought
about the harm caused to the wives and children of the workers they
exploited.

At this point, clearly, the idea of retribution has been stretched
beyond all recognition. It is in any case very incongruous for anarchists of this general persuasion to justify their actions in retributive
terms. We have seen that they are reluctant to hold ordinary criminals
responsible for their anti-social acts, seeing crime as the effect of
adverse social conditions. But if responsibility can be passed in this
way from individual to society in the case of the criminal, why not also
in the case of the bourgeois or state functionary, who is also a victim –
albeit a more pampered one – of a social system which has produced in
him the behaviour and the attitudes that he displays? Few anarchists
have faced this incongruity squarely, though its force has been
obliquely felt. 'It is not the rich and the powerful whom we devote to
destruction, but the institutions which have favoured the birth
and growth of these malevolent beings. It is the medium which it
behooves us to alter, and for this great work we must reserve all our
strength; to waste it in personal vindications were merest puerility,'
Reclus wrote.[14] While this stops short of saying that members of the
ruling class do not, as individuals, deserve retribution, it at least
acknowledges that personal revenge is pointless. Many anarchists
would tacitly echo this view.

The second justification of acts of terror sees them as instrumental
in the struggle between the ruling class and the proletariat. The basic
assumption here is that the state has such resources of indoctrination
and physical suppression at its disposal that it cannot be destroyed by
peaceful means. Single terrorist acts will not in themselves bring

about the destruction of the state, but they have three main uses in the conflict that precedes it: they are a means of defending the workers against particular oppressive acts by the state or the capitalist class; they help more generally to create a revolutionary consciousness in the proletariat; and they help to demoralize the ruling class, making it less willing to fight for its privileges.

To be useful in the first of these ways, acts of violence must be directed selectively against the perpetrators of oppression. The French anarchist Jean Grave made this point when he contrasted the burning of a factory owned by an 'average' employer and housing a large work-force, which would be counterproductive, with the execution of a particularly detested employer in the course of a strike, which he described as an 'intelligent deed'.[15] His advice was taken to heart by Alexander Berkman and Emma Goldman, who chose Frick for their assassination attempt because of his responsibility for the lock-out at Homestead, in the course of which several steel workers had been shot by Pinkerton men. 'A blow aimed at Frick would re-echo in the poorest hovel, would call the attention of the whole world to the real cause behind the Homestead struggle,' Goldman wrote.[16] On the other hand it might also create public sympathy for a man who did not deserve it and so rebound upon the assassins, as happened in this and many other cases.

The other uses were always more nebulous. The case for assigning revolutionary potential to acts of terror was that the proletariat were inherently prepared to rise against the state, but were cowed into submission by the power of the agencies of repression. Acts of violence directed against these agencies exposed their vulnerability and gave heart to their victims. As a Baader-Meinhof pamphlet put it, 'the urban guerrilla's aim is to attack the state's apparatus of control at certain points and put them out of action, to destroy the myth of the system's omnipresence and invulnerability'.[17] But here the anarchists faced an insurmountable difficulty. In order for the act of terror to convey the desired message, its meaning had to be conveyed to the masses – but how? In the absence of a mass revolutionary movement, there was no way in which the true significance of the deed could be put across. The anarchist press had a tiny circulation, and most workers acquired their political information from the 'bourgeois' press and later the state-controlled mass media. Johann Most, an ardent advocate of terrorist attacks in the 1880s, thought that a poster campaign might be used – but even this presupposed a large anarchist organization sufficiently co-ordinated to distribute the posters at the appropriate moment, whereas in fact most terrorist acts were per-formed by lone individuals who did not broadcast their intentions.[18]

What of the disheartening effect on the ruling class? It is clear that a terror campaign, even if only composed of a small number of incidents, can succeed in creating an atmosphere of public alarm, as the events in France in the 1890s show, and also the events in Germany in the 1970s. But rather than encouraging the powerful and the privileged to give up their advantages, the result is almost inevit-ably to make draconic measures against the terrorists publicly accept-able. In France the Chamber of Deputies passed measures making apology for crime a criminal act, and prohibiting all anarchist propa-ganda; these laws were then used to close down the anarchist press. In Germany, in the late 1970s, opinion polls revealed that, in the after-math of terrorist incidents, as many as two-thirds of the population were willing to accept limitations on their personal freedom for the sake of combating terrorism.[19]

In the light of these experiences, most anarchists have come to doubt the effectiveness of acts of terror in bringing the revolution nearer to hand. The case of Kropotkin is typical here. After having endorsed the insurrectionary strategy in the 1870s, and then indi-vidual acts of terror in the early 1880s, he had come by the 1890s to disapprove of acts of violence except those performed in self-defence in the course of a revolution.[20] This change of heart was caused partly by simple revulsion at acts such as the Barcelona theatre bombing and partly by an awareness that terrorism was hindering the anarchist cause – ordinary propaganda activities, for instance, were virtually impossible at the height of the 1890s campaign. Yet even Kropotkin continued to offer the third 'justification' for acts of terror – a justi-fication which is better described as an apology. This amounts to saying that such acts are the inevitable outcome of repressive social conditions, and their perpetrators are not to be condemned, for they are not fully responsible for what they have done. This 'justification' is found very widely in anarchist literature. An anonymous *Freedom Pamphlet*, published in 1893, is characteristic.

> Under miserable conditions of life, any vision of the possibility
> of better things makes the present misery more intolerable,
> and spurs those who suffer to the most energetic struggles to
> improve their lot, and if these struggles only immediately
> result in sharper misery, the outcome is often sheer despera-
> tion . . . Some natures in such a plight, and those by no means

119

the least social or the least sensitive, will become violent, and will even feel that their violence is social and not anti-social, that in striking when and how they can, they are striking not for themselves but for human nature, outraged and despoiled in their persons and in those of their fellow sufferers. And are we, who ourselves are not in this horrible predicament, to stand by and coldly condemn these piteous victims of the Furies and the Fates?[21]

This passage was quoted approvingly by Emma Goldman,[22] and similar sentiments (though with different nuances of emphasis) were expressed by Reclus, Kropotkin, Malatesta and many others.[23]

Despite this consensus among the luminaries of anarchism, the third 'justification' is peculiar in two respects. First, it depends on severing appraisal and prescription. The *Freedom Pamphlet* continues, on the following page, 'but we say to no man: "GO AND DO THOU LIKEWISE" '. Refusing to condemn acts of terror is thus not the same as urging people to commit them. But what, then, would the luminaries say to someone contemplating such an act who is seeking advice? It seems they are willing to say nothing beyond 'consult your own conscience'. But in view of the fact that they themselves regarded most such acts as justified neither on retributive nor on instrumental grounds, this is plainly unsatisfactory. Second, this 'justification' involves a kind of moral elitism. Those who offer it claim that they can see, from their detached point of view above the mêlée, that these acts of violence are unnecessary and ineffectual, but since those embroiled in the fight could not be expected to see as much, no judgments will be passed. This elitism comes out particularly clearly when the perpetrators of violent deeds are portrayed as 'noble savages' (by Reclus, for instance). Moral equality, on the other hand, implies that we should expect others to live by the standards that we set for ourselves.

To sum up, some anarchists have wanted to defend acts of terror on retributive and/or on instrumental grounds; but most have found these defences untenable, and have fallen back on the uncomfortable view that such acts are neither to be recommended in advance nor to be condemned in retrospect. On the other hand acts of violence which occur in the course of broader social struggles, and especially during revolutionary upheavals, are in a different category and require no special justification: while perhaps not desirable in themselves, they are the inevitable accompaniment of changes that are desirable. Thus, faced with a society that institutionalizes violence, there is no moral problem about the use of violence as such. But terrorist violence, even if an understandable reaction to oppression, is usually misdirected and nearly always counterproductive in its effects.

This has been the majority view among anarchists. My discussion would not be complete, however, without a brief look at the alternative view. Some anarchists have argued that their principles require a strategy that relies completely on non-violence. An extreme example is Tolstoy who, although repudiating the label, can reasonably be regarded as an anarchist in his later life. Tolstoy's anarchism and his rejection of violence both flowed from a radical interpretation of Christian doctrine. Christ's command, 'Thou shalt not kill', was for Tolstoy to be taken quite literally; it was not even permissible to kill a criminal about to murder a child.[24] By extension all acts of violence were morally prohibited, and government stood condemned as 'an organization for the commission of violence and for its justification'.[25] (Tolstoy's conversion to anarchism has been dated to the moment when he witnessed a public execution by guillotine in Paris.)[26] But it was not of course permissible to use violence to prevent violence (as the murderer/child example shows). Government could be undermined only by citizens refusing to co-operate with it and creating alternative institutions.

Tolstoy's rejection of violence stands or falls with his absolutist ethics, but other anarchists have tried to make out a case for non-violence that does not require such an extreme posture, even though moral revulsion against killing and wounding may form a part of it.[27] The case stands on two legs: strategies that employ violence are incapable of bringing into existence the kind of society that anarchists want; and moreover non-violent strategies are available that are sufficiently potent to challenge the might of the state. Let us consider these in turn.

One rather practical reason against using violent methods is that by doing so the revolutionary is challenging the state in an arena where it is almost bound to win. Latter-day anarchists, especially, have been impressed by the huge arsenal of weapons at the state's disposal, beside which the gun or the homemade bomb of the revolutionary look puny indeed. Moreover a violent attack on one of its outposts permits the state to respond in kind without moral compunction, and often with the approval of most of its citizens. However the case against violence does not rest there. The effects on the revolutionaries themselves must also be considered. Effective violence is likely to require a disciplined form of organization that contravenes anarchist principles and bodes ill for the kind of society that will emerge if the violence should succeed in its destructive task. If conducted on a large scale, a military hierarchy will be required, and we have already seen (in Chapter 7) the difficulties this poses from an anarchist point of view. Even on a smaller scale, however, analogous problems occur. A terrorist group needs to escape detection by the police, and in order to do so its members must adopt a clandestine life-style which prevents them from engaging in ordinary political activities – meetings, demonstrations and so forth. By so doing they cut themselves off from the broader movement of which they hope to form the spearhead, and begin to live in a closed world. The campaign of violence becomes an end in itself, losing any connection with wider political developments. (This can be seen very clearly in the case of the German terrorist groups of the 1970s, for instance.)[28] More speculatively, violence encourages certain traits of personality in those who employ it, which are not the traits that are needed to build an anarchist society. As the Dutch anarcho-pacifist Bart de Ligt put it, 'the violence and warfare which are characteristic conditions of the imperialist world do not go with the liberation of the individual and of society, which is the historic mission of the exploited classes. The greater the violence, the weaker the revolution, even where violence has deliberately been put at the service of revolution.'[29]

Conversely, a number of anarchists have come to see the potential of non-violent forms of resistance to the state.[30] Here the example of Gandhi's resistance to British rule in India has been very influential, though anarchists are unlikely to adopt wholesale the philosophy of life upon which Gandhi based his political strategy. What Gandhi essentially showed was that, in the right circumstances, a group willing to act illegally and accept punishment without resistance can wield great moral power, greater even than the physical power wielded by the authorities. The circumstances must include public sympathy for the cause the group is pursuing, and moral scruples on the part of those in power, so that eventually they are unwilling to continue punishing the dissenters. The forms of action which may be used are varied: illegal demonstrations, sit-ins, economic boycotts, strikes, work-ins, and so forth. The anarchist belief is that actions of this kind, initially undertaken by a small group with a specific objective – say the reversing of an unpopular government policy – may draw increasing numbers of sympathizers into the struggle, so that eventually there is mass disobedience on the scale that Gandhi achieved. At this point the institutions of the state will begin to crumble as they lose legitimacy in the eyes of the people, and the hope is that they can be replaced without violence by organs of popular self-government.

I think that anarchists who have taken this view have been right in one respect: a non-violent campaign can be carried out by a group organized consistently with anarchist principles whereas a campaign of violence almost certainly cannot. However, the chasm to be crossed is between a campaign with a specific objective (where the authorities may be able to give in without really weakening their overall position) and a head-on challenge to the state. Given their general point of view, anarchists are (of all people) the least likely to believe that the ruling class will give up its privileges without a fight. The question, then, is whether a non-violent campaign might be organized so effectively that it could topple the political authorities *even though* the latter were prepared to use the means of violence at their disposal against the revolutionaries. Perhaps if the state were in the hands of a very small and unpopular minority, and the revolutionary movement succeeded in uniting the rest of the population behind it, such an outcome would not be beyond the bounds of possibility – historical examples can be found where oppressive regimes have been swept from power with very little bloodshed on the revolutionary side. But most revolutions bear out Engels' verdict cited above:[31] ultimately they are contests of arms. If so, anarchists may have to choose once again between using means that are repugnant to their principles, and remaining pure but ineffectual.

9 Anarchism and Syndicalism

The term 'syndicalism' refers to the militant form of trade unionism which appeared in a number of countries during the first decades of this century. In France, especially, it quickly took root, and produced not only an organization powerful enough to cause the government serious alarm, but also an ideology which linked the everyday struggles of workers in the economic field to a final goal of 'emancipation' from capitalist society. To a greater or lesser extent both the organizational methods and the ideology of French syndicalism were borrowed by radical trade unionists elsewhere, so it is possible in these years to speak of an international syndicalist movement which competed with the parliamentary socialists for the allegiance of the working class. This movement was largely torpedoed by the outbreak of war in 1914, and thereafter syndicalism was only a pale shadow of its former self. There was one very important exception, however: in Spain, where syndicalist organization was comparatively weak until about 1917, it blossomed under the conditions of political instability which marked that country until the beginning of the civil war in 1936, and played a major part both in the social revolution that accompanied the outbreak of the war, and in the war itself. Thus if France was the main source of syndicalist ideology, Spain was its principal testing-ground.

It is not difficult to see why anarchists should have been attracted by the syndicalist movement. Following the frustrations of the insurrectionary period of the 1870s and the counterproductive results of the terror campaigns of the 1890s, anarchists seemed doomed to gather impotently in small groups of comrades, cut off from the industrial workers and the peasantry who were supposed to form the army of the revolution. Syndicalism was far from being an anarchist invention (though some of its principal theorists had anarchist backgrounds) but when it appeared, it seemed to provide an unprecedented opportunity for anarchists to make contact with the most militant sections of the working class, and to use the economic struggles of the syndicates as a means of conducting anarchist propaganda. Moreover the syndicalists' determination to have no truck with conventional parties or parliamentary politics corresponded exactly to the anarchists' long-standing policy of abstentionism. It is no surprise, then, that as early as 1890 we find a veteran of the movement like Kropotkin urging his comrades to enter the syndicates;[1] and by the time that syndicalism was a living force, in the early 1900s, this had almost become anarchist orthodoxy.[2]

At the same time, it is important not to conflate anarchism and syndicalism, or to suppose that syndicalism is merely one variety of anarchism. What one might call the 'core' of syndicalist ideology was not explicitly anarchist in character, even though it was possible (as we shall see) to gloss it in such a way that it seemed to point logically to an anarchist future. Moreover the anarchists who followed Kropotkin's advice differed considerably in the extent of their enthusiasm for syndicalist methods. To avoid confusion I shall begin by outlining the basic tenets of syndicalism, and next consider how these tenets were interpreted both by non-anarchists and by anarchists of different persuasions. I shall then survey the practical achievements of the syndicalist movement in an attempt to see whether those anarchists who placed their full faith in the movement were right to do so or not.

Syndicalist ideology began with a crude and simple view of the class war between the proletariat and the bourgeoisie.[3] The proletariat – both rural and urban – were exploited and impoverished. The bourgeoisie – the capitalist class and their functionaries, the politicians, administrators, judges, police and armed forces – were parasites who lived at the workers' expense but contributed nothing essential to social production. The interests of the two classes were diametrically opposed: the greater the power and wealth of the capitalists, the less that of the workers. No agreement or compromise could benefit both classes simultaneously. In the struggle between them, the ruling class had all the financial and military resources at its disposal. All that the working class had was its numerical strength and its capacity to control the process of production. But these resources could not be materialized unless the class was organized in the right way.

The details of syndicalist organization varied from country to country, but the main lines were the same everywhere. In any given place (town or rural district) workers should form themselves into syndicates on the basis of craft, profession or industry: organization by industry was the preferred form, but practical concessions were made where craft loyalties were strong. These syndicates, democratically controlled by their members, were to be the basic units of class action. They should be composed exclusively of workers and, even though they might appoint part-time officials from among their members, they should avoid creating a separate leadership. The syndicates were then to federate in two directions: first, horizontally with other syndicates in the same area, to create a local federation: second, vertically with other syndicates in the same branch of industry, to create a national federation (say of miners or railwaymen). Finally these federations were themselves to unite into an umbrella confederation to head the movement. None of this, however, was to threaten the autonomy of the local syndicates: the federations and the confederation were seen as devices for co-ordinating the actions of their component syndicates, but as having no rights of command.

In the immediate struggle with the capitalist class, over wages, hours of work, and so forth, the function of the local federations was to spread propaganda and to allow the workers in each area to support one another in times of hardship. The national federations would normally take the leading role in organizing strikes, conducting wage bargaining and so on – depending on whether the employers were also organized nationally. However the dual pattern of organization had another aspect as well: when the hour of the revolution came, and the capitalist class and its lackeys were driven from power, the syndicates would provide the basic framework for the new society. The national federations would plan and organize production: the local federations would arrange distribution in each district, and generally serve to maintain social order. Thus the proletariat, having thrown off its shackles, would find its own authentic form of organization ready to hand: there would be no leap into the void.

Next, the methods of struggle: here the idea popularized by the syndicalists was 'direct action'.[4] This meant, first, that the workers must be prepared to act on their own behalf and not leave the job to outsiders – especially not to politicians. Second, it meant that all effective forms of action should be used to combat the capitalist class, regardless of their legality. The four most commonly advocated methods were the strike, sabotage, the boycott and the 'label'. The effectiveness of the strike weapon is too familiar to need further comment. Sabotage was advocated as a way of harassing the employer without loss of pay, and as a means of preventing him from importing blacklegs to break a strike. Boycotting meant a concerted effort to prevent the sale of products made by recalcitrant employers, and labelling was its converse: a syndicate would allow 'approved' employers to stamp their goods with its label. In addition the syndicalists saw nothing wrong with using violence against the person or property of capitalists during a struggle, though they thought that isolated acts of violence were useless or worse.

These tactics had a dual purpose. Their immediate objective was to win concessions from the employers; their long-term aim was to create a fighting movement that would eventually unseat the capitalist class as a whole. This put an encouraging complexion on activities such as strikes. If they were successful, a small part of the capitalists' wealth would be expropriated; even if they were not, the workers became more aware of the absolute conflict of interests between themselves and their employers, and would be more resolute in the future. One syndicalist described the limited strike as 'a training session, a salutary exercise that will harden the proletariat for war, in preparation for a final struggle which will be the revolutionary general strike'.[5]

The revolutionary general strike: this was the means whereby the workers would finally emancipate themselves from the capitalist class. Provided that a large enough proportion of the workforce downed tools, neither the capitalists nor the political authorities would be able to provide basic services such as food, heat and lighting, and authority would pass inexorably into the hands of the only bodies able to do so: the syndicates in their federations. The authorities might try to use troops to force sections of the proletariat back to work, but the syndicalists counted on class solidarity between workers and ordinary soldiers, and their own anti-militarist propaganda efforts, to prevent his happening. The majority of syndicalists, however, gave little thought to how the general strike would usher in the new society. For most of them it was a distant goal which gave a more elevated meaning to their everyday trade-union activities.[6] Moreover in trying to describe the aftermath of the general strike, we reach a point at which anarchists and non-anarchist syndicalists part company.

To complete this short review of syndicalist ideology, a final word must be said about the syndicalists' adamant refusal to play any part in conventional politics. The syndicalists were not opposed to individual workers engaging in political activities, but they insisted that political commitments must be left behind when the worker participated in syndical debate, and they flatly refused to ally themselves with any political party. (Indeed in the three countries I shall consider later, there was active hostility between the syndicalist unions and the socialist parties which in appearance were their natural partners.) Three arguments were used to defend this position: first, political parties grouped people according to their beliefs, irrespective of class origin, whereas syndicates grouped people according to (class) interests, irrespective of beliefs. All parties, therefore, represented a compromise of some kind between classes; only the syndicates could be relied on to defend the authentic interests of the workers. Second, parliamentary politics inevitably corrupted even the best-intentioned of representatives – this was, of course, a venerable anarchist argument. Third, political action, even if successful, could only produce a change in legislation. But legislation was not the workers' friend; on the contrary, it was the capitalists who knew how to turn any legislation to their own advantage. What the workers needed was a clear field to carry on their direct-action struggle. Even so, the syndicalists did allow one form of political lobbying – which they called 'external pressure', meaning strikes or demonstrations against the government – as a method of blocking legislation which was clearly contrary to working-class interests.

All of this was very much to the anarchists' taste. But in order to reach a clear understanding of the relationship between anarchism and syndicalism, we need to chart the terrain rather carefully. I shall distinguish four interpretations of the syndicalist movement, though even these are no more than points on a spectrum which contained many intermediate shades of opinion.

The first view I shall call 'pure revolutionary syndicalism'. It was the view of Victor Griffuelhes, the leading figure in the French movement between 1902 and 1909, and also of several of the more moderate leaders of the Spanish C.N.T. (*Confederación Nacional de Trabajo*) in the 1930s. These men did not regard themselves as anarchists: indeed anarchism was seen as one among a number of competing political ideologies, and therefore as extraneous to the syndicalist movement proper. Syndicalism was sufficient unto itself: it was based purely on the material interests of the working class, and the consistent pursuit of these interests would one day lead the class into open and final conflict with the capitalists. What would happen next was a matter of speculation: the syndicates would no doubt organize production and distribution, but whether a new political entity would also be created was uncertain. Griffuelhes said that it was agreeable to speculate on these matters, but he would wait until he returned from a trip which allowed him to see the answers with his own eyes before pronouncing.[7]

The pure syndicalists were as willing as anyone to engage in militant struggle with the capitalist class, but their hazy vision of the future made it easier for them to conflate reformist and revolutionary action. A wage increase at the capitalists' expense, for instance, could be seen as a partial expropriation of the class itself. Thus in practice the pure syndicalists tended to behave in much the same way as their colleagues in the movement who were out-and-out reformists. This distressed the second group I want to distinguish, the anarcho-syndicalists, who regarded short-term gains as relatively trivial and saw the main point of limited trade-union action as preparation for the final struggle. Key figures here include Emile Pouget, a leading ideologist of the French C.G.T. (*Confédération Générale du Travail*), Pierre Monatte, who defended syndicalism in a famous debate with Malatesta at Amsterdam in 1907, and the historian of the movement, Rudolph Rocker.[8] Many other names might be added to this list.

The first assumption of the anarcho-syndicalists was that anarchists must break out of their exclusive circles and make contact with the masses; and the workers' syndicates were the obvious milieux for attempting this. Besides promoting their members' material interests in the short-term, they were training grounds where the workers learnt how to organize themselves and to practise solidarity. Their federal form of organization corresponded to anarchist principles; and so the syndicates could be seen as the embryos of a new, stateless social order. As Rocker put it,

> For the Anarcho-Syndicalists the trade union is by no means a mere transitory phenomenon bound up with the duration of capitalist society, it is the germ of the Socialist economy of the future, the elementary school of Socialism in general. Every new social structure makes organs for itself in the body of the old organism. . . . It therefore concerns us to plant these germs while there is yet time and bring them to the strongest possible development, so as to make the task of the coming social revolution easier and to insure its permanence.[9]

The anarcho-syndicalists realized, however, that the syndicates were not composed exclusively of revolutionary workers, much less of conscious anarchists; nor did they believe that it would ever be possible to achieve such a universal awakening of consciousness. Instead they thought that the syndicates would nurture a conscious minority of militants who could spearhead the revolution, drawing the apathetic masses in their wake. This necessitated some bending of the idea that syndicates should be democratically controlled by their members. Pouget, who took a fairly extreme view on this issue, contrasted 'le Droit Syndical' with 'le Droit Démocratique' and argued that conscious minorities, whose actions furthered the interests of their comrades, had no need to wait for majority approval before engaging in struggle.[10] In practice, as we shall see later, the desired result was achieved through the tutelage of a small group of anarchists who either held key posts in the syndicalist movement (as in the French case) or else used their own organization to guide the decisions of the wider movement (as in the Spanish case).

For the anarcho-syndicalists, then, anarchism and syndicalism were one and the same: or better, perhaps, syndicalism was anarchism come to maturity. The third view to be distinguished here rejected this identification, while still seeing in syndicalism an important means to the final goal of anarchy. This view was held during the apogee of syndicalism by older anarchists such as Kropotkin, Malatesta and Grave, and has since, with the decline in trade-union miltancy everywhere, become the predominant view once again. Its proponents in the early 1900s were often referred to as anarcho-communists to distinguish them from the anarcho-syndicalists (this was how the division was marked in Russia, for instance) but the label is misleading inasmuch as the anarcho-syndicalists were also, for the most part, aiming to create an anarcho-communist society. The debate between the two groups was primarily about revolutionary methods, not about goals.

What did the sympathetic critics of syndicalism have to say to their syndicalist comrades? In essence, while agreeing that syndical organization was a necessity for the workers, and moreover an excellent forum for anarchist propaganda, they insisted that it should not be confused with the anarchist movement itself. There were a number of reasons for this.[11] First, syndical organization unavoidably reflected the structure of the society that it was formed to combat. Each industry had its own union, and the immediate interests of workers in that industry were not necessarily identical with those of workers elsewhere. Union organization could thus become a means whereby the interests of one group were advanced at the expense of another. Second, the syndicates inevitably became caught up in the quest for immediate improvements in their members' living standards, and were thus liable to lose sight of the final revolutionary goal. Their leaders would find themselves impelled to make compromises to secure minor gains – especially in view of the conservatism of many unionized workers – and would in this way be drawn into class collaboration. Third, the organizational structure of the syndicates was not appropriate to a future society where production would be guided by need rather than profit. Some industries would disappear altogether; others would be completely reorganized to allow workers to move more easily from job to job and develop their skills in an all-round way. The syndicates, therefore, must disappear along with the society that had given birth to them; otherwise they would become a force of stagnation, and even, perhaps, the begetters of a new form of political authority. Finally, and as a generalization of the third point, advocates of syndicalism were in danger of losing sight of the many-sided nature of human existence and supposing that production was everything. Syndicates reflected people's roles as producers – no doubt a major part of their lives under capitalism – but people engaged in other activities besides, and they needed other forms of organization to reflect these. As Grave argued:

> Society teems with abuses; against each abuse, there must rise up the group of those who suffer most from it, in order to combat it. . . . Not only groups struggling against that which exists, but attempts to group together along the lines of the future, with a view to producing faith, well-being, solidarity, among like-minded individuals. We count too much on the inevitability of the revolution, forgetting that the latter only destroys that which clutters the ground, and that, once the destruction of oppressive forms has been accomplished, there will only develop those kinds of grouping which have already been tried out.[12]

The practical upshot of this sympathetic but critical view of the union movement was that anarchists should enter the syndicates to make propaganda, but should not submerge their anarchism in the movement itself. They should not hold office in the syndicates, and they should avoid becoming involved in the struggle for economic gains within the boundaries of capitalism, which were likely to be illusory in any case. They should retain their own separate organization, and they should not neglect opportunities for making propaganda in other fields through an obsession with the sphere of production. In short, anarchists in the syndical movement should act as gadflies, always trying to prevent the movement from succumbing to conservatism and pressing it forward to a revolutionary destination.

For a small minority of anarchists even this conceded too much to syndicalism. They preferred to stand completely aloof from the union movement and to continue associating in ideologically pure anarchist groups. Three arguments appear to have weighed with these dissidents.[13] First, they maintained even more rigidly than the anarchists whose views I have just outlined that the division of the social product between the capitalist and working classes was fixed, so any wage increase won by the workers in one industry was gained at the expense of the class as a whole.[14] Participating in a syndicate, therefore, was tantamount to trying to obtain a privileged position at the expense of comrades in other industries. Second, the dissidents claimed that syndical organization cramped the free individual and disciplined him to accept majority rule – whereas the anarchist affinity groups, as we have seen, were based on the principle that nobody was obliged to abide by a collective decision if he did not want to. Third, the class analysis which underlay syndicalist ideology was viewed with some suspicion. It appeared to assume that the organized factory worker had interests identical with the impoverished masses generally, and could be counted on to act on their behalf. In short, it resembled too closely the Marxist analysis of class conflict which anarchists had long since rejected.[15] The dissidents looked once more to 'the black mass, the mass of the unemployed and the starving' to spearhead the revolutionary movement.[16]

In the presence of a strong and apparently revolutionary trade-union movement, however, most anarchists saw this as ivory-tower purism. The majority were either out-and-out anarcho-syndicalists, or else took the more critical but still favourable view of Malatesta and Grave. But they could not of course hope to enjoy an ideological monopoly in the syndicates. They had to compete with the pure revolutionary syndicalists and, even further to the right, with reformists who saw the movement as merely a means of bettering the position of the working class within the limits of capitalism. Syndicalism was always an alliance between ideologically disparate elements. In view of this, there are at least three critical questions that need to be asked about the major syndical movements from an anarchist point of view. First, to what extent did the unions succeed in uniting the working class into a revolutionary force capable of challenging the bourgeoisie? Second, what in practice was the relationship between industrial action for immediate economic ends and the revolutionary general strike that was supposed to follow on? Third, was the general strike, when attempted, a genuinely revolutionary weapon as portrayed in syndicalist and anarcho-syndicalist ideology? I shall focus here on the C.G.T. in France and the C.N.T. in Spain, with a briefer look at the American International Workers of the World.

The C.G.T. can plausibly be seen as a revolutionary syndicalist body from its inception in 1902[17] until the outbreak of the First World War. The first generation of leaders – notably Griffuelhes, Pouget, Yvetot and Delesalle – were all syndicalists or anarcho-syndicalists, and although Jouhaux, who became general secretary in 1910, in practice took a somewhat more moderate line, his background was also anarchist. The Charter of Amiens, adopted in 1906, pledged the C.G.T. to syndicalist principles: class struggle, autonomous working-class action, political neutrality, the revolutionary general strike. The bipartite form of organization adopted in 1902 – one section uniting federations of workers in different branches of industry, the other uniting the Bourses du Travail, which served as local federations – corresponded to the syndicalist model. Furthermore the Confederation quickly established a reputation for militant action and for refusing to collaborate with employers or the government. Strikes were frequent, bitter and often violent, and occasionally widespread enough to create alarm in the minds of the middle classes and the government. Yet at no time did the long-awaited general strike materialize. The nearest the C.G.T. came to it was a campaign of strikes in 1906 for the eight-hour day, which was supposed to reach a climax on 1 May. But the government arrested the leadership and the strikes petered out without even achieving their objective, let alone bringing down the regime.

Why, despite its revolutionary pretensions, was the C.G.T. not more effective? To begin with, it never succeeded in unionizing more than a fraction of the French working class. At no stage was its membership more than 600,000, only about one-half of the total number of unionized workers, and a mere one-tenth of the workforce as a whole.[18] There is also some evidence that the radicalism of the leadership was not matched by the bulk of the members. The voting system used by the C.G.T. at its conferences – one syndicate, one vote, regardless of size – gave additional weight to small but radical syndicates such as the barbers'.[19] It took continual propaganda efforts from above to keep up the militancy of the rank and file; 'the work of propaganda and organization was in the hands of relatively few men, travelling from town to town, making key speeches at local conferences and public meetings, standing behind the more significant strikes'.[20] There were frequent complaints in leading circles about the apathy and 'egoism' of the ordinary members.

The C.G.T. did not, then, succeed in building up a mass revolutionary movement; it organized instead a sizeable body of workers who were willing to be led by revolutionaries so long as this helped them in their immediate battles with their employers. And this brings us to the second question: what relationship was there between the partial strikes that the Confederation organized and the general strike at which it was supposed to be aiming? According to syndicalist theory, any strike might, because of a heavy-handed response by the authorities, become generalized and lead to an all-out confrontation between the workers and the state. In the utopian novel written by Pataud and Pouget to illustrate this theory, a minor builders' strike in Paris leads to a battle between demonstrators and the police in which several workers are killed, then to a general strike of solidarity with the victims, and on to the final showdown.[21] In practice it was very different. The strikes called tended to be localized and quite short-lived, even though combative for as long as they lasted.[22] This was partly due to the C.G.T.'s organizational weakness: only in a few industries were the national federations strong enough to co-ordinate a country-wide strike. It was due also to the syndicates' policy of not amassing strike funds to see them through a long conflict, on the grounds that this would weaken the workers' fighting spirit. These factors encouraged each group of workers to take the initiative in declaring a strike (in line with syndicalist theory) but lessened the chances that the strike would spread beyond the group of factories concerned, or at most the local area (thus undermining the second part of the theory). There was also another possibility that the theory ignored. Strikes which ended in failure might demoralize the workers rather than increasing their militancy. There is evidence from the French case that, in a period when real wages fell slightly on average, the experience of strike action made many workers more cautious thereafter, and inclined them to accept compromise deals with their employers. Thus the C.G.T., towards the end of the period we are considering, found itself pushed into adopting more moderate tactics by its membership.[23]

Since the C.G.T. never succeeded in provoking a revolutionary general strike, it is idle to ask about the effectiveness of such a tactic in the French context. The question can be raised more sensibly with reference to the Spanish C.N.T. Before moving on to that body, however, I should like to insert a few words about the I.W.W. (or

'Wobblies'), an American union founded in 1904 and active until virtually suppressed by the government during the First World War. The I.W.W. was not at first authentically syndicalist in inspiration, but a split in the organization in 1908 created a syndicalist wing which wanted to detach itself from the socialist parties and from parliamentary activity generally. (Subsequent references to the I.W.W. are to this section.) Organizationally, however, the I.W.W. was considerably more centralized than the C.G.T., and in this respect departed from the federalist principles characteristic of syndicalism. All the emphasis was placed on organizing workers nationally into a dozen or so big industrial unions, and, although provision was made for the creation of local industrial councils, these were accorded much less importance. Not surprisingly, anarchist members of the I.W.W. tried to decentralize the organization, but without success.[24]

In contrast to the C.G.T., the I.W.W. had to compete with a powerful reformist trade union in the shape of the American Federation of Labor. The A.F.L. recruited skilled craftsmen in the cities, whereas most of the Wobblies' support came from the mining camps and the migratory farm workers of the West. The I.W.W. made a considerable impact during 1912 and 1913 through its participation in a number of strikes – the most notorious being at Lawrence, Massachusetts, where some 20,000 textile workers were out for two months – and in 'free speech fights' (confrontations with local authorities over revolutionary speech-making in public places). Even so, its membership never rose above 20,000 at the outside, whereas the A.F.L.'s was fast approaching the two million mark. This induced some syndicalists to argue that, rather than creating a separate organization, revolutionaries should try to infiltrate the big union and win it to their cause.[25] In the conditions prevailing in the U.S., it is difficult to believe that either strategy could have been successful. Trade unionism has only developed in a revolutionary direction where embittered workers have confronted high-handed employers. Such confrontations were common enough in France and Spain during this period, but in the U.S. they occurred only in certain specific places and industries (such as mining). The I.W.W. was a curiosity, and would have disappeared, or been absorbed, even if it had not been crushed politically.[26]

Spanish syndicalism had a firmer social basis. Indeed it had two bases, the more durable being the industrial workers of Catalonia, and the more volatile being the peasants and rural workers of Andalusia and the Levante. In both areas the proletariat was confronted with an employing (or landowning) class that was stubborn and often vindictive in the face of its demands. But even in Spain, it required the addition of a third ingredient – chronic political instability – to give revolutionary syndicalism its chance of success.

The origins of Spanish syndicalism have been traced back as far as the 1870s,[27] but its main development came with the founding of the C.N.T. in 1910. The union was banned shortly afterwards, and its major periods of activity were between 1917 and 1923 and 1930 and 1936 – periods divided by the dictatorship of Primo de Rivera and terminated by the Civil War. Its membership fluctuated greatly, but at its peak may have numbered as many as a million workers and peasants. This figure was matched by its main rival, the socialist U.G.T. (*Unión General de Trabajadores*). The two unions competed vigorously for support, and were almost always at loggerheads with each other, a factor which seriously weakened the workers' movement as a whole.

The C.N.T. changed its organizational structure several times in its history, but generally approximated to the syndicalist model. In contrast to the I.W.W., the local federations were strong, and the national industrial federations – in the periods when they were called into existence – were relatively weak. Thus the union was highly decentralized, and moreover had very little by way of a permanent bureaucracy. This made it resilient – it was able to survive underground even when declared illegal – but at the same time hampered its attempts to co-ordinate actions across the country.[28]

The leadership of the movement was always divided between more moderate syndicalist elements and more revolutionary anarchist elements. At first the syndicalists – led by Segui – were the stronger force, and the anarchists themselves were internally split into anarcho-syndicalists and 'pure' anarchists, the latter preferring to remain aloof from the materialism of day-to-day trade unionism.[29] The draw of the C.N.T. was strong, however, and even the purest syndicalists were very radical by comparison with trade unionists elsewhere,[30] so the Spanish anarchists came increasingly to see their future as lying with the C.N.T., while not confining themselves entirely to trade-union tactics. A congress held in Madrid in 1922 'resolved that all Anarchists should enrol in the C.N.T. and treat it as their special field of action'.[31] At about the same time power at the head of the union was shifting decisively towards the anarcho-syndicalists. Shortly afterwards the C.N.T. was forced to go underground, but during the period of the dictatorship an important development took place. In 1927 the *Federación Anarquista Ibérica* (F.A.I.) was formed. From the time that the C.N.T. was able to work openly again (in 1930), this body – which comprised some 10,000 militant anarchists, organized in federated affinity groups – began to exercise hegemony over the union. At first the moderates held on to key positions in the apparatus, but by late in 1931 they were fighting a rearguard action.[32] Some syndicates broke away from the C.N.T. in 1933 in response to F.A.I domination (the split was healed in 1936). From about the beginning of 1932, therefore, we can see in Spain the unique spectacle of a mass trade-union movement being led along the revolutionary path by a minority of conscious anarchists – the original anarcho-syndicalist strategy come to fruition.

The C.N.T. had little difficulty in persuading its members to engage in militant strike activities: throughout both the periods we are considering, the number of industrial stoppages was extremely high. Moreover on several occasions the union was able to turn limited strikes into general strikes – general, at least, to a particular city or region. And here we come to the C.N.T.'s major weakness as a revolutionary organization: it was unable to co-ordinate subversive action on a wide enough scale to pose a serious threat to the Spanish state. This can be demonstrated by a brief examination of some major episodes.

In Barcelona, in 1919, a strike by C.N.T. workers at the La Canadiense power plant virtually paralysed the city. Segui negotiated a return to work on very favourable terms, but the local representative of the military authorities was unwilling to release a number of workers held in prison, and a general strike was declared on 24 March. More than 100,000 workers participated, and at first the stoppage of work was total. But the authorities responded vigorously, declaring martial law, deploying troops and using the militia to provision the city. The strike had collapsed by 14 April.[33]

No other strike in the period up to 1923 was as impressive as the La Canadiense stoppage and its aftermath. General strikes were called by the C.N.T. in Barcelona in November and December 1920, but neither lasted more than a few days, their effectiveness being lessened by the U.G.T.'s refusal to collaborate. An attempt to call a general strike in Madrid on the day after Primo de Rivera assumed power in 1923 was likewise thwarted by U.G.T. non-co-operation.

In the later period, two episodes stand out. April and May 1933 witnessed a lengthy strike by the building workers of Barcelona, which later spread to other industries, and attracted sympathetic general strikes in Saragossa and elsewhere. The C.N.T. was simultaneously using demonstrations and rallies to campaign for the release of F.A.I.–C.N.T. prisoners. Neither form of action brought about the desired result.[34] In December of the same year, following the victory of the Right at the elections, the C.N.T. made its boldest attempt at an insurrectionary general strike. Despite a widespread withdrawal of labour, however, only the workers of Aragon and Rioja rose against the government, and these insurrections were put down by troops within four days. Significantly the Catalonian syndicates, exhausted by their earlier efforts, remained quiet on this occasion.[35]

The C.N.T. was of course to enjoy its hour of glory in 1936, when the revolt of large sections of the Army under General Franco left the union in effective control of a substantial area of Spain. Its constructive achievements when presented with this opportunity will be discussed in a later chapter. The fact remains that the Spanish syndicalists were unable to provoke a revolution on their own terms, and, by the same token, had to engage in social reconstruction in circumstances that were far from ideal – they failed to command the loyalty of the majority of the working class, and they were almost immediately involved in a bloody conflict with the fascists and an internecine struggle with the other Republican factions. Thus, although the C.N.T. came closer than any other trade union to fulfilling the anarcho-syndicalists' dreams, it did not in the end succeed in doing so. What lessons should we draw from this?

From an organizational point of view, first of all, no syndicalist union has succeeded in recruiting the bulk of the proletariat: the French and Spanish unions had at best half of the organized workforce, and the American I.W.W. far less. Although at times of crisis such a union might rally rather more workers than this behind its banner, it still faced competition from other working-class organizations which were unwilling to embark on what they saw as revolutionary adventurism. There was clearly a trade-off here between numbers and revolutionary spirit: the wider the union cast its net, the more it had to moderate its stance to draw in workers who were interested primarily in piecemeal gains. In syndicalist theory, of course, workers inducted in this way would have their consciousness raised by the experience of direct action: in practice this was not necessarily so.

This brings us to the second problem for syndicalists, the relationship between ordinary trade union activity and the final goal of a revolutionary general strike. The syndicalist position on this has been rehearsed above. There are two reasons for doubting it. Taking a long-term view, it is reasonable to suggest that the effect (though not the intention) of trade unionism has been to integrate the working class into capitalist society by providing a channel for its grievances and winning it some economic gains: this much is conceded by modern anarchists like Murray Bookchin.[36] In the French and Spanish cases, however, the unions were confronting employers and political authorities too recalcitrant to buy them off with concessions, and here a second difficulty occurred: the workers' fighting strength was sapped by repeated strikes and physical battles with the authorities, so that instead of an upward spiral of militant activity culminating in a general strike, we observe a patchwork of localized conflicts with no overall result.

Third, there is the problem of the general strike itself. The Spanish experience shows that a general strike of limited duration is less threatening to the authorities than syndicalist theory would have us believe. If the state responds firmly, the contest becomes a battle of wills which normally ends with the strike crumbling away. If, on the other hand, the strike is used as a springboard for an insurrection – the anarcho-syndicalist version of events – a revolutionary opportunity undoubtedly exists, but it can be suppressed fairly easily if confined to a few places. An organization such as the C.N.T., devoted to the principle of syndical autonomy, was poorly adapted for launching a general insurrection.

Finally, there is a specific moral for anarchists to be drawn from the Spanish case. In November 1936 an unprecedented event occurred: four anarchists became ministers in the socialist government of Largo Caballero. For many anarchists, reflecting on the event with hindsight, this represented the culmination of a process of collaboration with the state that had its roots in the F.A.I.–C.N.T. liaison. In Vernon Richards' words:

> The policy of making the C.N.T. 'their specific field of action' could only result in the F.A.I. losing its anarchist identity and independence, the more so when so many of the leaders of the C.N.T. were also leading members of the F.A.I. The outcome of this dual role was that by the end of 1936 the F.A.I. had ceased to function as a specifically anarchist organization . . .[37]

Thus the syndicalist movement, while on the one hand offering anarchists a unique opportunity to participate in a working-class

movement whose structure and aims were apparently in harmony
with theirs, might on the other hand represent a slippery slope at
whose foot lay reformism and political collaboration.

10   Anarchism and the New Left

The crushing of the anarcho-syndicalists in Spain – first by their
Republican allies and then finally by the forces of General Franco –
signalled the end of the organized anarchist movement. For the next
quarter-century, nothing was left but isolated groups of intellectuals
who continued to discuss the old anarchist ideas, but made virtually
no impact outside of their own circles. But then, quite unexpectedly,
anarchism was given a new lease of life. That diffuse movement of
protest and radical thought called the New Left, which swept through
most of the countries of the West in the late 1960s, appeared to revive
anarchism, along with Marxism and other revolutionary ideologies.
Whether this was really the case – whether the 'new' anarchism had
much in common with the older doctrine – is a question that will
require our careful attention.

The New Left appeared on an intellectual scene that had been
dominated, since the ending of the Second World War, by two major
ideologies – democratic socialism and orthodox Communism. It broke
with these ideologies in a number of respects. To begin with, New
Left thinkers were no more sympathetic to the Communist societies of
Eastern Europe than to the capitalist societies of the West. Their
revolutionary aim was to find a third alternative that avoided both the
traditional ills of capitalism and the bureaucratic deformities of the
Communist bloc. Moreover their critique of capitalism paid less
attention to the economic struggle between worker and employer, and
more attention to what might broadly be called cultural issues – to
questions about individual lifestyle, personal relationships, the relationship between man and his natural environment, and so forth.
Finally these critical ideas were often linked specifically to the youth
movement – students and other young people being seen as the
harbingers of revolutionary change.

What, then, was the relationship between anarchism and the New
Left as a whole? To begin with, traditional anarchism supplied some
of the raw material out of which the new theories were constructed.
Both the writings of the older anarchists and the experience of anarchist movements were drawn upon – often as a corrective to the

distorting lenses of orthodox Marxism. Furthermore a small number of intellectuals who were radicalized by the New Left began to describe themselves explicitly as anarchists, seeing their ideas as a continuation of the older tradition. Perhaps more significantly, however, other individuals and groups developed theoretical positions which had much in common with traditional anarchism, even though they refused the name itself.[1] This refusal probably stemmed from two sources: first, anarchism was sometimes equated with a cult of individual spontaneity and a corresponding unwillingness to organize collectively in pursuit of political ends; second, anarchism was also sometimes identified with a set of revolutionary tactics that were now outdated (with syndicalism, for instance). As we have seen, both of these identifications contain a grain of truth, but neither accurately reflects the mainstream of anarchism. Thus anarchism may have played a larger role in the diffuse intellectual movement I am considering than is apparent from the number of self-avowed anarchists present – as the following discussion will suggest.

Adherents of the New Left often called themselves revolutionaries, but was this more than a fashionable label? To be a revolutionary it is not enough to criticize existing society, however fundamentally: it is also necessary to have some reasonably coherent ideas about how it may be changed and what will replace it. This was not on the whole the New Left's strong suit, and we must be prepared to contemplate the possibility that the role played by its members was that of *social critic* – a more venerable avocation that than of revolutionary. The social critic condemns the real in the light of the ideal, but without necessarily putting forward any recipes for moving in the direction desired. By the same token we must ask whether the new anarchism remained a revolutionary ideology or whether it might not better be interpreted as a gesture of protest against a social and political system that was perceived to be intolerable. (This possibility lay behind my earlier question about the continuity between the older and the newer anarchism.)

There was, however, one important occasion on which the ideas of the New Left leapt beyond social criticism and became a moving force in a near-revolutionary situation: the May–June events in France in 1968. Anarchist ideas were especially prominent on this occasion. Reflection on these events may help us decide whether the emergent form of anarchism could realistically have formed the basis of a revolutionary movement, and indeed whether anarchism has any future in the advanced societies of the West.

The ideas of the New Left must be understood in the light of the enormous advances made by the Western economies in the period after 1945. Economic growth in this period dramatically raised the living standards of most workers, with two significant consequences. First, it was no longer possible to base a revolutionary movement on the material impoverishment of the working class, as both classical anarchism and classical Marxism had done. Second, the working class itself looked less and less like a cohesive revolutionary force, as affluence began to erode the old working-class communities and allowed increasing numbers of workers to emulate the lifestyle of the middle class. Thus radicals came to pay less attention to the sphere of production, to the exploitation of the worker by the capitalist and the pauperization of the former, and more attention to spheres of life outside of production, to domestic life, consumption, leisure and so forth. The focus also shifted to psychological questions, to the alleged mental and emotional poverty of most denizens of the advanced capitalist societies, as opposed to material questions. Moreover since most of the governments in these societies were unprecedentedly liberal in their dealings with their subjects, attention was switched away from the physically repressive character of the state towards its manipulative character – that is towards its role in conditioning its subjects to accept the constraints and routines of liberal capitalism. Again, the shift was from material issues to psychological issues.

Central to the new thinking, then, was the idea of a 'critique of everyday life', the title of an influential book by the French sociologist Henri Lefebvre.[2] Technological developments had allowed people to enjoy unprecedented material standards of living, but this had not been reflected in any improvement in the quality of their lives. Work was still alienating; leisure merely reproduced this alienation by assigning the consumer a passive role as recipient of commodities and of advertising designed to make him desire more commodities. The advertisers' claim was that these commodities would provide a more satisfying life, but the satisfaction was illusory. The central contradiction of advanced capitalism was between the possibilities for real satisfaction that technology opened up, and the poverty of actual life under the imperatives of such an economy.

Many different versions of this thesis were presented by New Left theorists – one of the most famous, of course, being Herbert Marcuse's *One-Dimensional Man*[3] – but I want to focus here on the extreme version developed by a small group of intellectuals, centred in France, who called themselves the 'International Situationists'.

143

The ideas of this group encapsulate better than any others the quality of New Left anarchism, and moreover they had an influence out of all proportion to the size of the group on the May–June events – above all on the colourful and disturbing slogans that appeared on the walls and buildings of Paris. The group itself had been formed a decade earlier, and its origins lay in the dissident artistic movements of the inter-war years, especially in Dadaism and Surrealism. The situationists came to believe that it was no longer possible to protest against modern society through artistic creation, however unconventional its form. Instead, the division between art and life had to be overcome, so that people would experience their surroundings in a new manner without entering some separate arena called 'the world of art'. The way to achieve this was held at first to be 'the construction of situations' (an idea from which the group's name was derived). These would be happenings involving a number of people in which each would be encouraged to act on his desires in unanticipated ways. There were also ideas for redesigning towns along emotional rather than functional lines:

> Everyone will live in their own cathedral. There will be rooms awakening more vivid fantasies than any drug. There will be houses where it will be impossible not to fall in love. Other houses will prove irresistibly attractive to the benighted traveller . . .[4]

From this fantastic vantage-point, an intellectual assault was launched on the banality of life in contemporary societies. A crucial concept was that of the 'spectacle'.[5] Modern existence was dominated by a series of spectacles created by the ruling hierarchy to condition and subdue the masses. The idea referred not only to the theatrical and media events that the term suggests, but (for instance) to conventional forms of politics and to the marketing and consumption of commodities generally. 'Spectacle' is meant to convey two things: first, the show is enacted before an audience of passive observers who merely drink in what is provided for them; second, the show is based on an illusion – the people or the things featured in it do not really have the qualities that they seem to have. For instance, politicians and entertainers are presented as having 'star' qualities, whereas in reality they may be the most undistinguished of individuals.[6] Commodities are presented as having life-enhancing qualities which, when they are purchased, they turn out not to have at all. In particular, 'the object which was prestigious in the spectacle becomes vulgar the moment it enters the house of the consumer, at the same time that it enters the house of all the others'.[7] Thus spectacles of all kinds, while captivating their audiences, cannot genuinely satisfy their desires.

The anarchism implicit in this position emerges when the spectacle is traced back to the power of a ruling class:

> The oldest social specialization, the specialization of power, is at the root of the spectacle. The spectacle is thus a specialized activity which speaks for the ensemble of the others. It is the diplomatic representation of hierarchic society in front of itself, where all other expression is banished. Here the most modern is also the most archaic.[8]

From this point of view, the difference between the capitalist societies of the West and the so-called socialist societies of the East is merely that the former embody a 'diffuse' spectacle (i.e. many different spectacles with different origins compete for our attention) whereas the latter embody a 'concentrated' spectacle (i.e. a single image of the good life is presented to the masses).

Given this analysis, how did the situationists propose to break out of the spectacular society? Here their thought moved along two apparently divergent tracks. On the one hand they looked to individual acts of subversion – as we have seen to 'the construction of situations' and other ways of breaking with the dominant form of consciousness. In this vein they looked to the young, to drop-outs, even to gangs of criminals (echoing here, of course, Bakunin's appeal to 'la masse noire'). On the other hand, the residual influence of Marxism showed itself in their belief that only a class-conscious proletariat could finally overthrow capitalist society – even while they admitted that the actual proletariat had to a very large extent become integrated into the system. In this vein they held up the idea of council communism as the only authentic vehicle of the revolutionary project, rejecting all Leninist and Trotskyist theories of the vanguard party.[9] Thus we are left with a curious mishmash of traditional revolutionary theory, which portrays the revolution as a transfer of power from one class to another, and the new idea of spontaneous individual protest against 'spectacular' society which seems to exclude any organized form of revolution at all. The tension, not to say contradiction, between these two themes appeared rather charmingly in some of the slogans of May 1968: 'Be realistic: demand the impossible.' 'Power to

145

the imagination.' 'The more I make love, the more I want to make the revolution. The more I make the revolution, the more I want to make love.'

The tension in question might nonetheless have been resolved on two provisos: first, that situationist-style revolt might inspire the working class to reclaim its revolutionary legacy; second, that the forms of organization which emerged from such a revolutionary undertaking were compatible with the aims of the new anarchists. The second proviso has never been put to the test, but the first can usefully be examined in the light of the May–June events in France. In appearance at least, a student revolt inspired by the extreme ideas of ultra-left groups, including the situationists, succeeded in detonating a working-class explosion that was not far from being a revolution. How accurate is that appearance?

Although the student revolt had multiple causes, some relating to the antiquated nature of the French system of higher education, there can be little doubt that left-wing ideas played a major part in giving the movement the direction that it took.[10] Indeed the origins of the revolt are sometimes traced back to the publication of a situationist pamphlet entitled 'The Poverty of Student Life' at the University of Strasbourg in 1966. The immediate cause was a confrontation between students and authorities at Nanterre (on the outskirts of Paris) early in 1968, from which was born the March 22nd movement, a coalition of Trotskyists and quasi-anarchists, including the notorious Daniel Cohn-Bendit.[11] Cohn-Bendit's ideas were ecletic, drawing on anarchism, situationism and to some extent Trotskyism, as he himself was perfectly willing to admit.[12] What is quite clear, however, is that he had seized upon precisely those ideas which differentiated the New Left from its precursors, and in that sense he is an archetypal representative of the new strain of anarchist thought.[13] So although the revolt had no single ideological inspiration, and indeed from its inception was marred by internal warfare between the different left groups, non-doctrinaire anarchism was a major influence, perhaps even *the* major influence as far as the style of the revolt was concerned.[14]

From Nanterre the March 22nd movement transferred to the Sorbonne, which was occupied early in May. There followed a series of confrontations with the police, which culminated in the 'night of the barricades' of 10–11 May, when thousands of students fought with the authorities for control of the streets of Paris. By this point two significant things had happened. First, a very large number of students had been radicalized, thus bearing out, in some measure, the claims of Cohn-Bendit and others that the students' position under advanced capitalism was inherently contradictory, and their political attitudes correspondingly unstable. Indeed the Sorbonne in these early days bore some resemblance to an anarchist utopia – even if a hard-headed observer could also see some likeness to an American nominating convention.[15] Some 20,000 people congregated together, governed only by a General Assembly and its various committees: intense debates were held on all kinds of subjects; parties, entertainments and other happenings occurred spontaneously.[16] It served as a beacon to many other, less spectacular, occupations, both in Paris and elsewhere in France. Second, the students had won the support of a large section of French society (indeed of four-fifths of Parisians, according to a public opinion poll). Tangible evidence of this support came on 13 May, when students and trade unionists joined forces in a massive demonstration against the government, leading an estimated 800,000 people through the streets of Paris.

This is not of course to say that the students had converted the population *en masse* to ultra-left ideas; no doubt the support was largely offered in response to the government's inflexible line on university reform and the brutal methods used by the police against the rioting students. Yet something more than liberal sympathy was involved, as is shown by the wave of workers' strikes that followed the student revolt. Between mid-May and mid-June nearly ten million workers went on strike, many of them also occupying their places of work. There is little doubt that the students' example was an important influence, even though that example would not have been sufficient in the absence of a number of long-standing economic grievances. It is difficult to say how far the students' revolutionary ideas penetrated into the factories: the established unions, especially the Communist-led C.G.T., did their best to prevent students and workers coming into contact, fearing that they might lose control of the movement.[17] In some places workers issued demands for a greater or lesser degree of self-management, but very rarely – to the chagrin of the anarchists – did they actually try to run the factories themselves.[18] This perhaps indicates the limitations of the workers' movement from a revolutionary point of view. By refusing to take the decisive step beyond 'bourgeois legality', they allowed the movement to be brought back, in time, to a trade-union contest for better wages and working conditions. Once the unions were back in the saddle, it was relatively easy to extract enough concessions from the employers to end the strikes.

In the meantime, however, the government of General de Gaulle had very nearly been unseated. For about a week at the end of May, it seemed that the government had lost its authority, and there was a real possibility that power would pass into the hands of one or other of the opposition leaders.[19] This would not, of course, have amounted to a revolutionary overthrow of the regime itself. Even so, it is a testament to the forces which the students unleashed that one of the most solidly entrenched of the Western leaders should almost have been driven from power. The moment passed, however, and a majority of Frenchmen, alarmed by the violence on the streets and the increasing disruption of the economy, turned back to offer de Gaulle their support. His party won a handsome victory in the elections called for June.

Perhaps the most important question, from an anarchist point of view, is not whether de Gaulle and his supporters could have been defeated (that question is specific to a time and a place) but whether the liaison between the students and the workers was or could have been genuine. The students were the bearers of New Left ideology, which as I have argued involved a shift of focus away from questions of production and towards questions of consumption and 'everyday life'. How interested were the workers? Some of them at least were interested in more than improvements in pay and conditions, which is what they had eventually to settle for. There is evidence that they were frustrated by the conservatism of the union leadership – this is shown in particular by their vehement rejection of the Grenelle Agreements, hammered out by the Prime Minister, the unions and the employers over the weekend of 25–27 May, and offering 'the biggest benefits secured for the working class since the Liberation'.[20] Yet perhaps what the students had tapped was not a wholesale rejection of 'spectacular society', but rather a latent demand for greater control over the workplace (possibly even for complete self-management) which would link the workers of 1968 to their syndicalist forebears sixty years earlier. If this speculation is correct, production still remained the crucial arena for the working class. It was only the students, themselves free from the constraints of a working day, who could dream about turning work into play and freeing the senses from the manacles of consumption. Both groups could talk about participatory democracy, but for the workers this meant something much more mundane than for the student anarchists.

This raises once more the question of whether the new anarchism was really a revolutionary ideology. As we have seen, the situationists and those they influenced tried to hinge together a critique of everyday life and an older idea of revolution, involving the proletariat and the creation of workers' councils. The May–June events suggest that these two projects remained far apart, even though an attempt to carry through the first sparked off, in another group of actors, some movement in the direction of the second. It is arguable whether the first by itself is a revolutionary project, if by revolution is meant a mass overthrow of social and political institutions which ushers in a new social order. For the change of consciousness and style of life which the situationists and others on the far left were calling for, revolution in this sense is neither necessary nor sufficient. Not sufficient, because how can any institutional change, however radical, ensure that a person's whole life-experience should alter in the way demanded? Not necessary, because individuals and groups seem able to break away from 'spectacular' society without revolutionary change, provided only that this society allows them the space and freedom to do so, as the hippies, drop-outs and commune-dwellers of the late 1960s proved.[21] In saying this, I do not at all mean to underestimate the radicalism of the New Left. It can plausibly be argued that the indictment of contemporary society offered by their spokesmen was more far-reaching than anything to be found on the older revolutionary Left. In that sense, they had every right to call their ideas 'revolutionary'. The point is merely that these ideas had fairly tenuous links with the traditional view of revolution (including the traditional anarchist view). Cohn-Bendit's slogan, 'C'est pour toi que tu fais la révolution', brings this out rather clearly.

The point just made about the situationists and their disciples can, I believe, be extended to other strands in recent anarchist thought and activity. Although it is hard to generalize about a heterogeneous phenomenon, one finds in most contemporary anarchism the same shift of attention to individual psychology, personal relationships, and forms of consciousness – and by implication the same break with the traditional idea of revolution. A recent anthology includes substantial sections on 'The liberation of self' and 'Anarcha-feminism' – the latter being an attempt to connect feminist critiques of patriarchy with the wider anarchist critique of hierarchical forms of authority.[22] This redirection of attention may be justified in its own terms, but it has two main effects. First, anarchism tends to lose its own distinct identity, and becomes merely one variation on a common theme – the cultural critique of modern capitalist society. Second, the aim of anarchist practice is no longer to overthrow capitalism and the state directly, but immediately to create a space in which individuals may develop alternative styles of life, and perhaps in the longer term to subvert contemporary society by the contagion of these lifestyles.[23]

Whether one regards this as a step forward or a step back depends of course on one's general verdict on anarchism as a revolutionary ideology, so this may be an appropriate point at which to take stock of what has gone before. Our discussion began from the problem of reconciling the anarchist belief in a society whose organization is in many respects diametrically opposed to that of contemporary society with the empirically observable facts of human nature. I argued in the fifth chapter that, despite some appearances to the contrary, the anarchist response to this problem does not fundamentally rest on a theory of historical progress. Instead most anarchists have looked to revolution as the means whereby humanity collectively transforms itself from its present benighted state into a condition of freedom and solidarity. But to achieve this purpose the revolution must take a certain shape: its means must be in conformity with its ends. This idea lay at the heart of the anarchist critique of Marxist revolutionary practice, which tried to usher in a society of freedom and equality through a class dictatorship guided by an elite party. The problem, however, was to find a strategy for revolution that avoided such a paradox while still retaining some chance of success. None of the three strategies subsequently examined – insurrection, terrorism, syndicalism – met this condition. In each case a relatively small group of conscious anarchists was trying, through revolutionary practice, to convert the mass of the population to its way of thinking and behaving. In no case was the attempt successful. The masses remained enmeshed in their old ideas and habits, so the anarchists were doomed either to remain isolated or to dilute their principles in order to work within larger, non-anarchist organizations. This is not of course to say that revolutions never occur, nor indeed that in the course of revolutions popular consciousness does not alter. It is rather to say that no revolution has taken place according to any of the anarchist recipes, and also that, in the revolutionary periods that have occurred, anarchist ideas have not prevailed.

These observations open the way for an anarchist critique of the idea of revolution. Indeed we have seen that, throughout its history, anarchism has included a number of thinkers (Godwin prominent among them) who have been critical of revolutions for reasons that the historical evidence appears to have confirmed. The exact nature of the critique will vary from person to person, but the central claim will be that the process of revolution is not such as to encourage those aspects of human nature upon which an anarchist society must be built. In Godwin's case, for instance, the argument is that revolution hinders the development of rational modes of thought. A recent variant by the American individualist David Friedman is that revolutions tend to bring to the fore those individuals who enjoy, and are good at, wielding power.[24] Both of these arguments seem to me persuasive.

If, for such reasons, an anarchist rejects the traditional idea of revolution, is he thereby condemned to be merely a social critic, in the sense indicated earlier? Not necessarily, though it should be said that some recent commentators have interpreted anarchism in this light.[25] An alternative is that anarchism should become reformist, even though the term itself would strike a jarring note in the ears of most anarchists. In place of a full-scale confrontation with the state, anarchists should attempt to create alternative, libertarian forms of association, which would allow people to by-pass the established institutions, and at the same time to develop habits and practices of co-operation that might eventually form the basis of a new society. Adherents of this view, of whom there have been a number,[26] are fond of quoting an aphorism from the German anarchist Gustav Landauer: 'The state is not something which can be destroyed by a revolution, but is a condition, a certain relationship between human beings, a mode of human behaviour; we destroy it by contracting other relationships, by behaving differently.'[27] The idea implicit in this remark is that the state may be undermined gradually, without a frontal assault of the kind that has up to now proved fruitless. Revolution might be unnecessary as well as counterproductive from an anarchist point of view.

If, then, we decide in the light of historical evidence that anarchism has failed as a revolutionary ideology, we need not infer that anarchist ideas are utterly worthless. We may still want to look at anarchism from a reformist point of view, as a source of ideas for social experimentation. I have argued in this chapter that the impact of New Left thinking on anarchism served to divert it from its revolutionary path, even though many of its new adherents were unaware of the fact. We see now that this was not necessarily a bad thing. What remains to be done is to look at the constructive achievements of anarchism, both in revolutionary and non-revolutionary periods, and to assess these in the light of anarchist ideals. We will then be in a position to pass a final verdict on the ideology we are considering.

Part III Assessing Anarchism

11   Constructive Achievements

The theme of the second part of my book was the relationship between revolutionary theory and practice in anarchism. The conclusion reached was that none of the strategies proposed by anarchists for realizing their ideals had proved to be satisfactory. In this final section I want to return to these ideals themselves, and to assess their strengths and weaknesses. An obvious starting-point is the attempts anarchists have made to implement their ideals on a small scale, in the absence of an all-encompassing revolution. These experiments do not constitute decisive evidence for or against anarchism – no such evidence could be decisive, because the background conditions will always be special in one respect or another – but they do provide relevant information which must be taken into account in any intelligent assessment. In this chapter I shall look at the lessons to be learned from the experiments themselves, and in the next extend the discussion to broader issues before delivering a final verdict on anarchism as a social theory.

The evidence I shall consider, besides being not fully decisive, may also be said to be incomplete. Anarchists themselves have often turned to the past history of human society for support for their views, pointing to the so-called 'stateless' societies found in early periods of human development, and also to the various forms of social organization – such as the village community – which have existed alongside (but independently of) the state in later periods.[1] This is taken to be evidence that social order, economic co-operation and other human objectives can be achieved without recourse to the centralized apparatus of the state. There are two difficulties with this evidence. First, although the evidence referred to does indeed show that the state is not a necessary condition for maintaining social order and so forth, it is much less clear that the methods of social control which are practised in these societies are compatible with anarchist ideals. The main point of contrast with the modern state is that, instead of a concentrated and formal system for enforcing social rules, there is a diffuse and informal system. The sanctions faced by potential rule-breakers include the threat of private retaliation, the threat to withhold co-operation in future, various kinds of social pressure (gossip, shaming and so forth), and the threat of supernatural punishment.[2] Anarchists may perhaps find these less obnoxious than the mechanical processes of law. Nevertheless it is difficult to avoid the conclusion that members of these societies have their freedom seriously restricted, both in the sense that many actions they might otherwise consider performing are rendered ineligible, and in the sense that the range of choices they might make about how to live their lives is drastically narrowed by the power of custom and tradition.[3]

The second difficulty is, if anything, still more serious. The traditional societies I have referred to embodied a world-view which has been irreversibly shattered by the transition to modern society. They were held together, in large measure, by a set of customary beliefs, taken on trust by each generation and characteristically backed up by religion. Such a world-view cannot be recreated at will, even if one should want to. Modern anarchism has to start with individuals whose outlook has been formed by the sceptical questioning of modern science and the moral pluralism of an open and fluid society. It has to solve the problem of social order without presupposing, at the outset, a strong set of shared beliefs about how life ought to be lived. For that reason it is much more revealing to look at anarchist experiments carried out under modern conditions than to delve into vanished forms of life, interesting though the latter may be from a scientific point of view.

I shall look at two pieces of evidence, the first being the various experimental communities that anarchists have established, mainly in the periods 1890–1910 and 1965–75, and the second being the anarchist-inspired collectivization programme that was carried out in the early months of the Spanish Civil War. The problems with both pieces of evidence are fairly obvious. The communities have had to deal with an unsupportive and often actively hostile environment; being so small in size and few in number, they could do little to help one another. Collectivization in Spain, although carried out on a much larger scale, was seriously hampered by the effects of the war, to say nothing of the political conflicts which divided the Republican camp. Even so, we may be able to reach some tentative conclusions about the viability of anarchist ideals by examining this material.

Most of the experimental communities were based on anarcho-communist principles, but by way of a preamble it is interesting to look briefly at the individualist experiments initiated by Josiah Warren earlier in the nineteenth century. Warren's ideal, it will be

recalled,[4] was a society based on the exchange of individually produced commodities at cost of production, through the use of labour
notes. He attempted to demonstrate its practicality in two ways, the
first being the 'Time Stores' that he ran in Cincinnati between 1827
and 1830 and in New Harmony between 1842 and 1844 (other similar
ventures were shorter-lived). Warren sold his goods at wholesale
prices, with a small percentage added to cover rent and overheads; in
addition he asked his customers for labour notes to cover the time he
spent on each transaction, as recorded by a clock hanging on the shop
wall. These were later to be redeemed either in goods or in labour.
The stores were apparently a success, not least because Warren's cash
prices undercut those charged by his competitors by some considerable amount.[5] It is less clear how successful the labour notes were.
One observer reports that Warren had difficulty with customers
overestimating the value of their labour.[6] Since, however, the notes
only played a supplementary role, alongside transactions that made
use of ordinary money, the idea of privately issued currency was not
put to a crucial test.

Warren's second initiative was the foundation of several colonies.
After two short-lived ventures at Spring Hill and Tuscawaras, he
started the 'Utopia' community on the Ohio river in 1847, and
'Modern Times' close to New York in 1851. Both were based on
separate landholding by individual families, some of these being
farmers and others artisans. The communities were differentiated
from conventional settlements by two features: the first was the lack
of any formal system of authority, and the second was the more or less
extensive use of labour notes for exchanges between the colonists. The
'Utopia' colony appears to have functioned successfully, although it
gradually lost members as cheap land became available in the West
later in the century.[7] 'Modern Times', on the other hand, achieved
notoriety of the wrong sort, and attracted a variety of eccentrics, some
of them with views decidedly at odds with Warren's.[8] Although it,
too, survived for several decades, the Warrenite element – the use of
labour notes – was of marginal importance after the early years.

When compared with the anarcho-communist experiments to be
discussed shortly, the individualist ventures seem relatively successful. On the other hand they broke less radically with existing social
practices: by basing themselves on individual ownership and production, they avoided the problems of co-operative labour which were to
dog the later communities. Even the direct exchange of labour was not
very far removed from the mutual aid which is likely to be found in

any pioneering agricultural community. Perhaps their greatest achievement was to show that social order can be maintained, at least on a small scale, without formal sanctions – in the case of undesirables the community simply refused to have any dealings with them, at which point they usually drifted away.

The early communist colonies were set up by groups of anarchists who hoped that they would serve as beacons to the remainder of society, demonstrating the validity of anarchist ideas. Examples can be found in Britain, France and the U.S.A., and no doubt in other countries too.[9] The colonies mostly lasted only a short while, the exceptions being cases where the communist system was abandoned in favour of private production. The same broad pattern can be found throughout. Funds were raised to purchase or lease a small agricultural holding. On this several families would settle and begin to erect buildings, engage in market-gardening or animal-breeding, and practise crafts of various kinds. The community would exchange its products with the outside world on a cash basis, but would practise communism internally. The financial position would remain precarious. In a short while disputes would break out among the colonists, and some of the founding generation would leave. Newcomers might be brought in, but the colony, always small in size, would become smaller still. Eventually just a single family would be left in possession, and the experiment would be terminated.

To fill out this theoretical sketch, let me describe a couple of cases in greater detail. The Clousden Hill colony was established close to Newcastle in 1895 by some disciples of Kropotkin. Twenty acres of land was rented, and the colonists – numbering about twenty at the peak – raised livestock and gardened under glass. Their produce was sold to the local Co-ops, and for a while the community was reasonably prosperous. Newcomers, however, were not necessarily as adept at horticulture as the founders, and disagreements within the group led to the break-up of the community in 1900.

In France, a colony was established by subscription at Vaux in 1903. Twelve hectares of land were eventually bought, and the colony, starting from a single family, rose in numbers to more than twenty. They grew vegetables, raised livestock and engaged in crafts – hosiery, shoemaking and tailoring. The colony was more or less able to support itself, but almost from the beginning there were personal dissensions. The founding member was accused of authoritarianism, and had to leave the colony in 1904 (he was called back shortly afterwards). The number of inhabitants declined in

1905, and the community was finally dissolved two years later.

Although the people involved in these experiments generally tried to make the best of what they had done, it is hard to describe the colonies other than as failures. Why was this so? Nearly all of them were undercapitalized, but this does not seem to have been the decisive factor. To begin with, they tended to attract individuals with strong personalities and equally strong convictions – not on the whole the most suitable material for a co-operative enterprise. They also had difficulty in creating in their members a lasting commitment to the community – people came and went, which reduced stability and made it hard to build up the various lines of work into anything substantial. Both of these factors do of course reflect the communities' position on the margin of capitalist society, and so one should be wary about drawing general lessons for anarchism on this basis. The remaining two difficulties, on the other hand, have a more general relevance. Being anarchistically inspired, the colonists would only undertake projects by unanimous agreement, and this was a major source of friction and inefficiency. The personal quarrels which loom so large in the records of these little communities must, I think, be attributed partly to this method of making decisions, which gave everyone a veto on common undertakings. Moreover there was a problem about getting each person to do his share of the community's work in the absence of personal incentives. This is, of course, an old objection to communist schemes, but in the cases I am considering it seems to have been borne out. The memoirs of disillusioned ex-colonists often refer to idleness as a reason for their community's downfall.

It is worth noting in this connection that two colonies of this period which outlasted their contemporaries by many years did so by foregoing communist production in favour of individual production, retaining only common meeting-places and certain other shared forms of consumption as tangible evidence of their communal character. The Whiteway colony in Gloucestershire, Tolstoyan in inspiration, gave up communism in its second year, but then survived for some thirty years as a loose community of anarchists.[10] In the U.S., the Home colony flourished between 1898 and 1917, also on the basis of individual possession of land and a limited range of common undertakings.[11] These ventures suggest that anarchists are not innately quarrelsome, but that they do best when not too much has to be decided collectively. Before reaching general conclusions, however, we should also take account of evidence from the more recent wave of communities.

In contrast to their predecessors, modern commune-dwellers are unlikely to see themselves as flag-bearers for an ideology, and much more likely to see their experiment as a means of personal salvation.[12] This makes it more difficult to identify particular communes as anarchist-inspired – instead anarchism is often an element in the commune-dwellers' world-view, along with vegetarianism, ecological concern, feminism and a few other ingredients.[13] Many communes, however, approximate to the anarcho-communist model internally – no one is forced to do anything, all collective undertakings must be agreed upon unanimously, and most goods are shared on the basis of need. We should therefore expect to find some of the same difficulties as were experienced by the older communities.

The first of these is instability of membership. Modern communes are nearly always short-lived, and their individual members tend to come and go still more quickly. In the absence of any underlying ideological commitment, there is nothing to hold anyone inside a commune besides the personal fulfilment achieved at any time.[14] This in itself makes it difficult for a commune to organize its productive work effectively. A second problem, once again, is the lack of an effective procedure for making decisions. The unanimity rule tends to be a recipe for stagnation. Here, for instance, is an account of a recent Californian commune:

> All personal decisions were made by individuals. The community met once a week on Sunday evenings to discuss group issues, but if someone refused to abide by the consensus of the group, there was no way to enforce the decision, and generally nothing happened. It ran counter to the wishes of the group to force any individual to conform or to demonstrate more commitment than he was willing to give. As a result, problems of getting the work done around the commune were never solved. The members of the commune 'tried everything we could think of', including encounter groups and rotating leadership, but nothing worked.[15]

Many communes have also experienced difficulty in inducing their members to perform the often laborious tasks that need to be undertaken if the commune is to be economically self-sufficient. In practice most have relied on personal savings, social security handouts and casual earnings outside the commune to keep themselves going.[16] In this respect there are advantages as well as drawbacks to living on the margin of an affluent capitalist society. These deficiencies do not of course detract from the personal fulfilment which many commune-dwellers have found in their shared forms of life, albeit only for a comparatively short period in most cases. They are relevant only as being indicative of the kinds of problems which the anarcho-communist would face if he tried to implement his ideals under modern conditions. Here it is interesting to compare both the recent communes and the older anarchist colonies with the comparatively stable utopian communities that were formed in the U.S. earlier in the nineteenth century. Sociologists making this comparison have pointed to a number of contrasts between the stable communities and their ephemeral counterparts.[17] The former employed what Kanter has called 'commitment mechanisms' – practices which bound the members to the community and cut them off from the outside world – to maintain stability. They developed their own peculiar rituals – styles of dress, patterns of sexual and other behaviour – to mark themselves off from the rest of society. They discouraged any contact with the outside world. They had a well-developed system of authority, and powerful methods – such as group criticism – for enforcing the rules of the community. Finally the community was held together by a common belief-system, which in practice meant a common religion.[18]

This strongly suggests that communities can only remain stable, under modern conditions, by structuring themselves in a way that anarchists would find repugnant. The virus of individualism has taken a deep hold. To eradicate it requires a stringent method of subjecting the individual to group discipline. Anarchists will protest, of course, that the freedom they value is not the freedom of the wilful individualist who turns his back on his social obligations, but the freedom which manifests itself in social solidarity. As Kropotkin put it, their goal is 'the individuality which attains the greatest individual development possible through practising the highest communist sociability in what concerns both its primordial needs and its relationship with others in general'.[19] But this development is supposed to occur spontaneously through ordinary contact between person and person, not to be brought about deliberately through a set of conditioning mechanisms.

Let me turn now to the other main piece of evidence for the constructive possibilities of anarchism, the collectives in the Spanish revolution. The importance of this evidence is that it throws light not only on the internal strengths and weaknesses of communities built upon anarcho-communist lines, but also on the problem of establishing relationships between these communities without relying either on a market regime or on central planning. It should be said straight away that this experiment in collectivization was carried out under the most unfavourable circumstances. Although the anarchists were the most powerful single force in several areas of Spain at the outbreak of the Civil War, they had always to compete with other Republican factions – especially the Socialists at first and the Communists later on – and their influence was waning almost from the beginning of the revolution. The collectives, therefore, had to contend with increasing hostility from the Republican government, and by the middle of 1937 the experiment was more or less at an end, only a year after it had begun. There was barely time to consolidate the internal arrangements of the communes and the factories, let alone to develop institutions for co-ordinating their activities.

We may begin with the collectives in the countryside. I have already drawn attention (in Chapter 7) to the difficulty of deciding how far collectivization in the rural areas was voluntary, and how far it was imposed by the anarchist militias as they moved forward. We have to rely on eye-witness accounts, and these are prejudiced by the political sympathies of the observer. For the same reason it is hard to reach definite conclusions about the success of the collectives.[20] It is also hard to generalize across different regions of Spain, because the enthusiasm of peasants and rural workers for collectivization was strongly influenced by the previous pattern of landholding, which varied significantly between the regions.[21] Despite these difficulties, I shall try to describe the main features of the rural communes.

More than one thousand collectives were formed in all; in Aragon about three-quarters of the land was managed in this way. The collectives varied considerably in size, from under a hundred persons to several thousand.[22] Authority was shared between the general assembly of the town or village and the political committee, formed under the auspice of whichever faction was dominant in the locality (in the cases we are concerned with this was, of course, the anarchist-inspired C.N.T.). The relationship between the two bodies is one of those issues on which observers are prone to disagree, but it is uncontroversial to say that the day-to-day running of the collective was in the hands of the committee. Work itself was undertaken by teams of workers – usually about ten in number – who would choose a delegate to represent them at the local committee. Land was acquired either by expropriating large estates or by collectivizing the smallholdings of the peasantry, depending on the region in question. Tools and raw materials were also pooled.[23] In most places 'individualists' were allowed to continue working their own plots of land, provided they did not attempt to hire labour. Relations between the 'collectivists' and the 'individualists' seem to have varied a great deal: from some places there are reports of peaceful co-existence (and even of 'individualists' being given access to the services of the collective); in other cases private owners were virtually forced by economic pressure to hand over their property to the collective.[24]

All of the collectives moved some way towards the communist ideal of distribution according to need, but the schemes adopted varied considerably in points of detail. In some places the community's goods were simply placed in a central storehouse and each member allowed to take what he or she needed – Borkenau describes such an arrangement in the poverty-stricken Andalusian village of Castro.[25] But few villages were able to sustain such a libertarian system overall, and practised it only with respect to a few basic commodities such as bread and wine. Other goods were distributed either by rationing, or, more commonly, against an allowance paid to each family in the collective, calculated on the basis of the number of persons in the household. Many towns and villages decided to print their own currency or vouchers to replace the Spanish peseta, which was felt to be redolent of the old system. In this case people who wanted to travel outside the village were provided with pesetas by the local committee.[26]

The internal economy of the towns and villages appears to have functioned quite smoothly. Regular services such as medical care and hairdressing were simply provided free, while requests for tools, machinery and so forth were passed to the local committee, which would then pass them on to the delegate of the appropriate trade. There does not seem to have been much of a problem with slackers. No doubt revolutionary élan and the need to combat the fascists played their part here, but in addition the assembly retained the ultimate right to expel any member who failed to meet his obligations. This sanction was hardly ever used: the community was effectively self-policing.

Evidence about the economic performance of the collectives is harder to come by. Hugh Thomas's review of the available figures suggests, however, that overall production of agricultural goods increased somewhat between 1936 and 1937, and this is borne out by a study of one small town which left a detailed stock inventory.[27] Given the circumstances of civil war, which seriously disrupted the economy and carried off large numbers of young workers to the front line, it was an impressive achievement. Clearly the revolution released the energies of the Spanish peasantry, and this showed itself in their willingness to cultivate the lands they had inherited more intensively than under the old landowners (there was no doubt much room for improvement here). Reports speak, for example, of peasants planting potatoes between their rows of orange trees, and of intercropping wheat and rice.[28] A number of modernizing projects were also carried through: new threshing machines were bought, fields were irrigated, roads and schools were built, and so forth.[29] Improvements such as these would not generally feature in the economic statistics.

The collectives succeeded internally because they evolved a form of organization – the local committee and the delegate system – which was adequate to its task. The same cannot be said of relations between the collectives. It is very difficult to form an accurate picture here: the reports that are available are confusing and sometimes even contradictory. Clearly there are three ways in which inter-community relations might have been conducted: through straightforward cash transactions, through bartering goods for goods (this was the solution traditionally favoured by anarcho-communists in non-ideal conditions), or through reciprocal giving with the aim of equalizing the position of the various communities. In practice all three methods were used, but it is hard to tell in what proportions. There are many reports of villages bartering their surplus produce with one another; yet the obvious defects of this method (what if village A has surplus wheat which village B wants, but B has nothing in surplus that A wants?) must have underlain the growing belief, in anarchist circles, that a uniform national currency was after all a good thing. Proposals for the establishment of a collectivist bank were advanced both in Aragon and the Levante.[30] Meanwhile the peseta continued to be used for a number of transactions.

As far as gifts are concerned, the evidence suggests that rural communities were more likely to send their surpluses to the militias on the front and to the cities than to one another. In theory it should have been possible to organize redistribution between collectives. In both Aragon and the Levante – the two major areas in which collectivization was able to proceed relatively unhindered – regional federations were created that saw this as one of their primary tasks. Inter-village storehouses were established to hold food surpluses, and the federal committee informed of the contents. It is very doubtful, however, whether the system really worked as it was supposed to on paper. Even the most sympathetic of commentators, Gaston Leval, admits that 'the generalization of the egalitarian levelling up, which corresponded to the spirit of general solidarity, could not be realized because of the attack by the Stalinist armed forces in August 1937 . . .'[31] Thomas's more critical inquiry reveals that living standards in the various communities, as measured by the family wage, varied a great deal: in collectives in the Madrid region working couples received twelve pesetas per day, while (at the other end of the scale) the rate for such couples in a collective near Cuenca was only four pesetas.[32] Such variations no doubt reflected historical inequalities of wealth, but at the same time the redistributive impact of the federation had clearly been slight.

The problems of collectivization in the cities were in many respects greater than those encountered in the countryside. Collectivization followed one of two paths, depending on whether the previous owner of the factory or workshop in question stayed put or fled. If he stayed, the C.N.T. encouraged him to continue with his management functions, while installing a 'control committee' of its own members to supervise the general running of the enterprise. If he left, the union quickly developed its own management structure, promoting technicians and skilled workers to positions of responsibility. These measures appear to have struck a sensible balance between industrial democracy and the requirements of efficient production, and eyewitness accounts (such as Borkenau's) testify to their success. After visiting the workshops of the Barcelona bus company, he wrote that, 'it is an extraordinary achievement for a group of workers to take over a factory, under however favourable conditions, and within a few days to make it run with complete regularity. It bears brilliant witness to the general standard of efficiency of the Catalan worker and to the organizing capacities of the Barcelona trade unions. For one must not forget that this firm has lost its whole managing staff.'[33] In addition, whole branches of industry were reorganized. Contrary to what one might have expected, this took the form of combining small workshops and businesses into larger establishments. For instance in Barcelona the number of plants in the tanning industry was reduced from seventy-one to forty, and in glass-making from one hundred to thirty; over nine hundred barber's shops and beauty parlours were consolidated into some two hundred large shops.[34]

Barcelona was the main scene of urban collectivization, though a number of other cities (such as Alcoy) also witnessed developments of a similar kind.[35] In the Catalonian capital it embraced all forms of transport, the major utilities, the telephone service, the health service, the textile and metal industries, much of the food industry, and many thousands of smaller enterprises. Orwell has left us a memorable picture of life in a city 'where the working class was in the saddle'.[36] As a demonstration of the creative capacities of that class when left to organize industry by itself, it is surely impressive. As a vindication of anarcho-communist theory, however, it is less so. There were two major sources of difficulty. The first was the problem of co-ordinating the work of different enterprises. Industry, unlike agriculture, depends on a complex chain of supply between different stages in the productive process, and this proved difficult to maintain. The ordinary banking system was paralysed at the outbreak of the revolution. In its place two institutions were created: an Economic Council and a Central Labour Bank. The former was supposed to plan and supervise production generally, while the latter was to arrange credit for enterprises that needed it and to conduct transactions between enterprises. In reality, however, inter-enterprise relations were arranged haphazardly, through some combination of cash purchases and requisitioning of raw materials. Many factories were unable to obtain the materials that they needed and had to work part-time.

The other difficulty was that the workers who took over the various factories and workshops found themselves in very different economic circumstances. Some had funds in reserve, others were badly in debt. These inequalities persisted in the revolutionary period, despite the efforts of the Economic Council, so workers were able to enjoy markedly different incomes. A C.N.T. commission observed that 'the immoderate concern to collectivize everything, especially firms with monetary reserves, has revealed a utilitarian and petty bourgeois spirit among the masses . . . By regarding each collective as private property, and not merely as its usufruct, the interests of the rest of the collective have been disregarded.'[37] The communist goal of equalizing personal incomes (except in respect of differences in need) proved to be as elusive in the cities as it had in the countryside.

These manifest weaknesses in the collectivization programme aided the Socialists and the Communists in demanding greater government control over the economy. Anarchists would no doubt claim that the problems would have resolved themselves in due course, given time and freedom from outside interference. It is difficult, however, to believe that this was really so. The decentralized form of organization favoured by the anarchists was effective for certain purposes – for running individual factories and villages, and for equalizing the incomes of their members – but it was not up to handling complex economic processes or to removing long-established inequalities between branches of industry and between regions. Indeed this points us towards a general difficulty in anarcho-communist theory, which I shall consider at greater length in the next chapter.

It is instructive to compare the Spanish collectives with the experimental anarchist communities that we examined earlier. A major problem for the communities was to find a form of organization that would enable their members to work together effectively. The collectives largely avoided this problem, partly because they based themselves on pre-existing associations (villages and factories) and partly because an organizational structure was ready to hand in the shape of the C.N.T. The constructive achievements of the Spanish revolution would have been impossible without the syndicates. These events provide strong backing for the view that a social revolution can only be carried through if alternative forms of organization are available to replace the established ones – a vindication of the anarcho-syndicalist position against the purer anarchism of some of its critics.

But were these advantages purchased at the expense of individual freedom? The experimental communities seem to embody more perfectly the ideal of individual autonomy, of each person only doing what his own inclinations and moral conscience advise him to do. The collectives, by contrast, display what might be called a system of voluntary authority. No one was forced to join or remain a member of a collective against his will – though as we have seen the costs of non-membership were often considerable. Once inside, however, he was subject to the authority of the general assembly, in principle, and in practice quite often to that of the local committee. These bodies had substantial sanctions at their disposal – they controlled the issuing of food coupons, for example – but they rarely needed to impose them. We may surmise that this was partly because the people concerned knew and trusted their committee members, and partly because they were morally committed to the collective system. Individualism had not completely disappeared (as is shown by reports of defections from the collectives) but it was a less insidious problem than in the case of the communities.

This brings home the point that we have been dealing with two very different groups of people. On the one hand we have been looking at people who have come together for personal or ideological reasons, trying to evolve a form of communal living and working that meets their aspirations; on the other, at people already associated trying to transform their association in the light of a shared ideal – an ideal that in the Spanish case had been germinating for over half a century. It is easy to see that the Spanish collectivists had the better chance of success. At the same time the problems of the communities seem closer to our own. Could an anarchist movement today draw on the solidarity that characterized the villages of rural Spain, or the loyalty of the syndicalists in the towns?[38]

If we were to draw up a final balance sheet on the evidence we have examined, there would be several entries on the credit side. To begin with, we should have to include the personal fulfilment felt by many participants both in the communities and the collectives – the sense that here at last they had found the brotherhood they had been seeking. We should also want to include the evidence that these experiments provide about human creativity: they show that people can take on quite new tasks and fulfil them with distinction – that, indeed, conventional society makes much less than full use of its members' potential. Third, the evidence bears out the anarcho-communist claim that people do not require individual incentives in order to carry out their share of society's work – or at least not incentives of the crude monetary kind. Finally the collectives in particular show that industrial democracy of quite a radical kind is not a pipedream, given the appropriate background conditions.

There would also, however, be a number of entries on the debit side. The familiar tension between the demands of individual autonomy and those of social solidarity seems not to have been over-come – the communities, broadly speaking, enjoying autonomy at the expense of solidarity, and the collectives solidarity at the expense of some autonomy. The question of structure has not been fully resolved: the collectives, which were better organized than most of the communities, were too short-lived for us to say whether the structure they adopted would not in time have ossified into a new form of hierarchical authority. Third, there is very little in this evidence to suggest how equality within a small group can be translated into equality across a large society without recourse to a central authority to maintain such a distributive pattern. Fourth, the evidence also fails to assuage critical doubts about how the economy is to be organized under anarchy: the communities existed on the margins of capitalist society, and the collectives, although breaking to some extent with the market economy, failed to devise a viable alternative means of co-ordinating their activities.

Anarchists, therefore, can find some support for their claims in the constructive experiments considered in this chapter; but their critics will also find several of their doubts confirmed. I shall look more closely at these doubts in the final chapter.

12   Critical Questions

So far in this book I have looked at anarchism from the inside (as it were), raising critical questions only when such questions have occurred naturally to anarchists themselves. It is now time to relax this self-imposed limitation and to take a harder look at the consistency and realism of anarchist ideas. There are many questions that might be asked under this rubric: no doubt most readers will already have formulated their own.[1] My discussion will be fairly selective, and in particular it will avoid tackling head-on an issue which crops up at a fairly early stage in most critical assessments of anarchism: namely whether 'human nature' is good enough to permit anarchy to function successfully. My reason for avoiding this is that I share the anarchists' view that 'human nature' is not a fixed quantity, but rather something that varies (within limits) according to the social and political context in which particular members of the species find themselves. On the other hand the issue cannot be ducked entirely, because a number of my critical comments are to the effect that anarchists cannot simultaneously advocate A and B (two social ideals), and such comments make tacit assumptions about human nature – I hope assumptions that are not too controversial.

We saw in the first part of the book that anarchist ideas are not all of a piece, and my first critical questions have to be addressed separately to individualist and communist anarchists. (These views, as I suggested, represent the two poles around which anarchist ideas tend to cluster.) Later I raise issues that apply to anarchists of all kinds, stemming as they do from the shared idea of the abolition of the state.

The individualist ideal is one of personal sovereignty in the market place. It holds that all of society's business can be conducted through exchange and contract, along with charitable aid to those who for one reason or another are unable to fend for themselves. A question that arises immediately is whether the benefits of the market, as they appear to us today, do not depend on the existence of other institutions whose workings follow a different principle. In particular, is the state not an indispensable prerequisite for a successfully functioning market economy?

169

There is at least one basic reason for believing that it is. Market transactions presuppose a number of background features whose very familiarity makes us inclined to take them for granted. Among these are an agreed definition of property rights (so that each person knows precisely which goods are his to dispose of), a set of rules governing contracts (for instance rules prohibiting fraudulent descriptions of commodities), a common currency (to enable non-simultaneous exchanges to occur) and general protection against invasion, assault and theft. Without these features we would not have a market, but something more akin to a Hobbesian war of all against all. But can their emergence be explained without reference to the state? They are all to some degree public goods: goods which benefit everyone but which no individual has a private incentive to provide. From each separate participant's point of view, the best state of affairs is for others to contribute to the cost of providing the goods, while he merely enjoys the benefits they create. The question, then, is whether such goods can be provided in the absence of an agency which compels people to contribute to their cost.

Broadly speaking there are two alternatives to political compulsion. One is the emergence of social norms, where each person plays his part in ensuring that others keep to the conventions that have been adopted. Thus, it might be suggested, rules for determining property rights and so forth will emerge over time, and it will then be in each person's interest to exert pressure on other people to abide by them. But, as I will argue later, this solution is only likely to work in small communities, not in large societies. The other alternative is for an entrepreneurial agency to supply the benefits in question only to those who agree to pay for them. This is a possible solution if the goods are of such a nature that non-contributors can be prevented from enjoying them (and so undermining the rationale for signing up). But in the case of such basic features of a market economy as an agreed definition of property rights and a common currency, there is no way of compartmentalizing the benefits and excluding non-contributors.

I suggested earlier that individualist anarchists might in the last resort dispose of the public goods problem by saying that it was better for such goods not to be provided than for a Leviathan to be created with the object of supplying them.[2] This riposte might be adequate in the case of familiar goods such as harbours and parks which are useful or enjoyable rather than essential. But the framework of the market falls into a different category: without it the very mechanism on which individualists are relying to get society's productive business done is put in jeopardy.

The critical question for individualists, therefore, is whether in attempting to convert all human relations into market relations, they are not cutting away the ground on which the present market economy is built. The question for anarcho-communists is rather different. They wish to abolish the market altogether, without at the same time replacing it with central planning on the Soviet model. The difficulty here is to see how productive activity can be co-ordinated at all. As we saw in the last chapter, the problem is not necessarily one of motivating people to work. Given suitable conditions – essentially a number of small productive units, each of which is able to discipline its own members by some combination of moral pressure and informal sanctions – it does seem possible to organize production without personal rewards. The difficulty is rather one of co-ordinating the activities of different units, and of aligning production with the needs of consumers. We saw in Chapter 4 that the anarcho-communists hoped to alleviate this problem by localizing production as far as possible. Each commune would then be responsible for informing groups of producers in its area about the needs of the local population, and for harmonizing the activities of the various groups. This still says very little about the actual mechanics of such local planning; but in addition it fails to come to terms with a basic precondition for an advanced industrial economy. Such an economy (which the anarchists presuppose, for they assume that goods will be produced in greater abundance than under capitalism) requires a high degree of specialization on the part of producers. It is impossible (for instance) for a single factory to make television sets using only basic raw materials such as wood and iron. Instead each enterprise depends on incorporating the manufactured products of other factories into its own output. Thus an industrial economy is inconceivable without a vast network of exchange between different enterprises. A large measure of local self-sufficiency may be possible in an economy made up of peasant farmers and artisans, but not in one composed of high technology industries.

I am not arguing here that the units of production in an advanced economy need themselves be large: it may well be possible to break down complex technological processes in such a way that each unit can be managed effectively by its own workers. But the more this is done, the more each unit becomes dependent on its suppliers and/or its customers. Co-ordination becomes increasingly vital, and there appear only to be two ways in which it can be achieved: by the market (each enterprise sells its products to the next and regulates its output by considerations of profit) and central planning (a central agency instructs each enterprise to produce a certain output using given inputs). No anarchist has devised a plausible third alternative.

We may say, in short, that neither of the major schools of anarchism has developed an adequate economic theory. The individualists are stymied by the public goods problem, the communists by the problem of co-ordination. Proudhon's mutualism, representing a compromise of sorts between market and communitarian ideals, is perhaps the most plausible of anarchist theories from an economic point of view; but even here it is necessary to ask whether the system proposed does not require the support of the state at a number of crucial points.[3]

I turn next to the related issue of distribution. Individualists and communists hold markedly different views about distributive justice, but both face the difficulty that a central agency seems necessary to maintain any society-wide distribution of resources. Anarcho-individualists might well deny that they adhered to an idea of distributive justice in the sense just indicated. They might, like Nozick, espouse an 'entitlement' theory of justice, according to which any distribution of resources may be considered just, provided it has arisen by just procedures, of which a paradigm case would be voluntary exchange in the market.[4] However it is difficult to believe that even the most tough-minded of individualists could remain wholly indifferent to the question of distribution. If inequalities are very large, and the worst-off members of society are as a result quite badly off, the prospects for a stable market system will not seem very bright. To meet this objection, individualists have in practice relied on two claims: first, that a genuinely free market would generate less inequality between participants than the state-manipulated markets with which we are familiar; second, that in the absence of the state, the springs of private charity would flow more freely, taking adequate care of those unable to compete in the market. Both of these claims rest on somewhat flimsy evidence. The first presupposes that state intervention does little except create monopoly power, whereas in fact such intervention often occurs in response to monopoly or oligopoly that is rooted directly in the characteristics of advanced technology. The second overlooks the fact that people may be more willing to contribute to the relief of poverty through a tax system that weighs fairly on everyone, than through unco-ordinated private giving.[5]

Considerations such as these have led enthusiasts for the free market such as Hayek to argue that a state-administered safety net for the poor is essential to the stability of such an economy.

There is no doubt at all that anarcho-communists are wedded to a distributive ideal, namely one of distribution according to need. It is possible to implement such an ideal at least approximately within a small community, and indeed we saw in the last chapter that both the anarchist communities and the collectives in Spain had gone some way towards achieving this goal. There are major difficulties, however, in attempting to realize it *between* communities (again our evidence confirmed this). First of all there is a problem of co-ordination. Suppose, as seems reasonable, that each of the many communities that make up a large society achieves a different level of *per capita* production. Unless all consumer goods are to be centrally pooled and distributed back to the communities – an arrangement which seems inconceivable in the absence of the state – there will have to be a complex set of transfers from richer to poorer communities to achieve an overall pattern of distribution according to need. How, one may ask, is this set of transfers to be organized? There is also a problem of establishing mutual trust. Within a small community, each person will help to ensure that the others pull their weight in carrying out productive work, and the assurance that this is so encourages people to concur in a distribution of goods according to need. Between communities, however, there can be no such assurance. How can we be certain that the neighbours to whom we transfer some of our goods are worse off because of poorer natural endowments, say, rather than because they have chosen to work less hard than us? It seems unlikely that a system of voluntary transfers could survive such doubts.

The problem I have just identified – that of reconciling distributive ideals with a decentralized form of social organization – is not exclusive to anarchists. Many liberals and socialists also wish to combine a devolved system of authority with a society-wide pattern of distribution. The regional inequalities that currently exist in countries (such as Yugoslavia) whose governments claim to be pursuing egalitarian ideals show how intractable the problem may turn out to be in practice. By advocating the complete abolition of central authority, however, anarchists are forced to confront the problem in its most acute form.

I want now to consider some difficulties in reconciling the anarchist ideal of freedom with the idea that anti-social behaviour can be controlled without recourse to a formal system of law. Although their respective analyses of the problem are different in important ways, both individualist and communist anarchists believe that social life is to a large extent self-regulating, and that where this self-regulation breaks down deviant individuals can be disciplined by private means – by protective agencies seeking compensation in the case of the individualists or by the local commune in the case of the communists. Social life is self-regulating because for the most part people will adhere voluntarily to the moral rules that make it possible.[6]

But under what conditions can people be expected to behave in this way? When people act morally they do so partly because they have come to accept certain rules as binding in themselves, and partly because they are aware of the reactions of those around them; they anticipate approval and reward if they keep to the rules, and disapproval and punishment (in an informal sense) if they break them. No doubt there are some very conscientious people who would keep the rules even if no one else knew what they were doing; but they are not all that common, and they are usually sustained by religious belief ('for God's all-seeing eye surveys, thy secret thoughts and words and ways'). Most of us need to be kept up to the mark by the gentle pressure of our neighbours.

This moralizing force must, however, vary in strength according to how much we interact with those whose approval we seek and whose disapproval we fear. It will be strongest where we are tightly bound into a small community whose responses we must live with for the rest of our lives. To the extent that we can isolate ourselves from a particular community or, more realistically, escape from that community and join another, we will have less compunction about breaking the rules of morality. Consider, for instance, the individualist argument that one important reason people have for keeping their contracts is that anyone who fails to do so will rapidly find himself running out of contractual partners. This argument applies most forcefully where a person has only a limited number of partners to choose from, and where knowledge that he has defaulted on a contract will spread rapidly through the community. It would be a weighty consideration in a village, less weighty in a town, and less weighty still in a large society where a malefactor can move on whenever he is found out. Much the same can be said about the anarcho-communist view that people will fulfil their social responsibilities because of the solidarity they feel with those around them.

The anarchist view that social order can largely be achieved through moral self-regulation therefore looks most plausible when considered in the context of a small, stable community – the kind of community, in fact, that has characteristically been eroded by the liberalization and industrialization of society. Now whatever virtues such communities may have had, personal freedom was not prominent among them. To be more specific, the freedom which is crucially lacking in such a community is the freedom to withdraw from an established pattern of life and to create a new one in association with others whom one finds congenial and sympathetic. This is not a freedom which has always been valued, but it is widely valued nowadays, not least by anarchists who often contrast the 'free associations' and 'affinity groups' that would form in a stateless society with the rigid organizations that exist in the present one. But the presupposition of such freedom is an open and fluid society containing a multiplicity of groups, embodying many different views about how life ought to be lived, so that a person may gravitate towards the group whose outlook he finds most attractive.

The critical question now is whether legal regulation is not the price we pay for the benefits of such an open society. For, as I have argued, moral regulation is likely to be much weaker in a social order of this kind. Instead of having a stable set of other people on whose good opinion we depend, we find that we can easily drift from group to group. In addition, we may find that moral attitudes differ from one group to the next, and this will further erode our conscientious scruples. To keep people within the boundaries of social behaviour, a more impersonal system of control is necessary. The elaborate structure of legal rules, police, courts and prisons serves to meet this need. (I shall ask in a moment whether this structure is not also valuable for other reasons.)

This raises the further question whether anarchism is not, as some critics have claimed, a backward-looking, pre-industrial ideology. I think it is clear that anarchists have not consciously wished to return to an idealized era in the past. Some of them, it is true, have used the experience of pre-industrial societies as a point of contrast to conditions under industrial capitalism, but so have many other critics (including socialists like Marx) whose attitudes are usually regarded as progressive. From one point of view anarchism can be regarded as the extreme expression of the modernizing ideals of the French Revolution – liberty, equality and fraternity carried to their logical conclusion. It is also true, however, that the main formulation of anarchist theory took place at a time when the older communities still survived, or at least fell within living memory; its adherents were often villagers

175

or first-generation industrial workers. Assumptions that reflected pre-industrial conditions took their place alongside the modernizing ideals, and created internal tensions within anarchism, such as the one I have just diagnosed. So anarchism is neither straightforwardly backward-looking nor straightforwardly forward-looking. It depicts a radical future, but the vision it presents depends on social mechanisms that flourished in the simpler and more stable communities of the past.

We have looked already at the anarchist idea of moral self-regulation; anarchists concede, however, that more explicit sanctions may have to be imposed on people who fail to respond to social pressure. In the individualist case this means extracting compensation from people who violate other people's property rights – say by theft or by breach of contract. In the communist case it means restraining people who are dangerous to others and (in the last resort) excluding from the community people who fail to pull their weight or to abide by the local rules. In neither case is there any attempt to apply uniform rules or to administer justice impartially, as this notion is understood in liberal societies. Indeed anarchists have usually been critical of legal systems for their abstractness, for their failure to take account of the particular circumstances of each individual case.

What might be said against such informal procedures for sanctioning deviant behaviour?[7] One problem is that people may not know where they stand. In the absence of a uniform body of rules, they may be unsure which activities are permitted and which are not. Take first the individualists' proposal for enforcing justice through voluntary agencies. Even if there is overall agreement about which personal rights should be protected, there may well be substantial disagreement about how precisely these rights are to be construed, and about how compensation is to be assessed. Each time that I find myself in dispute with another person, the uncertainty starts afresh, because I have no way of knowing what practices the agencies he favours will follow. There is no reason to believe that the agencies will spontaneously converge on a uniform set of rules; they are supposed to be competitors, and they may decide to follow different practices in order to appeal to particular kinds of client.

For the anarcho-communists, the final court of appeal is presumably to be an assembly of the people who form each commune. This assembly is not, however, a legislative body: it lays down no general rules to govern its future decisions. It will decide each case on its merits. What reason is there to think that uniformity will result from such a procedure? Even if the decisions taken are all good ones, how can anyone be certain in advance what criteria will be applied to his case if he decides on a particular course of action?

Anarchists may retort that the certainty I am talking about is valued only by people who have been brought up in a law-ridden society.[8] Why should predictability matter if I can be assured that any case in which I am involved will be settled fairly? I agree that (in contrast to some of the other critical issues raised in this chapter) certainty about the future is not a value to which anarchists themselves attach much weight. It is, nonetheless, an important consideration for most people, because such predictability makes it possible to plan one's life and one's projects knowing that they will not be interfered with. A regime of legal rights, harsh though it may be in some of its effects, does give this assurance.

A second problem with informal settling of disputes and punishing of offences is that the arbitrating authority may know too much about the parties involved. To an anarchist this might seem an astonishing criticism to make: the failing of legal punishment, he would claim, is that it takes only a superficial view of the offender; it is unable to penetrate to the real source of his anti-social behaviour. This claim is often well founded. On the other hand, it is a virtue of legal systems of punishment that they attempt to punish people only for what they have done. In particular, people are not punished for faults of character or for moral offences that are not also legal offences (in principle at least; in practice evidence about a person's character produced to establish guilt or innocence may bias the verdict that is returned). An important means of achieving this is to ensure that the person charged is not known personally to those who stand in judgment on him, so that their verdict is based solely on facts produced as evidence for the offence. The danger inherent in systems of communal justice is that the verdict returned will be some kind of overall verdict on the person in question ('Is he a good man by our standards?'). This is a danger so long as one wants to maintain a distinction between crimes and other kinds of moral misdemeanours (rudeness or irresponsibility, for instance).

Other problems will flow from the particular method of arbitration chosen. The individualist proposal that parties to a dispute should resort to a commercial arbitration agency seems open to the obvious objection that the agency is liable to favour the party with the larger bank balance at his disposal. The fact that many disputes are currently settled by private arbitration to the apparent satisfaction of both parties does not remove this objection, because arbitration now occurs within a framework established by law. This has two effects. Both parties know that their resort to arbitration is conditional, and that in the last instance they can press their case in the public courts. They therefore have an incentive to patronize agencies that can be expected to reach a visibly fair decision. Second, the agencies themselves are likely to model their verdicts on those reached in the courts, on the similar grounds that they want their customers to accept their decisions as final. Law, therefore, forms a nucleus around which less formal methods of settling disputes can cluster, but these other methods could not be expected to work in the same way in the absence of any authoritative guidelines to follow.

The anarcho-communist idea of administering justice by general assembly faces a rather different problem. The danger here is that discussion of a particular case may be distorted by disagreements of a more general kind. Suppose, for instance, that a community is divided into two sections, one favouring longer hours of work and a higher standard of living and the other favouring shorter hours and a lower standard. Suppose that a prominent member of the second section is called before the assembly on the grounds that he is work-shy. In his defence he may argue that he is working as hard as he thinks that he should, and that if others would follow his example everyone would be better off as a result. It is clearly impossible here to disentangle the culpability of the person concerned from the general issue at stake. The problem arises because no distinction has been made between legislation – laying down general rules to cover all cases – and adjudication – applying the rules to a particular case. It is theoretically possible, of course, for a body made up of the same people to act at one time as a legislative body and at another time as a judicial body; but such a separation will clearly be difficult to maintain in practice, and it is no accident that those who have favoured the separation of powers have also argued that the powers in question should be divided between several independent bodies.

I have offered, in effect, a defence of the rule of law (as this notion has traditionally been understood) against the anarchist idea that disputes can be settled by informally arranged arbitration and discipline. One further point may be worth adding. The informal method seems most likely to be successful in those small and stable communities where (as I argued earlier) moral self-regulation will in any case be most effective. For in such communities, the decisions that are reached in contested cases may amount, over time, to a kind of common law which can then be applied to new cases as they arise. This is likely to happen, in particular, because there will be substantial agreement about the principles to be applied in each case. In an open and fluid society such agreement is unlikely to emerge; so there will be no basis on which case law can be built up. In such a society, the advantages of authoritative legislation which is then enforced as impartially as possible by professional judges seem very striking.

Most of my observations up to this point have concerned the difficulty of achieving certain valued objectives (economic efficiency, distributive justice, the control of anti-social behaviour) in the absence of a state. I want now to suggest, rather more speculatively, a reason that people may have for wanting to be associated politically within a state – a reason, in other words, for rejecting anarchy even if the problems I have mentioned could somehow be resolved. This has to do with the connection between the state and nationality.

The fact of national identity will not, I think, be denied. For most people it is an important part of the answer to the question 'Who am I?' to say that they belong to a particular nation, with its own culture, outlook and historical record. One might add that it has become more important to the extent that other sources of identity have been eroded by the break-up of smaller communities (villages and so forth) within each country. People clearly feel a need to locate themselves in relation to something beyond their own immediate environment, and national identity meets this need, even if the sources of that identity are often rather doubtful (I should not deny that nationality can to some extent be manufactured by politicians and others who wish to make use of the forces so released).

Given that nationality exists, what does this imply about the state? People for whom national identity matters will also feel that they want to be self-governing. This is for two reasons. First, the state, provided it is made up of co-nationals, may be expected to serve as the guardian of national identity. It may act, for instance, to protect the national culture against being swamped by foreign influences. Second, and perhaps more important, the state may *express* the nation's will through its actions. As bearers of national identity, in other words, people see themselves not just as passive recipients of a culture and a tradition, but as actors – for instance in relation to other nations. But the nation as such is an amorphous mass, unable to act on its own accord. The state serves as the executive arm of the nation, and people come to regard its actions (or some of them at least) as their own.

The views just presented are (as I have admitted) speculative.

On the other hand, unless something like this is true, how are we to account for the manifest desire of people everywhere to be self-governing, even when there is no reason to believe that self-government will mean better government when measured in ordinary material terms?[9]

Anarchists will be very hostile to the idea that these observations provide any justification for the existence of the state. How might they respond? They might dismiss the whole idea of nationality as fraudulent; or they might accept that idea, but deny that it had the political implications outlined above.

The first response reveals something of the narrowness of the anarchist view of human nature. It is true that a great deal that is mythical may be incorporated into the idea of national identity: history may be rewritten to emphasize the past glories of the nation; old legends and folklore may be artificially revived and embellished; and so forth. But none of this would be possible if the idea did not answer a deep-seated human need: the need to see oneself as part of a larger whole with an identity, a history, and quite possibly a mission to the future as well. This need can be met by means other than nationality: by religion, for instance, or by ethnic identity (though the latter often turns in due course into a form of nationalism). The anarchist, however, offers nothing to replace the nation: his ideal society is devoid of any features which might serve as a focus of identity. It will of course possess an ideology – a set of beliefs justifying its social arrangements – so perhaps the thought is that ideological commitment itself can fulfil the need we are discussing. But commitments of this kind are too abstract and bloodless to fit the bill, unless they can be linked to actual groups of people, as happened to a degree with socialism and the nineteenth-century working class, and with Marxism–Leninism and the Soviet Union: in these cases loyalty could be given to a concrete section of humanity regarded as the bearers of an ideal. The all-embracing anarchist utopia would allow no room for such sectional loyalties.

The second response concedes that people will go on thinking of themselves as Germans, Frenchmen and so forth, but maintains that this need imply nothing about the continuing existence of the state.[10] It is certainly a mistake to confuse nation and state. People may regard themselves as forming a nation without possessing their own form of government, or alternatively their sense of national identity may include political ideals which do not correspond to the institutions that they presently have (for instance they may regard themselves as a 'democratic people'). Nevertheless, as I suggested earlier, the idea of nationhood does quite naturally lead to a demand for self-government, for a unitary body embracing all the people able to express their will in active form. Without such a body the nation remains inchoate and directionless.

Anarchists have seen only the repressive aspects of the state: they have seen it as an enemy of personal freedom and as an upholder of economic exploitation. Consequently they have been amazed to discover that it could attract the loyalty even of those subjects who profit from it least; in particular they have been bewildered at the ease with which national loyalties have displaced class loyalties in time of war. Faced with this evidence, their only response has been to point to the vast propaganda machine that the state has at its disposal for whipping up nationalistic fervour. What they fail to see is that the tune can only evoke such a reaction because it strikes a sympathetic chord in the heart of the hearer. National sensibilities can be artificially inflamed, but they cannot be created out of nothing. Their blindness to this fact and its political implications may be a major factor in explaining the anarchists' failure to win many converts among the masses of modern Europe and America.

We have reached a pessimistic conclusion about the prospects of anarchism as an ideology. Anarchists have been signally unsuccessful in translating their ideals into a coherent programme of change. Either they have relied on rational persuasion, and found very few listeners willing to take them seriously; or they have taken the path of revolution, and found a seemingly unbridgeable chasm between the organization and methods needed to carry through a revolution successfully and the kind of society that they hope to see emerging in its aftermath. On those few occasions when they have been given a chance to apply their ideals constructively, they have had some unexpected successes, but they have also encountered intractable problems, particularly the problem of co-ordinating the activities of many independent social units without recourse to central authority. Finally the critical questions I have raised in this chapter suggest some serious deficiencies in anarchism from a theoretical point of view.

Should we then simply consign anarchism to the historical dustbin as one of the more bizarre offshoots of nineteenth-century liberal and socialist ideologies? It is hard to believe that a mass anarchist movement could now be created in the advanced societies of the West, or, indeed, that if such a movement were to be created it would provide a realistic alternative to the major ideologies now on offer. The problems that we currently face seem to underline ever more emphatically our dependence upon one another both within societies and increasingly between them; and much as we may regret the steady growth of state regulation of social life and look for ways of counteracting it, the idea of abolishing the state entirely must strike us as utopian. We have come a very long way from the largely self-sufficient village community where anarchism found its natural home.

Yet I believe two things are worth salvaging from the wreck. They are not versions of anarchism, but ideas which anarchists have expressed more clearly and vigorously than anyone else. The first of these is simply the imperfection of all relations of power. Anarchists have had a keen sense of the way in which the power of one man over another corrupts the first and degrades the second. They have, it is true, often been oblivious of differences between kinds of power – of the difference, for instance, between power in the form of coercion and power in the form of authority which is willingly accepted by those over whom it is exercised; or again, between power that is exercised according to the arbitrary whims of individuals and power that is exercised through a stable set of legal rules. Their failure to make these distinctions is a major weakness, but it is matched by a corresponding strength. They have never been tempted to regard power as anything other than what it is; they have never supposed that because power is exercised by people with whose aims they sympathize, it somehow changes its nature and becomes innocuous. Thus, unlike many others, including many socialists, they have never become the fellow-travellers of oppressive regimes. Indeed they have often been the first to condemn the authoritarianism of regimes whose intentions appear to be good but whose later performance bears out all that the anarchists have said.

Although one-sided, this view is an important corrective to a tendency to which all of us are prone; namely to suppose that the 'social problem' could be solved if only power were placed in the right set of hands or channelled through the right set of institutions. We may not share the anarchist view that the power of one man over another is always a bad thing, but we ought at least to admit that it is always dangerous; in general, the less we have of it, the better.

The second idea which I want to extract from anarchist thinking is the mirror-image of the first: the ideal of free, uncoercive social relationships. I have given a number of reasons for thinking that this ideal cannot be applied universally: a certain amount of centralized authority seems to be unavoidable under modern conditions. At the same time the anarchist ideal can still serve to guide us in forming relationships on a small scale. In fact we have examined not one ideal but two: the idea of independent individuals related by contract, and the idea of a solidaristic group working freely together and sharing its resources according to need. As pure types these two ideas are radically opposed; in practice they can be juxtaposed in various ways (for instance communitarian groups can themselves be related contractually). Both ideas, however, contrast markedly with the predominant form of organization in modern society, which is that of bureaucratic hierarchy. So it is possible to accept the existence of central authority for some purposes, but at the same time to work to reconstruct social relationships either on contractual or on communitarian lines. An obvious area in which these ideas might be applied is that of work. Instead of organizations governed by a chain of command from superior to subordinate, one might move either towards associations of independent contractors or towards federations of small collectives – or indeed towards some combination of these models. Such changes might contribute a very great deal to human fulfilment in the advanced societies.

As I noted earlier, a good deal of recent anarchist thought has turned in this direction. Rather than attacking the state frontally, it has seemed more profitable to urge the gradual reconstruction of social life, partly for its own sake and partly so that people may eventually come to depend less on central authority. One can find much to sympathize with in anarchism of this kind. Indeed a very good reason for rescuing it from the historical dustbin is to use it as a source of evidence for such a project. We can learn a great deal from the experience of anarchists both about the abuses of power and about the problems and possibilities of free social relationships. That in the end is why they are still worth studying.

Notes

1. What Is Anarchism?

1. See, for instance, James Joll, *The Anarchists* (2nd ed., London, Methuen, 1979); D. Guerin, *Anarchism* (New York, Monthly Review Press, 1970); R. Rocker, *Anarcho-Syndicalism* (London, Secker and Warburg, 1938). George Woodcock's *Anarchism* (Harmondsworth, Penguin, 1963) follows the same general pattern when dealing with anarchism as an idea, though some attention is paid to the individualists in the section on anarchism in the U.S.A.

2. A classic analysis and defence of the idea of the state as presented here is provided by Hobbes in *Leviathan*, first published in 1651 and reprinted many times since. But note that the anarchist critique applies not only to the absolute state defended by Hobbes, but to the milder versions advocated by his constitutionalist, liberal or democratic successors. These do not challenge the idea of the state as such, but merely alter its institutional form.

3. John Locke, *Two Treatises of Government*, ed. P. Laslett (New York, Mentor, 1965), p. 372.

4. P.-J. Proudhon, *General Idea of the Revolution in the Nineteenth Century*, trans. J.B. Robinson (London, Freedom Press, 1923), p. 294.

5. M. Bakunin, *God and the State*, ed. G. Aldred (Glasgow and London, Bakunin Press, 1920), p. 42. The whole pamphlet is a good illustration of Bakunin's attitude to religion.

6. S. Dolgoff (ed.), *Bakunin on Anarchy* (New York, Vintage Books, 1972), p. 319.

7. ibid., p. 284.

8. The details of Proudhon's scheme vary from book to book. In his first *Mémoire* on property, published in 1840, he argued that producers should only possess, rather than own, their means of production, meaning in effect that they should have permanent rights of use, but no rights of transference, and he also argued forcefully that the wages of associated workers should vary only according to hours worked, not according to differences in skill and responsibility. (See *What Is Property?*, trans. B.R. Tucker, London, William Reeves, n.d., First Memoir.) He later abandoned both of these positions, the former after recognizing how badly it had been received by the French peasantry. These amendments are to be found in, for instance, *Idée générale de la révolution au XIXe siècle*, published in 1851, and *De la capacité politique des classes ouvrières*, published posthumously in 1865. (The former is available in English as

General Idea of the Revolution in the Nineteenth Century, trans. J.B. Robinson, London, Freedom Press, 1923).

9. He opened the Banque du Peuple early in 1849, but it lasted only a few months and was not a financial success. See G. Woodcock, *Pierre-Joseph Proudhon* (London, Routledge and Kegan Paul, 1956), pp. 141–4; R.L. Hoffman, *Revolutionary Justice: the Social and Political Theory of P.-J. Proudhon* (Urban, University of Illinois Press, 1972), pp. 124–8.

2. *Philosophical Anarchism*

1. See H.D. Thoreau, 'Civil Disobedience', reprinted in H.A. Bedau (ed.), *Civil Disobedience: Theory and Practice* (New York, Bobbs-Merrill, 1969). As a comment on Thoreau himself this is slightly harsh, since he appears to have believed that his acts of disobedience would encourage others to behave likewise, although this was not their primary purpose.

2. For an interpretation of this kind, see A. Ritter, *Anarchism: A Theoretical Analysis* (Cambridge, Cambridge University Press, 1980), esp. pp. 65–71.

3. Of course an anarchist may and probably will recognize that a given state has authority *in the eyes of the majority of its subjects*. This is a recognition of fact, not to be confused with morally recognizing the state oneself. The distinction is sometimes made by contrasting *de facto* and *de jure* authority. For the philosophical anarchist there is never *de jure* authority, and there is only *de facto* authority while there remain misguided subjects.

4. See, for instance, Bakunin, *God and the State*, ed. G. Aldred (Glasgow and London, Bakunin Press, 1920), pp. 19–21. The distinction between the two kinds of authority is discussed in R.B. Friedman, 'On the Concept of Authority in Political Philosophy' in R. Flathman (ed.), *Concepts in Social and Political Philosophy* (New York, Macmillan, 1973); A. Carter, *Authority and Democracy* (London, Routledge and Kegan Paul, 1979); R.T. De George, 'Anarchism and Authority' in J.R. Pennock and J.W. Chapman (eds.), *Nomos XIX: Anarchism* (New York, New York University Press, 1978).

5. This contrast was made by Max Weber in the course of his justly famous analysis of types of authority. See M. Weber, *The Theory of Social and Economic Organization* (New York, Free Press, 1964), Part III.

6. This was shown in a famous series of experiments carried out by Stanley Milgram. His subjects were instructed by the experimenter to inflict electric shocks of increasing severity on a 'learner' whenever he answered questions wrongly, and many willingly obeyed these instructions, notwithstanding the cries of anguish emitted by their victims and their own knowledge that the shocks might possibly be lethal. (It should be added that both the shocks and the screams were simulated, though the subjects did not of course know this.) See S. Milgram, *Obedience to Authority* (London, Tavistock, 1974).

7. W. Godwin, *Enquiry Concerning Political Justice*, ed. I. Kramnick (Harmondsworth, Penguin, 1976), p. 175.

8. ibid., p. 169. Fénelon was a celebrated French educationalist and political thinker, a precursor of the *philosophes*; Godwin had no doubt that his readers would share his view about which man should be rescued.

9. ibid., pp. 207–8.

10. ibid., p. 253. For a discussion of Godwin's critique of representative democracy, see R. Garrett, 'Anarchism or Political Democracy: The Case of William Godwin', *Social Theory and Practice*, 1(3) (Spring 1971), 111–20.

11. See ibid., pp. 198–208. For further discussion see J.P. Clark, *The Philosophical Anarchism of William Godwin* (Princeton, Princeton University Press, 1977), Part II.

12. Empirical support for this view can be found, for instance, in J. Piaget, *The Moral Judgement of the Child* (London, Kegan Paul, 1932). The view itself is a very old one: we find it expressed in Aristotle's *Ethics* and Hume's *Treatise of Human Nature*, for example.

13. Godwin, *Enquiry*, p. 208.

14. M. Stirner, *The Ego and His Own*, trans. S.T. Byington (London, Jonathan Cape, 1921).

15. ibid., pp. 137–42, 254–5.

16. ibid., pp. 256–7, 299–300.

17. ibid., pp. 233–4.

18. I claim no originality in detecting this. Both R.W.K. Paterson, *The Nihilistic Egoist: Max Stirner* (London, Oxford University Press, 1971) and J.P. Clark, *Max Stirner's Egoism* (London, Freedom Press, 1976) tackle the problem at greater length than I am able to here. Paterson's is an especially good general treatment of Stirner which brings out the difficulties in assimilating him to full-blooded anarchism.

19. Of course if Stirner really believed that each person would be better off if everyone else behaved egoistically, the paradox could be avoided. But it is surely fantastic to believe this in general, even though it may be true in certain segments of social life. There is some evidence that Stirner was influenced by Adam Smith's arguments for economic competition, and it is just possible that he thought these could be applied universally.

20. Stirner, *Ego*, p. 394. The verse is from Goethe's *Wilhelm Meister*.

21. R.P. Wolff, *In Defense of Anarchism* (New York, Harper Colophon, 1976).

22. It is not Kantian, for Kant regarded autonomy as a presupposition of morality rather than as a substantive duty, though it is clearly inspired by Kant's idea of the self-legislating moral agent. See P. Riley, 'On the "Kantian" Foundations of Robert Paul Wolff's Anarchism' in Pennock and Chapman (eds.), *Nomos XIX: Anarchism*. Wolff himself has shown awareness of the difficulty of using Kant in this manner in *The Autonomy of Reason* (New York, Harper, 1973), pp. 177–81.

23. Wolff, *Defense*, p. 19.

24. See the acute critique of Wolff by Grenville Wall, 'Philosophical Anarchism Revisited' in Pennock and Chapman (eds.), *Nomos XIX: Anarchism*.

25. See Wolff, *Defense*, pp. 29, 41–2.

3. *Individualist Anarchism*

1. The phrase is Benjamin Tucker's, but the idea is to be found in Steven Pearl Andrews, *The Science of Society*, first published in 1851, and it is echoed in a recent book by Murray Rothbard. See B.R. Tucker, *Instead of a Book* (New York, B.R. Tucker, 1893), p. 14; S.P. Andrews, *The Science of Society* (London, C.W. Daniel, 1913), p. 37; M.N. Rothbard, *For a New Liberty* (New York, Collier, 1978), pp. 7–8.

2. A nineteenth-century example is Lysander Spooner; see, for example, his *Letter to Grover Cleveland* (Boston, B.R. Tucker, 1886). A twentieth-century example is Murray Rothbard; see his *For a New Liberty*, ch. 2.

3. For the impact of egoism on Tucker and his associates, see J.J. Martin, *Men Against the State* (DeKalb, Ill., Adrian Allen, 1953), pp. 243–6. A recent defence of egoism can be found in Ayn Rand, *The Virtue of Selfishness* (New York, Signet, 1964). Strictly speaking Rand's position is minimal-statist rather than anarchist, but she has influenced a number of latter-day anarcho-individualists.

4. Rothbard, for instance, although formally a believer in natural rights, has been at pains to show that the market tends always to maximize social utility, whereas action by the state tends to reduce it. See his *Power and Market* (Kansas City, Sheed Andrews and McMeel, 1977), ch. 2. A more openly utilitarian argument for individualist anarchism is D. Friedman, *The Machinery of Freedom* (New York, Harper, 1973).

5. See J. Warren, *Equitable Commerce* (New York, Fowlers and Wells, 1852), pp. 40–8, 61–78, 107–9; Andrews, *Science of Society*, esp. chs. 2–4. Andrews's book provides a more systematic presentation of Warren's ideas. For discussion see B.N. Hall, 'The Economic Ideas of Josiah Warren, First American Anarchist', *History of Political Economy*, 6 (1974), 95–108. Warren's credentials as an anarchist have sometimes been questioned, but in *Equitable Commerce*, at least, he makes a sweeping attack on the idea of government and envisages that a regime of equitable commerce will render it unnecessary; see pp. 22–40 and 99–103. The evolution of Warren's ideas is discussed in Martin, *Men Against the State*, chs. 1–3.

6. See Warren, *Equitable Commerce*, pp. 80–93 and 108–9.

7. See Andrews, *Science of Society*, pp. 232–6. Warren himself appears to have been opposed to people associating for the purposes of production, his views remaining firmly within the farmer/artisan context.

8. B.R. Tucker, 'State Socialism and Anarchism' in *Individual Liberty*, ed. C.L. Schwartz (New York, Vanguard Press, 1926) (also included in *Instead of a Book*).

9. Tucker, *Instead of a Book*, pp. 11–13.

10. ibid. p. 311.

11. ibid., p. 404. 'Manchesterism' was the term commonly used to describe laisser-faire liberalism.

12. ibid., p. 332.
13. ibid., p. 347.
14. See Rothbard, *For a New Liberty* and *Power and Market*; also Friedman, *The Machinery of Freedom*.
15. Rothbard, *Power and Market*, ch. 3.
16. Rothbard, *For a New Liberty*, p. 154.
17. See Rothbard, *Power and Market*, esp. pp. 13–16, 228–34.
18. See, for instance, Tucker, *Instead of a Book*, pp. 21–3.
19. See Rothbard, *Power and Market*, ch. 3; Friedman, *The Machinery of Freedom*, chs. 7 and 21.
20. This reply presupposes, of course, that the goods in question *can* be supplied to particular individuals in return for payments. The difficulties which occur in cases where this is not so – with so-called 'public goods' – are discussed below, pp. 41–3.
21. The distinction between obligations of justice, which are enforceable, and acts of charity, which are not, was drawn clearly by Lysander Spooner in *Natural Law; or the Science of Justice* (Boston, A. Williams, 1882), p. 6. For a critique of state-administered relief programmes, see Rothbard, *For a New Liberty*, ch. 8.
22. L. Spooner, *No Treason, No. VI. The Constitution of No Authority* (Boston, L. Spooner, 1870).
23. ibid., pp. 27–8.
24. Rothbard, *Power and Market*, pp. 20–2.
25. For a crude statement of this view, see Spooner, *Natural Law*, pp. 16–20. See also Rothbard, *For a New Liberty*, ch. 3.
26. L. Spooner, *A Letter to Grover Cleveland*, pp. 104–6; Tucker, *Instead of a Book*, pp. 32–7; Rothbard, *Power and Market*, ch. 1. and *For a New Liberty*, ch. 12; Friedman, *The Machinery of Freedom*, chs. 28–32.
27. R. Nozick, *Anarchy, State and Utopia* (Oxford, Blackwell, 1974), chs. 2–6. For a critique of Nozick from the anarchist point of view, see E. Mack, 'Nozick's Anarchism' in J.R. Pennock and J.W. Chapman (eds.), *Nomos XIX: Anarchism* (New York, New York University Press, 1978).
28. I discuss this issue more fully in ch. 12 below.
29. See, for instance, Rothbard, *For a New Liberty*, ch. 11; Friedman, *The Machinery of Freedom*, ch. 15.
30. This difficulty is recognized by Friedman in *The Machinery of Freedom*, pp. 186–7. For general discussion of this and other solutions to the public goods problem, see M. Olson, *The Logic of Collective Action* (Cambridge, Mass., Harvard University Press, 1965); J.M. Buchanan, *Demand and Supply of Public Goods* (Chicago, Rand McNally, 1968); N. Frolich *et al.*, *Political Leadership and Collective Goods* (Princeton, Princeton University Press, 1971); M. Taylor, *Anarchy and Co-operation* (London, Wiley, 1976). M. Laver, *The Politics of Private Desires* (Harmondsworth, Penguin, 1981) provides a helpful overview of the area.
31. A bogus public good is not necessarily a provision that benefits nobody; it may simply be a provision whose cost to the community (in tax revenues,

say) is greater than its benefit (a more stringent requirement would be that a genuine public good must make *everyone* better off on balance).

32. Rothbard, *For a New Liberty*, pp. 309–12.

4. Communist Anarchism

1. E. Malatesta, *Anarchy* (London, Freedom Press, 1974), p. 41.
2. A good account of the rise and fall of the First International can be found in G.D.H. Cole, *Socialist Thought: Marxism and Anarchism 1850–1890* (London, Macmillan, 1954), chs. 6 and 8.
3. See for example his *Revolutionary Catechism* of 1866, reprinted in S. Dolgoff (ed.), *Bakunin on Anarchy* (New York, Vintage Books, 1972), pp. 76–97. For interpretations which play down the difference between Bakunin and the anarcho-communists, see the note by James Guillaume excerpted in Dolgoff (ed.), *Bakunin on Anarchy*, pp. 158–9; and E. Pyziur, *The Doctrine of Anarchism of Michael A. Bakunin* (Milwaukee, Marquette University Press, 1955), pp. 41 and 134–9.
4. For a similar view, see N. Walter, *About Anarchism* (London, Freedom Press, 1969), pp. 20–2.
5. Kropotkin perceptively used the case of Rothschild – who once offered to restore to the exploited people of Europe the amount he had taken from them (which turned out to be four shillings per head) – to make the point that the economic problem could not be solved by dividing up the fortunes of the rich. See P. Kropotkin, *The Conquest of Bread* (New York, Vanguard Press, 1926), pp. 34–5.
6. See, for instance, P. Kropotkin, 'Anarchism: Its Philosophy and Ideal' in R.N. Baldwin (ed.), *Kropotkin's Revolutionary Pamphlets* (New York, Dover, 1970), pp. 126–30; V. Richards (ed.), *Errico Malatesta: His Life and Ideas* (London, Freedom Press, 1965), pp. 93–5; A. Berkman, *What Is Communist Anarchism?*, ed. P. Avrich (New York, Dover, 1972), ch. 5.
7. See Kropotkin, *Conquest of Bread*, ch. 1; E. Malatesta, *A Talk about Anarchist Communism between Two Workers* (London, Freedom Press, 1894), pp. 4–7.
8. See especially Berkman, *What Is Communist Anarchism?*, chs. 3–4.
9. For instance E. Goldman, *Anarchism and Other Essays* (Port Washington, N.Y., Kennikat Press, 1969), pp. 60–2.
10. For instance P. Kropotkin, *Wars and Capitalism* (London, Freedom Press, 1914).
11. For instance M. Bookchin, 'Post-Scarcity Anarchism' in his *Post-Scarcity Anarchism* (London, Wildwood House, 1974).
12. P. Kropotkin, 'Le Gouvernement Représentatif' in his *Paroles d'un Révolté* (Paris, Flammarion, 1885), p. 169 (my translation).
13. Malatesta, *Anarchy*, pp. 20–1.
14. ibid., p. 18.
15. P. Kropotkin, *The State: Its Historic Role* (London, Freedom Press, 1911) and 'Le Gouvernement Représentatif'.

16. On this aspect, see also P. Kropotkin, *Mutual Aid* (London, Heinemann, 1910), chs. 5–6.

17. See P. Kropotkin, 'Les Droits Politiques' in *Paroles d'un Révolté*.

18. See Kropotkin, 'Le Gouvernement Représentatif'; Berkman, *What Is Communist Anarchism?*, ch. 10; E. Goldman, 'Socialism: Caught in the Political Trap' in A.K. Shulman (ed.), *Red Emma Speaks* (New York, Vintage Books, 1972).

19. Kropotkin, *Mutual Aid*, passim. Kropotkin's analysis is examined below in ch. 5; I have assessed it critically in *Social Justice* (Oxford, Clarendon Press, 1976), ch. 7.

20. Malatesta, *Anarchy*, pp. 37–8.

21. Compare Kropotkin, *Conquest of Bread*, chs. 3, 5, 13 with Malatesta, *A Talk about Anarchist Communism*, pp. 26–7 and Richards (ed.), *Errico Malatesta*, pp. 34–8, 102–5.

22. Kropotkin, *Conquest of Bread*, pp. 58–9. See also Berkman, *What Is Communist Anarchism?*, ch. 29.

23. Kropotkin, *Conquest of Bread*, p. 60.

24. Kropotkin, *Conquest of Bread*, chs. 5–6; Berkman, *What Is Communist Anarchism?*, ch. 29.

25. Anyone familiar with the literature of Utopia will have noticed how regularly its apostles announce the number of hours per day which must be worked to provide for the needs of mankind. Among the anarchists, Kropotkin put the figure at five hours per day, Berkman at three, and Godwin, best of all, at half an hour. The variety of these claims is only matched by the scientific assurance with which they are advanced.

26. See P. Kropotkin, *Fields, Factories and Workshops* (London, Nelson, 1912); M. Bookchin, 'Towards a Liberatory Technology' in his *Post-Scarcity Anarchism*.

27. See Kropotkin, *Conquest of Bread*, ch. 11; G. Woodcock, *Railways and Society* (London, Freedom Press, 1943), chs. 6–8. Later anarcho-communists, influenced by syndicalism, tended to see trade unions as having an important role to play in this area.

28. Kropotkin, *Conquest of Bread*, chs. 8–10.

29. ibid., pp. 156–7.

30. Malatesta, *A Talk about Anarchist Communism*, p. 25.

31. For the anarchist idea of federation see, for instance, Bakunin's *Revolutionary Catechism* in Dolgoff (ed.), *Bakunin on Anarchy*. A classic analysis of the liberal idea is A.V. Dicey, *An Introduction to the Study of the Law of the Constitution* (10th ed., London, Macmillan, 1959), ch. 3.

32. P. Kropotkin, 'Anarchist Communism: Its Basis and Principles' in Baldwin (ed.), *Kropotkin's Revolutionary Pamphlets*, pp. 65–9; Malatesta, *Anarchy*, pp. 35–40.

33. I do not mean that there will be no difficulties about the supply of public goods. There may well be problems in identifying common benefits, in establishing priorities among them, and in deciding who shall play what part in the provision of the goods. On anarcho-communist assumptions, however, there is not the difficulty of inducing egoists to contribute to

collective benefits that we found in the case of the individualists.
34. See P. Kropotkin, 'Law and Authority' and 'Prisons and Their Moral Influence on Prisoners' in Baldwin (ed.) *Kropotkin's Revolutionary Pamphlets*; E. Goldman, 'Prisons: A Social Crime and Failure' in Shulman (ed.), *Red Emma Speaks*.
35. Berkman, *What Is Communist Anarchism?*, p. 198.
36. See Berkman, *What Is Communist Anarchism?*, ch. 22; Kropotkin, *Conquest of Bread*, ch. 12.
37. For a negative answer, see A. Ritter, *Anarchism: A Theoretical Analysis* (Cambridge, Cambridge University Press, 1980), pp. 65–71.
38. Malatesta, *A Talk about Anarchist Communism*, p. 29.
39. See the use of this question in the fictional dialogue between an individualist and a communist anarchist in J.H. Mackay's novel, *The Anarchists: A Picture of Civilization at the Close of the Nineteenth Century*, reprinted in L.I. Krimerman and L. Perry (eds.), *Patterns of Anarchy* (New York, Anchor Books, 1966), pp. 16–33 (the question is asked on p. 31). This dialogue gives the reader a good sense of the differences between individualists and communists.
40. See B.R. Tucker, *Instead of a Book* (New York, B.R. Tucker, 1893), pp. 383–408, especially p. 400.
41. See, for instance, P. Kropotkin, 'Modern Science and Anarchism' in Baldwin (ed.), *Kropotkin's Revolutionary Pamphlets*, pp. 171–4; Richards (ed.), *Errico Malatesta*, pp. 31–2; Berkman, *What Is Communist Anarchism?*, pp. 211–13; D. Wieck, 'Anarchist Justice' in J.R. Pennock and J.W. Chapman (eds.), *Nomos XIX: Anarchism* (New York, New York University Press, 1978).
42. The relationship between the two schools has been somewhat variable. Each has been aware of ground shared with the other, both theoretical (the critique of the state, etc.) and practical (mutual support in the face of political oppression of anarchists, resistance to conscription, etc.). At the same time, the ideological distance between the two views has been more or less clearly recognized. My own intuition is that the schools have become more estranged, as the individualists have come to support capitalism more openly (see above, pp. 31–6), while the communist position has hardened into an all-out critique of 'bourgeois society'. Recent exchanges between individualists and communists have certainly tended to be more abusive than the relatively courteous discussions in the pages of Tucker, Kropotkin and the other nineteenth-century anarchists.

5. Human Nature and Historical Progress

1. Another view is possible here. It may be said that anarchists' aspirations to realize their ideals should not be interpreted too literally. Anarchists are essentially moral critics of society as it now is, and their utopias are intended merely to highlight the defects of that society. The contribution of anarchism, in this view, is that it counteracts the centralizing tendencies of modern society, and exerts pressure in the direction of a freer and

more dispersed social order. This view is taken by, for instance, George Woodcock in his 'Anarchism Revisited', *Commentary*, 46 (2) (August 1968), 54–60. Whatever its merits as an interpretation of the 'latent function' of anarchism, it does not square with the intentions either of the major anarchist thinkers of the past, or of the movements they helped to inspire. Their revolutionary ideas were meant in earnest.

I shall return to this issue in the third part of the book.

2. M. Weber, 'Politics as a Vocation' in H.H. Gerth and C. Wright Mills (eds.), *From Max Weber* (London, Routledge and Kegan Paul, 1970), p. 125.

3. W. Godwin, *Enquiry Concerning Political Justice*, ed. I. Kramnick (Harmondsworth, Penguin, 1976), Book I, ch. 4.

4. See above, ch. 2, pp. 18–19.

5. Godwin, *Enquiry*, p. 140. For a good discussion of Godwin's view of human nature, see J.P. Clark, *The Philosophical Anarchism of William Godwin* (Princeton, Princeton University Press, 1977), ch. 3.

6. Godwin, *Enquiry*, Book I, ch. 8.

7. ibid., p. 402.

8. ibid., pp. 279–80.

9. ibid., p. 794.

10. ibid., Book VI, ch. 1.

11. ibid., Book IV, ch. 2.

12. ibid., Book IV, ch. 3.

13. ibid., p. 273.

14. See the discussion in Clark, *William Godwin*, ch. 11.

15. L. Spooner, *Natural Law; or the Science of Justice* (Boston, A. Williams, 1882).

16. M. Rothbard, 'Society without a State' in J.R. Pennock and J.W. Chapman (eds.), *Nomos XIX: Anarchism* (New York, New York University Press, 1978); *For a New Liberty* (New York, Collier, 1978), chs. 2 and 8.

17. Rothbard, 'Society without a State', p. 194.

18. S.P. Andrews, *The Science of Society* (London, C.W. Daniel, 1913), Part I.

19. Rothbard, *For a New Liberty*, p. 317.

20. P.-J. Proudhon, *De La Justice dans La Révolution et dans L'Église* (Paris, Marpon and Flammarion, n.d.), Première Étude, ch. 3. A valuable discussion is A. Ritter, *The Political Thought of Pierre-Joseph Proudhon* (Princeton, Princeton University Press, 1969), ch. 2.

21. Proudhon, *De La Justice*, Neuvième Étude, chs. 3–4.

22. M. Bakunin, *Dieu et L'État* in *Oeuvres* (Paris, Stock, 1895), p. 275 (translated in S. Dolgoff, ed., *Bakunin on Anarchy*, New York, Vintage Books, 1972, p. 236).

23. ibid., p. 274 (trans. Dolgoff, *Bakunin on Anarchy*, p. 236).

24. M. Bakunin, *Étatisme et Anarchie*, ed. A. Lehning (Leiden, E.J. Brill, 1967), p. 226 (translation amended from Dolgoff, *Bakunin on Anarchy*, p. 335).

25. Bakunin proclaimed himself a materialist. But for him idealism implied a

belief in God, in metaphysical free will, and in an idea of the person as a preformed, presocial atom. In my sense, his interpretation of history was predominantly idealist in character, as emerges clearly in his critique of Marx's historical materialism, which we shall examine below in ch. 6. It is also true, however, that Bakunin gave greater weight than Proudhon to material factors in explaining the genesis of revolution. See M. Bakunin, *God and the State*, ed. G. Aldred (Glasgow and London, Bakunin Press, 1920).

26. P.-J. Proudhon, *Théorie de la Propriété* in S. Edwards (ed.), *Selected Writings of Pierre-Joseph Proudhon* (London, Macmillan, 1970), p. 229.

27. Bakunin, *Dieu et L'État*, in *Oeuvres*, p. 287 (my translation).

28. P.-J. Proudhon, *General Idea of the Revolution in the Nineteenth Century*, trans. J.B. Robinson (London, Freedom Press, 1923), pp. 15–17, 172–3.

29. See Proudhon, *General Idea of the Revolution*, esp. pp. 40–6; Dolgoff (ed.), *Bakunin on Anarchy*, p. 114.

30. See, for instance, P. Kropotkin, 'Anarchism: Its Philosophy and Ideal' in R.N. Baldwin (ed.), *Kropotkin's Revolutionary Pamphlets* (New York, Dover, 1970).

31. Their quarrel was always with the use made of Darwin's ideas by some of his followers rather than with Darwin himself. Both spoke of Darwin with great respect. Kropotkin claimed that Darwin had been the first to point to natural human sociability as the origin of morality. For Reclus's favourable attitude, see M. Fleming, *The Anarchist Way to Socialism: Elisée Reclus and Nineteenth-Century European Anarchism* (London, Croom Helm, 1979), pp. 150–1. The contrasting uses made of Darwin's ideas in this period are analysed in G. Himmelfarb, 'Darwinism, Religion and Morality: Politics and Society' in L.M. Marsak (ed.), *The Rise of Science in Relation to Society* (New York, Macmillan, 1964).

32. Quoted in Fleming, *The Anarchist Way to Socialism*, p. 150. Kropotkin extended the argument to animals as well. See P. Kropotkin, *Mutual Aid* (London, Heinemann, 1910), chs. 1–2. I have examined his use of animal evidence in 'Kropotkin', *Government and Opposition*, 18 (1982–3), 319–38.

33. P. Kropotkin, 'Law and Authority' in Baldwin (ed.), *Kropotkin's Revolutionary Pamphlets*.

34. See P. Kropotkin, *Modern Science and Anarchism* (London, Freedom Press, 1912), ch. 1.

35. See P. Kropotkin, 'Anarchist Communism: Its Basis and Principles' in Baldwin (ed.), *Kropotkin's Revolutionary Pamphlets*; Kropotkin, *Mutual Aid*, chs. 7–8.

36. Kropotkin, 'Anarchist Communism: Its Basis and Principles', pp. 57–9. Kropotkin's view of history thus combined idealist and materialist elements.

37. ibid., p. 47. The opposing view – that the struggle between authority and liberty is perennial – can be found in the closing pages of his *The State: Its Historic Role* (London, Freedom Press, 1911).

38. E. Reclus, *Evolution and Revolution* (London, International Publishing Co., 1886).

39. See above, p. 64.
40. On Reclus, see Fleming, *The Anarchist Way to Socialism*, ch. 11; on Kropotkin, see G. Woodcock and I. Avakumović, *The Anarchist Prince* (New York, Schocken Books, 1971), ch. 5, esp. pp. 243–6.
41. See V. Richards (ed.), *Errico Malatesta: His Life and Ideas* (London, Freedom Press, 1965), pp. 257–68.
42. E. Malatesta, *Anarchy* (London, Freedom Press, 1974), pp. 28–30. It must be said, however, that Malatesta also spoke of the steady advance of the sociable instincts throughout human history and, like Kropotkin, argued that this process had been accelerated by the interdependence created by modern technology. The substantial difference between them was not great, therefore, and Malatesta's principal objection must have been to Kropotkin's attempt to present his interpretation of history as a 'scientific law', with the fatalistic implications which followed from that.
43. N. Walter, *About Anarchism* (London, Freedom Press, 1969), p. 7.

6. Anarchism and Marxism

1. Here I am considering the relationship between Marxism and collectivist and communist anarchism. Readers of ch. 3 will soon observe that the relationship between Marxism and individualist anarchism is more distant, though it is worth remembering that Tucker placed Marx together with Warren and Proudhon as a founding member of the socialist tradition to which he belonged. All that Tucker took from Marx, however, was the labour theory of value as the basis of a theory of exploitation.
2. This verdict applies even to the recent book by Paul Thomas, *Karl Marx and the Anarchists* (London, Routledge and Kegan Paul, 1980) which, although useful as a source for Marx's attacks on Stirner, Proudhon and Bakunin, never really grasps the force of the anarchist critique of Marxism.
3. See K. Marx and F. Engels, *Selected Works* (London, Lawrence and Wishart, 1968), pp. 181–5. It is impossible here to tackle the complex question of how representative the Preface is of Marx's thought. We need only say that it has become the received version of the Marxist theory of history.
4. See M. Bakunin, 'The International and Karl Marx' in S. Dolgoff (ed.), *Bakunin on Anarchy* (New York, Vintage Books, 1972) and *Étatisme et Anarchie*, ed. A. Lehning (Leiden, E.J. Brill, 1967), esp. pp. 308–10; P. Kropotkin, *Modern Science and Anarchism* (London, Freedom Press, 1912), esp. chs. 8 and 13.
5. P.-J. Proudhon, Letter to Karl Marx in S. Edwards (ed.), *Selected Writings of Pierre-Joseph Proudhon* (London, Macmillan, 1970), pp. 150–1.
6. Bakunin, 'The International and Karl Marx', p. 302.
7. M. Bakunin, *God and the State*, ed. G. Aldred (Glasgow and London, Bakunin Press, 1920), pp. 28–34.
8. Kropotkin, *Modern Science and Anarchism*, pp. 77–9.

9. See P. Avrich, *The Russian Anarchists* (Princeton, Princeton University Press, 1967), ch. 4; M. Nomad, *Rebels and Renegades* (New York, Macmillan, 1932), pp. 206–8.
10. See, for instance, his letter to Lafargue in Marx, Engels, Lenin, *Anarchism and Anarcho-Syndicalism* (Moscow, Progress Publishers, 1972), pp. 47–8.
11. See the editor's Preface to Marx, Engels, Lenin, *Anarchism and Anarcho-Syndicalism*; G. Plekhanov, *Anarchism and Socialism* (Chicago, Charles Kerr, 1907), *passim*.
12. K. Marx, 'The Conspectus of Bakunin's book *State and Anarchy*' in Marx, Engels, Lenin, *Anarchism and Anarcho-Syndicalism*, p. 150.
13. Editor's Preface to Marx, Engels, Lenin, *Anarchism and Anarcho-Syndicalism*, p. 16.
14. M. Bakunin, 'Letter to *La Liberté*' in Dolgoff (ed.), *Bakunin on Anarchy*, pp. 281–2.
15. Bakunin, 'The International and Karl Marx', pp. 314–18.
16. M. Bakunin, 'The Paris Commune and the Idea of the State' in Dolgoff (ed.), *Bakunin on Anarchy*, p. 263.
17. Marx, 'Conspectus of *State and Anarchy*', p. 151. See also Gramsci's analysis in his 'Address to the Anarchists' in A. Gramsci, *Selections from Political Writings*, ed. Q. Hoare (London, Lawrence and Wishart, 1977).
18. F. Engels, Letter to Cuno in Marx, Engels, Lenin, *Anarchism and Anarcho-Syndicalism*, p. 71.
19. For Marx, see R. Miliband, 'Marx and the State' in T. Bottomore (ed.), *Karl Marx* (Oxford, Blackwell, 1979); J.M. Maguire, *Marx's Theory of Politics* (Cambridge, Cambridge University Press, 1978). For the anarchists, see above, ch. 4, pp. 47–50.
20. Bakunin, 'The International and Karl Marx', p. 294.
21. Bakunin, 'The International and Karl Marx', p. 294; *Étatisme et Anarchie*, pp. 346–7 (translated in Dolgoff, ed., *Bakunin on Anarchy*, pp. 330–1).
22. See E. Goldman, 'Socialism: Caught in the Political Trap' in A.K. Shulman (ed.), *Red Emma Speaks* (New York, Vintage Books, 1972), p. 83.
23. See A. Berkman, *What Is Communist Anarchism?*, ed. P. Avrich (New York, Dover, 1972), pp. 237–8; E. Goldman, 'Syndicalism: Its Theory and Practice' in Shulman (ed.), *Red Emma Speaks*, p. 75.
24. M. Bookchin, 'Listen, Marxist!' in his *Post-Scarcity Anarchism* (London, Wildwood House, 1974), p. 189.
25. K. Marx, 'The Eighteenth Brumaire of Louis Bonaparte' in Marx and Engels, *Selected Works*, p. 172.
26. ibid., p. 138. This refers to the Parisian lumpenproletariat.
27. ibid., pp. 138–40. On the general theme, see Plekhanov, *Anarchism and Socialism*, ch. 8.
28. Even Lenin, whose political activities were set in the context of a predominantly peasant society, argued that 'only the proletariat – by virtue of the economic role it plays in large-scale production – is capable of being the leader of *all* the working and exploited people . . .' V.I. Lenin, *The*

State and Revolution (Moscow, Progress Publishers, 1969), p. 25.

29. M. Bakunin, 'Federalism, Socialism, Anti-Theologism' in Dolgoff (ed.), *Bakunin on Anarchy*, p. 145.

30. G.P. Maximoff (ed.), *The Political Philosophy of Bakunin* (New York, Free Press of Glencoe, 1964), p. 218.

31. See, for instance, Bakunin, 'The Paris Commune and the Idea of the State'; V. Richards (ed.), *Errico Malatesta: His Life and Ideas* (London, Freedom Press, 1965), pp. 141–8; Berkman, *What Is Communist Anarchism?*, ch. 28.

32. P. Kropotkin, 'Revolutionary Government', in R.N. Baldwin (ed.), *Kropotkin's Revolutionary Pamphlets* (New York, Dover, 1970), pp. 247–249. See also P. Kropotkin, *The State: Its Historic Role* (London, Freedom Press, 1911), section X.

33. See his 'Message to the Workers of the West' in P. Avrich (ed.), *The Anarchists in the Russian Revolution* (London, Thames and Hudson, 1973) (also printed as 'The Russian Revolution and the Soviet Government' in Baldwin, ed., *Kropotkin's Revolutionary Pamphlets*).

34. See Bakunin, 'Letters to a Frenchman' in Dolgoff (ed.), *Bakunin on Anarchy*, pp. 213–17; 'The International and Karl Marx', pp. 289–90; Maximoff (ed.), *Political Philosophy of Bakunin*, pp. 289–94.

35. Maximoff (ed.), *Political Philosophy of Bakunin*, p. 215.

36. See Goldman, 'Socialism: Caught in the Political Trap', pp. 80–2.

37. P. Kropotkin, 'Le Gouvernement Représentatif' in his *Paroles d'un Révolté* (Paris, Flammarion, 1885), pp. 190–7.

38. Berkman, *What Is Communist Anarchism?*, p. 118. Ch. 13 *passim* contains a good general statement of the anarchist position.

39. Kropotkin, 'Le Gouvernement Représentatif', pp. 197–200.

40. See. A.R. Carlson, *Anarchism in Germany (Vol. I: The Early Movement)* (Metuchen, N.J., Scarecrow Press, 1972), ch. 6; Berkman, *What Is Communist Anarchism?*, ch. 13.

41. See the passage from Bakunin cited above, ch. 1, pp. 10–11; and Kropotkin, 'Revolutionary Government'.

42. For a non-partisan account of this, see Avrich, *The Russian Anarchists*, ch. 5.

43. E. Goldman, *My Disillusionment in Russia* (London, C.W. Daniel, 1925), p. 245.

44. For this charge, see Berkman, *What Is Communist Anarchism?*, pp. 163–5; Goldman, *My Disillusionment in Russia*, pp. 248–9; Bookchin, 'Listen, Marxist!', pp. 200–8.

45. Cited in Avrich (ed.), *Anarchists in the Russian Revolution*, p. 147. The letter was written in March 1920.

46. Cited in ibid., pp. 102–6.

47. Cited in ibid, pp. 122–5. See also Avrich, *The Russian Anarchists*, pp. 190–4.

48. See Avrich, *The Russian Anarchists*, chs. 7–8.

49. F. Engels, 'On Authority' in Marx, Engels, Lenin, *Anarchism and Anarcho-Syndicalism*, p. 105.

50. See K. Marx and F. Engels, 'The Alliance of Socialist Democracy and the International Working Men's Association' in Marx, Engels, Lenin, *Anarchism and Anarcho-Syndicalism*, pp. 109–11; F. Engels, 'The Workingmen of Europe in 1877' in ibid., p. 161.
51. K. Marx and F. Engels, 'The Alliance of Socialist Democracy and the International Working Men's Association', p. 118. On the relationship between Bakunin and Nechaev, see below ch. 7, note 2.
52. Plekhanov, *Anarchism and Socialism*, chs. 8–9.
53. V.I. Lenin, 'The Attitude of the Workers' Party to Religion' in Marx, Engels, Lenin, *Anarchism and Anarcho-Syndicalism*, pp. 231–2. A more subtle view was taken by Gramsci, who distinguished anarchist ideologues from anarchist workers, and argued that the latter, whose real quarrel was with the *bourgeois* state, not the state as such, could be absorbed into the Communist movement. See Gramsci, 'Address to the Anarchists', pp. 187–8.
54. F. Engels, 'The Bakuninists at Work' in Marx, Engels, Lenin, *Anarchism and Anarcho-Syndicalism*, pp. 129–47; V.I. Lenin, 'Anarchism and Socialism' and 'Report on the Question . . .' in ibid., pp. 185–8.
55. Marx, 'The Conspectus of Bakunin's book *State and Anarchy*', p. 152.

7. Revolutionary Organization and Strategy

1. See, for example, B.R. Barber, *Superman and Common Men: Freedom, Anarchy and the Revolution* (New York, Praeger, 1971); I. Kramnick, 'On Anarchism and the Real World: William Godwin and Radical England', *American Political Science Review*, 66 (1972), 114–28.
2. Consideration of Bakunin's ideas here is complicated by his relationship with Sergei Nechaev, a young Russian who for a time exercised a strong influence on the older man. The *Catechism of the Revolutionary*, which presents a lurid picture of the revolutionary as a man fanatically dedicated to his cause and without ordinary moral scruples, is now thought to have been largely if not wholly Nechaev's work. At the same time Nechaev's extremism undoubtedly struck a sympathetic chord in Bakunin, and it would be wrong to dismiss Bakunin's work of this period as completely aberrant. See P. Avrich, *Bakunin and Nechaev* (London, Freedom Press, 1974) and A. Kelly, *Mikhail Bakunin* (Oxford, Clarendon Press, 1982), chs. 5–6, for discussion.
3. M. Bakunin, 'The Programme of the International Brotherhood' in S. Dolgoff (ed.), *Bakunin on Anarchy* (New York, Vintage Books, 1972), pp. 154–5.
4. ibid., p. 155.
5. M. Bakunin, 'Letter to Albert Richard' in Dolgoff (ed.), *Bakunin on Anarchy*, p. 180.
6. For a defence by a disciple, see Dolgoff's Introduction to *Bakunin on Anarchy*.
7. P. Kropotkin, 'Les Minorités Révolutionnaires' in his *Paroles d'un Révolté* (Paris, Flammarion, 1885).

8. E. Goldman, 'Minorities versus Majorities' in her *Anarchism and Other Essays* (Port Washington, N.Y., Kennikat Press, 1969).
9. Quoted in J. Maitron, *Le Mouvement Anarchiste en France* (Paris, Maspero, 1975), vol. I, p. 118 (my translation).
10. This was exacerbated by the fact that the new International contained a federalist group led by de Paepe as well as anarchists. See G.D.H. Cole, *Socialist Thought: Marxism and Anarchism 1850–1890* (London, Macmillan, 1954), pp. 202–10; Maitron, *Le Mouvement Anarchiste en France*, Part I, ch. 6; D. Stafford, *From Anarchism to Reformism* (London, Weidenfeld and Nicolson, 1971), chs. 2–3.
11. See P. Avrich, *The Russian Anarchists* (Princeton, Princeton University Press, 1967), chs. 5–7.
12. E. Goldman, *My Disillusionment in Russia* (London, C.W. Daniel, 1925), pp. 251–2.
13. M. Bakunin, Letter to the Comrades of the Jura Federation in Dolgoff (ed.), *Bakunin on Anarchy*, p. 352.
14. 'La Propagande par le fait', published in the *Bulletin* of the Jura Federation and reprinted in slightly abbreviated form in J. Guillaume, *L'Internationale: Documents et Souvenirs*, vol. IV (Paris, Stock, 1910), pp. 224–7. Kropotkin's participation in the writing of this article is probable but not certain.
15. Guillaume, *L'Internationale*, vol. IV, pp. 226–7 (my translation).
16. ibid., p. 116.
17. See R. Hostetter, *The Italian Socialist Movement I: Origins (1860–1882)* (Princeton, Van Nostrand, 1958), pp. 339–44.
18. Ceccarelli, one of the leaders of the band, cited in Hostetter, *Italian Socialist Movement*, p. 377.
19. See Hostetter, *Italian Socialist Movement*, pp. 376–84.
20. Stafford, *From Anarchism to Reformism*, pp. 86–7.
21. See Maitron, *Le Mouvement Anarchiste en France*, vol. I, p. 83. Kropotkin spoke at this time of 'la révolte permanente par la parole, par l'écrit, par le poignard, le fusil, la dynamite . . .' It is possible, however, that he was still thinking of the use of these methods within the context of a general insurrection. Those who read him were often not.
22. Full accounts can be found in P. Arshinov, *History of the Makhnovist Movement (1918–21)* (Black and Red, Detroit/Solidarity, Chicago, 1974) and D. Footman, 'Nestor Makhno' in *St Antony's Papers, Number 6: Soviet Affairs* (London, Chatto and Windus, 1959); shorter accounts in Avrich, *The Russian Anarchists*, ch. 8 and G. Woodcock, *Anarchism* (Harmondsworth, Penguin, 1963), ch. 13. I have relied on these sources for what follows.
23. See Arshinov, *History of the Makhnovist Movement*, p. 96.
24. See Footman, 'Nestor Makhno', p. 113.
25. Cited in Footman, 'Nestor Makhno', p. 116.
26. See Arshinov, *History of the Makhnovist Movement*, esp. pp. 85–91, 148–155, 239–54; Footman, 'Nestor Makhno', esp. pp. 105–12; Woodcock, *Anarchism*, pp. 395–7; Avrich, *The Russian Anarchists*, pp. 213–19.

27. See G. Brenan, *The Spanish Labyrinth* (Cambridge, Cambridge University Press, 1969), p. 162; M. Bookchin, *The Spanish Anarchists: The Heroic years 1868–1936* (New York, Free Life Editions, 1977), pp. 118–19. Brenan puts the size of the force at 4,000, but Bookchin maintains that only about 500 actually entered the city.
28. Peirats, cited in S.J. Brademas, *Revolution and Social Revolution: A Contribution to the History of the Anarcho-Syndicalist Movement in Spain: 1930–37* (D.Phil. thesis, University of Oxford, 1953), p. 151.
29. F. Borkenau, *The Spanish Cockpit* (London, Faber, 1937), p. 98.
30. ibid., p. 102.
31. See B. Bolloten, *The Grand Camouflage: The Communist Conspiracy in the Spanish Civil War* (London, Hollis and Carter, 1961), pp. 73–5 for examples. Bolloten argues that the Communist Party – hitherto a negligible force in Spanish politics – was able to gather support rapidly by posing as the defender of small private property in town and country.
32. See Brademas, *Revolution and Social Revolution*, pp. 408–9 for the regulations. Rule 2 read, 'He [the militiaman] may not act on his own in military matters, and he will fill unquestioningly the posts and places assigned to him, both at the front and in the rearguard.'
33. G. Orwell, *Homage to Catalonia* (Harmondsworth, Penguin, 1962), pp. 29–31. Orwell was attached to a militia of the P.O.U.M. – a Trotskyist group whose attitudes were in practice very close to those of the anarchists.
34. See Bolloten, *The Grand Camouflage*, ch. 19 for some striking examples.
35. Cited in Brademas, *Revolution and Social Revolution*, p. 411.
36. See P. Broué and E. Témime, *The Revolution and the Civil War in Spain* (London, Faber, 1972), pp. 219–20. For the resistance of one famous anarchist militia – the 'Iron Column' – to militarization, see Bolloten, *The Grand Camouflage*, ch. 24.

8. Anarchism, Violence and Terror

1. For a fuller account of the affair, see J. Joll, *The Anarchists* (2nd ed., London, Methuen, 1979), pp. 123–5.
2. The Kaiser's assailants, Hoedel and Nobiling, are sometimes described as anarchists, but it seems more likely that they were dissident Social Democrats, frustrated by the moderation of the party. For a description of the assaults, see A.R. Carlson, *Anarchism in Germany (Vol. I: The Early Movement)* (Metuchen, N.J., Scarecrow Press, 1972), chs. 4–5.
3. Indeed we have seen that anarchist intellectuals such as Kropotkin were urging the use of violent methods as early as 1880.
4. For fuller accounts, see J. Maitron, *Le Mouvement Anarchiste en France* (Paris, Maspero, 1975), Part II, ch. 5; E.A. Vizetelly, *The Anarchists; Their Faith and Their Record* (London and New York, John Lane, 1911), chs. 6–8; M. Fleming, 'Propaganda by the Deed: Terrorism and Anarchist Theory in Late Nineteenth-Century Europe' in Y. Alexander and

K.A. Myers (ed.), *Terrorism in Europe* (London, Croom Helm, 1982).

5. The story is told in E. Goldman, *Living My Life* (New York, Alfred Knopf, 1931), vol. I, chs. 8–9.

6. See J. Quail, *The Slow Burning Fuse* (London, Paladin, 1978).

7. See Vizetelly, *The Anarchists*, chs. 9–10.

8. Mention might also be made here of the Weathermen, who carried out a series of bombings in the U.S.A. in the early 1970s, but identifying their ideological make-up is complicated by their alignment with the Black Power movement – thus the enemy was not merely the state and the capitalist class, but 'whites' generally. See J. Weinstein, *Ambiguous Legacy: The Left in American Politics* (New York, Franklin Watts, 1975), pp. 151–9.

9. I have drawn here upon J. Becker, *Hitler's Children: The Story of the Baader-Meinhof Terrorist Gang* (London, Michael Joseph, 1977); B. Baumann, *Terror or Love?* (London, John Calder, 1979); G. Pridham, 'Terrorism and the State in West Germany during the 1970s: A Threat to Stability or a Case of Political Over-Reaction?' in J. Lodge (ed.), *Terrorism: A Challenge to the State* (Oxford, Martin Robertson, 1981).

10. See P. Furlong, 'Political Terrorism in Italy: Responses, Reactions and Immobilism' in Lodge (ed.), *Terrorism*; R. Drake, 'The Red Brigades and the Italian Political Tradition' in Alexander and Myers (eds.), *Terrorism in Europe*. The latter particularly illuminates the relationship between anarchism and the ideology of the Brigate Rosse.

11. For a full account, see G. Carr, *The Angry Brigade* (London, Gollancz, 1975).

12. His defence is reproduced in G. Woodcock (ed.), *The Anarchist Reader* (London, Fontana, 1977), pp. 189–96.

13. ibid., p. 195.

14. E. Reclus, *An Anarchist on Anarchy* (London, Liberty Press, 1897), p. 14.

15. J. Grave, *Moribund Society and Anarchy* (San Francisco, A. Isaak, 1899), pp. 125–6.

16. E. Goldman, *Living My Life*, p. 87.

17. Rote Armee Fraktion (R.A.F.), *Das Konzept Stadtguerilla*, translated in W. Laqueur (ed.), *The Terrorism Reader* (London, Wildwood House, 1979), p. 178.

18. See Most's articles in *Freiheit*, translated in Laqueur (ed.), *The Terrorism Reader*, pp. 100–8.

19. See Pridham, 'Terrorism and the State in West Germany during the 1970s', pp. 42–3.

20. See G. Woodcock and I. Avakumović, *The Anarchist Prince* (New York, Schocken Books, 1971), pp. 246–9.

21. Anon., *Anarchism and Outrage* (London, C.M. Wilson, 1893), pp. 6–7.

22. E. Goldman, 'The Psychology of Political Violence' in A.K. Shulman (ed.), *Red Emma Speaks* (New York, Vintage Books, 1972), pp. 210–33.

23. For Reclus, see M. Fleming, *The Anarchist Way to Socialism: Elisée Reclus and Nineteenth-Century European Anarchism* (London, Croom Helm, 1979), ch. 10; for Kropotkin, Woodcock and Avakumović, *The Anarchist*

Prince, pp. 246–9 and M.A. Miller, *Kropotkin* (Chicago, University of Chicago Press, 1976), pp. 173–5; for Malatesta, V. Richards (ed.), *Errico Malatesta: His Life and Ideas* (London, Freedom Press, 1965), pp. 61–7.

24. See L. Tolstoy, 'Letter on Non-Resistance' in L. Tolstoy, *Essays and Letters*, trans A. Maude (London, Henry Froude, 1903), pp. 177–88.

25. L. Tolstoy, 'Patriotism and Government' in Tolstoy, *Essays*, p. 258.

26. See G. Woodcock, *Anarchism* (Harmondsworth, Penguin, 1963), ch. 8.

27. For an excellent exploration of this case, see A. Carter, 'Anarchism and Violence' in J.R. Pennock and J.W. Chapman (eds.), *Nomos XIX: Anarchism* (New York, New York University Press, 1978).

28. See especially the reflections of Bommi Baumann in *Terror or Love?*, pp. 104–20. I have examined this problem in greater depth in my paper, 'The Use and Abuse of Political Violence', *Political Studies* (forthcoming).

29. B. de Ligt, *The Conquest of Violence* (London, Routledge, 1937), p. 75.

30. See de Ligt, *Conquest of Violence*, esp. chs. 6–7; N. Walter, *Nonviolent Resistance: Men Against War* (London, Nonviolence 63, 1963); G. Woodcock, *Civil Disobedience* (Toronto, Canadian Broadcasting Corporation, 1966). There is a helpful discussion of the different forms of non-violent direct action in A. Carter, *Direct Action* (London, Housemans, 1970).

31. p. 92.

9. Anarchism and Syndicalism

1. See J. Maitron, *Le Mouvement Anarchiste en France* (Paris, Maspero, 1975), vol. I, p. 266.

2. Almost but not quite. As we shall see, a small minority of anarchists remained resolutely hostile to syndicalism.

3. For the account that follows I have drawn on E. Pouget, *Les Bases du Syndicalisme* (Paris, Bibliothèque Syndicaliste, n.d.); E. Pouget, *Le Syndicat* (Paris, Bibliothèque Syndicaliste, n.d.); V. Griffuelhes, *L'Action Syndicaliste* (Paris, Marcel Rivière, 1908); G. Yvetot, *A.B.C. Syndicaliste* (Paris, L'Espérance, 1911); and the very helpful discussion in F.F. Ridley, *Revolutionary Syndicalism in France* (Cambridge, Cambridge University Press, 1970). A later exposition is R. Rocker, *Anarcho-Syndicalism* (London, Secker and Warburg, 1938), ch. 4.

4. See, for instance, Yvetot, *A.B.C. Syndicaliste*, ch. 5; Ridley, *Revolutionary Syndicalism*, pp. 95–134.

5. Yvetot, *A.B.C. Syncialiste*, p. 40 (my translation).

6. Georges Sorel, who was not an active participant in the syndicalist movement but who for a time regarded syndicalism as the best expression of the heroic and military virtues that he wished to see flourish, called the general strike a 'myth'. The syndicalists could not of course have seen it in that way themselves, though many of them shared Sorel's distaste for 'scientific' theories of the revolution, and like him preferred to place their trust in the untutored instincts of the proletariat. For Sorel's views see

G. Sorel, *Reflections on Violence* (London, Collier-Macmillan, 1961).

7. Griffuelhes, *L'Action Syndicaliste*, p. 4.
8. See Pouget, *Les Bases du Syndicalisme* and *Le Syndicat*; P. Monatte, Speech at Amsterdam, translated in G. Woodcock (ed.), *The Anarchist Reader* (London, Fontana, 1977), pp. 213–19; Rocker, *Anarcho-Syndicalism*. Other defences of anarcho-syndicalism can be found in E. Goldman, 'Syndicalism: Its Theory and Practice' in A.K. Shulman (ed.), *Red Emma Speaks* (New York, Vintage Books, 1972); (G.P. Maximoff, *Constructive Anarchism* (Chicago, Maximoff Memorial Publication Committee, 1952); G. Woodcock, *Anarchy or Chaos* (London, Freedom Press, 1944).
9. Rocker, *Anarcho-Syndicalism*, p. 89.
10. Pouget, *Les Bases du Syndicalisme*, pp. 20–4.
11. I have drawn here especially upon Malatesta's reply to Monatte at Amsterdam, translated in Woodcock (ed.), *Anarchist Reader*; V. Richards (ed.), *Errico Malatesta: His Life and Ideas* (London, Freedom Press, 1965), pp. 113–33; J. Grave, *Le Syndicalisme dans L'Évolution Sociale* (Paris, Temps Nouveaux, 1908). For Kropotkin's view, see M.A. Miller, *Kropotkin* (Chicago, University of Chicago Press, 1976), pp. 176–7.
12. Grave, *Le Syndicalisme*, p. 9 (my translation).
13. See Maitron, *Mouvement Anarchiste*, vol. I, pp. 275–9.
14. An alternative view, rather more sinister in its implications, was that union activity might indeed win small economic gains for workers, but this would only have the effect of accommodating them to capitalism and prolonging its existence. See Maitron, *Mouvement Anarchiste*, vol. I, p. 276 for an example of this view.
15. See above, ch. 6, pp. 84–5.
16. Maitron, *Mouvement Anarchiste*, vol. I, p. 275.
17. The C.G.T. was actually founded in 1895, but its major significance dates from the time when it merged with the Fédération des Bourses du Travail and organized itself along 'classic' syndicalist lines. For the pre-history, see Ridley, *Revolutionary Syndicalism*, pp. 63–71.
18. See Ridley, *Revolutionary Syndicalism*, pp. 77–9; V.R. Lorwin, *The French Labor Movement* (Cambridge, Mass., Harvard University Press, 1966), p. 43. Both consider that the claimed membership of 600,000 is exaggerated.
19. See Ridley, *Revolutionary Syndicalism*, pp. 176–8.
20. ibid., p. 183.
21. E. Pataud and E. Pouget, *Syndicalism and the Co-operative Commonwealth (How we shall bring about the Revolution)* (Oxford, New International Publishing Co., 1913).
22. See P.N. Stearns, *Revolutionary Syndicalism and French Labor* (New Brunswick, N.J., Rutgers University Press, 1971), pp. 25–33.
23. ibid., ch. 3.
24. See P.F. Brissenden, *The I.W.W.: A Study of American Syndicalism* (New York, Columbia University, 1920), pp. 305–19.
25. See Brissenden, *The I.W.W.*, pp. 299–305 for this argument.

26. A similar pessimistic assessment of the prospects of revolutionary syndicalism in the U.S. can be found in J. Weinstein, *Ambiguous Legacy: The Left in American Politics* (New York, Franklin Watts, 1975), pp. 6–19.
27. See M. Bookchin, *The Spanish Anarchists: The Heroic Years 1868–1936* (New York, Free Life Editions, 1977), ch. 3.
28. cf. S.J. Brademas, *Revolution and Social Revolution: A Contribution to the History of the Anarcho-Syndicalist Movement in Spain: 1930–37* (D.Phil. thesis, University of Oxford, 1953), p. 18.
29. See G. Meaker, *The Revolutionary Left in Spain, 1914–1923* (Stanford, Stanford University Press, 1974), ch. 6.
30. One symptom of this is that, in Spain, there appears to have been little disagreement between syndicalists and anarcho-syndicalists about the movement's final goal – *comunismo libertario*, as it was called. The pure syndicalists argued, however, that the mass of Spanish workers were not yet prepared to make the revolution to achieve this goal, so that the C.N.T. should for the time being be concerned with limited gains and with educating its members, while the anarcho-syndicalists thought that the workers could be catapulted into revolution by initiatives taken by 'audacious minorities'.
31. G. Brenan, *The Spanish Labyrinth* (Cambridge, Cambridge University Press, 1969), p. 183.
32. The so-called *treintista* declaration of August 1931 was a manifesto issued by thirty leaders of the C.N.T. who rejected the policies of the F.A.I. in favour of pure revolutionary syndicalism. See Brademas, *Revolution and Social Revolution*, chs. 5–6, for a well-documented account of these power struggles.
33. For further accounts, see Meaker, *Revolutionary Left in Spain*, pp. 153–163; Brenan, *Spanish Labyrinth*, pp. 70–1.
34. See Brademas, *Revolution and Social Revolution*, pp. 155–8; Bookchin, *The Spanish Anarchists*, pp. 249–50.
35. See Brademas, *Revolution and Social Revolution*, pp. 171–3; Brenan, *Spanish Labyrinth*, pp 270–1.
36. M. Bookchin, 'Listen, Marxist!' in his *Post-Scarcity Anarchism* (London, Wildwood House, 1974), p. 186.
37. V. Richards, *Lessons of the Spanish Revolution* (London, Freedom Press, 1953), p. 137.

10. Anarchism and the New Left

1. I have already argued for this view in the case of the terrorist groups of the 1970s which sprang from the New Left – see above, chapter 8, pp. 113–14.
2. H. Lefebvre, *Critique de la vie quotidienne* (2nd ed., Paris, L'Arche Editeur, 1958–61)
3. H. Marcuse, *One-Dimensional Man* (London, Routledge and Kegan Paul, 1964).

4. Gilles Ivain, cited in C. Gray (ed.), *Leaving the 20th Century: The Incomplete Work of the Situationist International* (London, Free Fall Publications, 1974), p. 19.
5. See especially G. Debord, *Society of the Spectacle* (Detroit, Black and Red, 1970).
6. Debord, *Society of the Spectacle*, sections 60–61.
7. ibid., section 69.
8. ibid., section 23. The situationists did not describe themselves as anarchists, for the general reasons cited above. See ibid., sections 92–4 for Debord's verdict on traditional anarchism.
9. For a brief history of this idea and its appropriation by the situationists, see R. Gombin, *The Origins of Modern Leftism* (Harmondsworth, Penguin, 1975), ch. 4.
10. For a good discussion of the general background, see D. Goldey, 'A Precarious Regime: The Events of May 1968' in P.M. Williams, *French Politicians and Elections, 1951–1969* (Cambridge, Cambridge University Press, 1970).
11. The events are chronicled in some detail in P. Seale and M. McConville, *French Revolution 1968* (Harmondsworth, Penguin, 1968).
12. 'I am not, and do not want to be, anything but a plagiarist when it comes to the preaching of revolutionary theory and practice.' G. and D. Cohn-Bendit, *Obsolete Communism: The Left-Wing Alternative* (Harmondsworth, Penguin, 1969), pp. 18–19.
13. See ibid., esp. pp. 103–12 and 249–56.
14. For a much fuller consideration of the role of anarchism in the May–June Events, see R. Gombin, 'The Ideology and Practice of Contestation seen through Recent Events in France', *Government and Opposition*, 5 (1969–1970), 410–29.
15. Goldey, 'A Precarious Regime', pp. 248–9.
16. See Seale and McConville, *French Revolution*, pp. 101–10 for a good description.
17. See ibid., ch. 10; Cohn-Bendit, *Obsolete Communism*, Part III, ch. 2.
18. This failure is lamented in, for instance, M. Bookchin, 'The May–June Events in France' in *Post-Scarcity Anarchism* (London, Wildwood House, 1974).
19. See Seale and McConville, *French Revolution*, ch. 14; Goldey, 'A Precarious Regime', pp. 253–60.
20. Seale and McConville, *French Revolution*, p. 176.
21. A counter-argument here would be that life-experiences cannot really be changed until the constraints of existing society are abolished. Revolution is a *sine qua non* of authentic experience. This reply strikes me as implausible in the face of the available evidence.
22. H.J. Ehrlich, C. Ehrlich, D. DeLeon and G. Morris (eds.), *Reinventing Anarchy* (London, Routledge and Kegan Paul, 1979). Admittedly these interests were prefigured to some extent in earlier anarchist writing – for instance in Alex Comfort's psychological study *Authority and Delinquency in the Modern State* (London, Routledge and Kegan Paul, 1950) and in

Emma Goldman's essays on women (see A.K. Shulman, ed., *Red Emma Speaks*, New York, Vintage Books, 1972, Part II).

23. Somewhat similar assessments of the new anarchism can be found in G. Woodcock, 'Anarchism Revisited', *Commentary*, 46 (2) (August 1968), 54–60; D. Apter, 'The Old Anarchism and the New – Some Comments', *Government and Opposition*, 5 (1969–70), 397–409; M. Lerner, 'Anarchism and the American Counter-Culture', *Government and Opposition*, 5 (1969–70), 430–55.

24. D. Friedman, *The Machinery of Freedom* (New York, Harper, 1973), ch. 37.

25. For example Apter, 'The Old Anarchism and the New'; J. Joll, *The Anarchists* (2nd ed., London, Methuen, 1979), ch. 10.

26. Good examples are Paul Goodman and Colin Ward: see, for instance, P. Goodman, *People or Personnel* (New York, Vintage Books, 1968) and C. Ward, *Anarchy in Action* (London, Allen and Unwin, 1973). Both of these writers explore ways in which the centralized institutions of modern society might be replaced by decentralized and participatory forms of organization. Among the areas treated in their work are the education system, the structure of industry, and town planning. Ward is firmly located within the anarchist tradition, whereas Goodman is rather more of a maverick – a decentralizer and a pluralist, with a high regard for the American past, who nonetheless draws a good deal of inspiration from the classics of anarchism.

27. Cited in Ward, *Anarchy in Action*, p. 19. The popularity of this view among the British anarchists influenced by the journal *Anarchy* (which Ward edited) is noted in D. Stafford, 'Anarchists in Britain Today', *Government and Opposition*, 5 (1969–70), 480–500, esp. pp. 487–9.

11. Constructive Achievements

1. A classic example is Kropotkin's *Mutual Aid* (London, Heinemann, 1910). Two recent discussions, both sympathetic to the anarchist position but more guarded than Kropotkin's, are M. Taylor, *Community, Anarchy and Liberty* (Cambridge, Cambridge University Press, 1982), chs. 2–3 and H. Barclay, *People without Government* (London, Kahn and Averill with Cienfuegos Press, 1982).

2. I borrow this classification from Taylor, *Community, Anarchy and Liberty*, ch. 2.

3. These points are effectively conceded by Taylor in ibid., pp. 158–9 and 161.

4. See above, ch. 3, pp. 32–3.

5. They are described in J.J. Martin, *Men Against the State* (DeKalb, Ill., Adrian Allen, 1953), chs. 1–2.

6. See J.H. Noyes, *History of American Socialisms* (Philadelphia, Lippincott, 1870), p. 97.

7. See Martin, *Men Against the State*, pp. 57–64.

8. ibid., pp. 67–87.
9. For Britain, see D. Hardy, *Alternative Communities in Nineteenth Century England* (London, Longman, 1979), ch. 5; W.H. Armytage, *Heavens Below: Utopian Experiments in England 1560–1960* (London, Routledge and Kegan Paul, 1961), Part IV, chs. 2, 4 and 5; J. Quail, *The Slow Burning Fuse* (London, Paladin, 1978), ch. 12. For France, see J. Maitron, *Le Mouvement Anarchiste en France* (Paris, Maspero, 1975), Part III, ch. 4. For the U.S., see L. Veysey, *The Communal Experience: Anarchist and Mystical Counter-Cultures in America* (New York, Harper and Row, 1973), chs 1–2.
10. See Hardy, *Alternative Communities*, pp. 199–207.
11. For an account of the colony, see S. Holbrook, 'Anarchists at Home', *The American Scholar*, 15 (1945–6), 425–38.
12. This does not mean that they do not hope that others might follow their example, or have any vision of an alternative society, but these aims are in most cases secondary. For a classification of British commune-dwellers on the basis of motivation, see A. Rigby, *Alternative Realities: A Study of Communes and Their Members* (London, Routledge and Kegan Paul, 1974).
13. Some evidence of the variety can be found in Rigby, *Alternative Realities* and (for the U.S.), J. Jerome, *Families of Eden: Communes and the New Anarchism* (London, Thames and Hudson, 1975).
14. As one commune-dweller put it: 'Why are any of us here *except* to self-indulge? No one came here or stays here for anyone but themselves. That is good. We have enough martyrs in the world, too many unhappy people doing things for someone else' (cited in Jerome, *Families of Eden*, p. 245). This point needs to be qualified, however, in the case of communes set up for specific purposes – say to provide a service of some kind to the local community, or to advance a political cause. These tend to be somewhat more cohesive. See P. Abrams and A. McCulloch, *Communes, Sociology and Society* (Cambridge, Cambridge University Press, 1976), ch. 2 for a discussion.
15. R.M. Kanter, *Commitment and Community: Communes and Utopias in Sociological Perspective* (Cambridge, Mass., Harvard University Press, 1972), p. 181.
16. See Rigby, *Alternative Realities*, ch. 9; Jerome, *Families of Eden*, ch. 4.
17. See Kanter, *Commitment and Community*, esp. ch. 4; C.J. Erasmus, *In Search of the Common Good* (New York, Free Press, 1977), ch. 5.
18. Even in the contemporary world, the most stable communities are usually those with a religious basis, or with ideological commitments that serve as a substitute for religion, such as the Israeli kibbutzim. This is obviously related to the point made in n. 14 above that members need to have reasons for staying in the community that go beyond personal gratification.
19. Letter to Nettlau, cited in Kropotkin, *Selected Writings on Anarchism and Revolution*, ed. M.A. Miller (Cambridge, Mass., M.I.T. Press, 1970), p. 297.

20. Sometimes the same village is painted in very different colours by observers of different political persuasions. For an example, see the competing anarchist and Communist accounts of Calanda in Aragon reproduced in Broué and Témime, *The Revolution and the Civil War in Spain* (London, Faber, 1972), pp. 160–1.
21. This is brought out rather clearly by Borkenau. See *The Spanish Cockpit* (London, Faber, 1937), *passim*.
22. See H. Thomas, 'Anarchist Agrarian Collectives in the Spanish Civil War' in M. Gilbert (ed.), *A Century of Conflict 1850–1950* (London, Hamish Hamilton, 1966); Broué and Témime, *Revolution and Civil War*, pp. 156–60.
23. See Peirats' account, cited in S. Dolgoff (ed.), *The Anarchist Collectives* (Montreal, Black Rose Books, 1974), pp. 112–20.
24. Peaceful co-existence is described by Peirats on pp. 112–13 and by Souchy on p. 130 of Dolgoff (ed.), *Anarchist Collectives*. Evidence of private owners being squeezed is provided by B. Bolloten, *The Grand Camouflage: The Communist Conspiracy in the Spanish Civil War* (London, Hollis and Carter, 1961), pp. 70–3.
25. Borkenau, *The Spanish Cockpit*, pp. 166–7.
26. For the variety of distributive practices adopted by the collectives, see G. Leval, *Collectives in the Spanish Revolution* (London, Freedom Press, 1975), esp. ch. 8.
27. Thomas, 'Anarchist Agrarian Collectives', pp. 253–7.
28. Leval, *Collectives in the Spanish Revolution*, p. 162.
29. ibid., *passim*. Dolgoff (ed.), *Anarchist Collectives*, pp. 115–18.
30. Dolgoff (ed.), *Anarchist Collectives*, p. 75.
31. Leval, *Collectives in the Spanish Revolution*, p. 88.
32. Thomas, 'Anarchist Agrarian Collectives', pp. 258–9.
33. Borkenau, *The Spanish Cockpit*, pp. 90–1.
34. I have taken these figures from Bolloten, *The Grand Camouflage*, p. 51. See also Souchy's description in Dolgoff (ed.), *Anarchist Collectives*, pp. 86–96.
35. For Alcoy, see Leval, *Collectives in the Spanish Revolution*, pp. 231–9.
36. G. Orwell, *Homage to Catalonia* (Harmondsworth, Penguin, 1962), esp. ch. 1.
37. Cited in Broué and Témime, *Revolution and Civil War*, p. 163.
38. This question raises once more the issue that I broached at the beginning of the chapter: whether anarchist ideals do not presuppose a social and moral order that has been irretrievably eroded by the transition to modern society. Many commentators on Spanish anarchism have related it to the 'backward' (by European standards) character of that country. I shall consider the issue further below.

12. Critical Questions

1. Two informative discussions are B. Russell, *Roads to Freedom: Socialism,*

Anarchism and Syndicalism (London, Allen and Unwin, 1918) and J. Plamenatz, *Karl Marx's Philosophy of Man* (Oxford, Clarendon Press, 1975), Part III. The latter ranges more widely than its title may suggest.

2. See above, ch. 3, pp. 42–3.
3. See my discussion in ch. 1, pp. 11–12.
4. See R. Nozick, *Anarchy, State and Utopia* (Oxford, Blackwell, 1974), ch. 7, section I. I have exposed some of the difficulties of such a theory in 'Justice and Property', *Ratio*, 22 (1980–81), 1–14.
5. They will think like this if they regard the obligation to relieve poverty as a collective obligation that falls on everyone in a particular society and if they are unwilling to put themselves at a competitive disadvantage by fulfilling the obligation when others do not.
6. A few anarchists have been egoists, holding that people do as a matter of fact always act selfishly, but that this need be no obstacle to social harmony because each person's interests, when properly understood, coincide with everyone else's. The view seems to me too fantastic to be worth rebutting at length.
7. I have drawn here upon the fuller discussion in Plamenatz, *Karl Marx's Philosophy of Man*, ch. 14.
8. They may also retort that in practice people may well *not* know where they stand under a legal system. The law may be uncertain because of conflicting decisions taken in different courts; it may be difficult for poor and ill-educated people to find out what their legal rights are; and success in a lawsuit may depend on the financial resources at one's disposal. All of these points are well taken, and finally it is a matter of weighing up the relative merits of two imperfect systems of administering justice. (I am grateful to April Carter for reminding me of them.)
9. Self-government here means government by people recognized as members of one's own national community. This should not be confused with democratic government, even though the demand for national self-government and the demand for democracy are often associated. For a much fuller discussion of such issues, see J. Plamenatz, *On Alien Rule and Self-Government* (London, Longmans, 1960).
10. Few anarchists have chosen to respond in this way, but one who did was Gustav Landauer. Landauer saw the nation as part of an ascending series of forms of community, which began with the family and culminated in humanity as a whole. He drew a sharp distinction between nation and state, and argued that nations as such should naturally co-exist peacefully as equals. Landauer's anarchism was of an unusual sort – in particular his stress on national identity meant that class antagonisms were played down to the point of extinction – but it is not less interesting for that. Very little of his work has been translated from the German, but there is a useful account in E. Lunn, *Prophet of Community: The Romantic Socialism of Gustav Landauer* (Berkeley and Los Angeles, University of California Press, 1973). I am grateful to James Joll for drawing this aspect of his thought to my attention.

Select Bibliography

Listed below are some of the major sources for those wishing to read further in this area. A wider range of references will be found in the footnotes. Books marked with an asterisk also contain more extensive bibliographies. There is a useful article bibliography in *Political Theory*, 4 (1976), 113–27.

General Anthologies

Woodcock, G. (ed.), *The Anarchist Reader* (London, Fontana, 1977).
Krimerman, L.I. and Perry, L. (eds.), *Patterns of Anarchy* (New York, Anchor Books, 1966).
Horowitz, I.L. (ed.), *The Anarchists* (New York, Dell Publishing Co., 1964).

General Histories

*Woodcock, G., *Anarchism* (Harmondsworth, Penguin, 1963).
Joll, J., *The Anarchists*, 2nd ed. (London, Methuen, 1979).
*Guérin, D., *Anarchism* (New York, Monthly Review Press, 1970).

Critical Studies

*Carter, A., *The Political Theory of Anarchism* (London, Routledge and Kegan Paul, 1971).
Ritter, A., *Anarchism: A Theoretical Analysis* (Cambridge, Cambridge University Press, 1980).
Taylor, M., *Community, Anarchy and Liberty* (Cambridge, Cambridge University Press, 1982).
*Pennock, J.R. and Chapman, J.W. (eds.), *Nomos XIX: Anarchism* (New York, New York University Press, 1978).
*Apter, D.E. and Joll, J. (eds.), *Anarchism Today* (London, Macmillan, 1971). (Reprints papers from *Government and Opposition*, vol. 5, no. 4).

Works by Individual Anarchists (in English)

Godwin, W., *Enquiry Concerning Political Justice*, ed. I. Kramnick (Harmondsworth, Penguin, 1976).
Warren, J., *Equitable Commerce* (New York, Fowlers and Wells, 1852).

Stirner, M., *The Ego and His Own*, trans. S.T. Byington (London, Jonathan Cape, 1921).

Spooner, L., *Natural Law; or the Science of Justice* (Boston, A. Williams, 1882).

Proudhon, P.-J., *Selected Writings of Pierre-Joseph Proudhon*, ed. S. Edwards (London, Macmillan, 1970).

—— *General Idea of the Revolution in the Nineteenth Century*, trans. J.B. Robinson (London, Freedom Press, 1923).

—— *What Is Property?*, trans. B.R. Tucker (London, William Reeves, n.d.).

Bakunin, M., *Bakunin on Anarchy*, ed. S. Dolgoff (New York, Vintage Books, 1972).

—— *The Political Philosophy of Bakunin*, ed. G.P. Maximoff (New York, Free Press of Glencoe, 1964).

—— *God and the State*, ed. G. Aldred (Glasgow and London, Bakunin Press, 1920).

Reclus, E., *An Anarchist on Anarchy* (London, Liberty Press, 1897).

—— *Evolution and Revolution* (London, International Publishing Co., 1886).

Kropotkin, P., *Kropotkin's Revolutionary Pamphlets*, ed. R.N. Baldwin (New York, Dover, 1970).

—— *The Conquest of Bread* (New York, Vanguard Press, 1926).

—— *The State: Its Historic Role* (London, Freedom Press, 1911).

—— *Modern Science and Anarchism* (London, Freedom Press, 1912).

—— *Mutual Aid* (London, Heinemann, 1910).

Malatesta, E., *Errico Malatesta: His Life and Ideas*, ed. V. Richards (London, Freedom Press, 1965).

—— *Anarchy* (London, Freedom Press, 1974).

Tucker, B.R. *Instead of a Book* (New York, B.R. Tucker, 1893).

Goldman, E., *Red Emma Speaks*, ed. A.K. Shulman (New York, Vintage Books, 1972).

—— *Anarchism and Other Essays* (Port Washington, N.Y., Kennikat Press, 1969).

Berkman, A., *What Is Communist Anarchism?*, ed. P. Avrich (New York, Dover Publications, 1972).

Rocker, R., *Anarcho-Syndicalism* (London, Secker and Warburg, 1938).

Maximoff, G.P., *Constructive Anarchism* (Chicago, Maximoff Memorial Publication Committee, 1952).

Walter, N., *About Anarchism* (London, Freedom Press, 1969).

Ward, C., *Anarchy in Action* (London, Allen and Unwin, 1973).

Bookchin, M., *Post-Scarcity Anarchism* (London, Wildwood House, 1974).

Rothbard, M.N., *For a New Liberty: The Libertarian Manifesto* (New York, Collier, 1978).

—— *Power and Market: Government and the Economy* (Kansas City, Sheed Andrews and McMeel, 1977).

Friedman, D., *The Machinery of Freedom* (New York, Harper, 1973).

Wolff, R.P., *In Defense of Anarchism* (New York, Harper Colophon, 1976).

Biographies and Critical Studies

Locke, D., *A Fantasy of Reason: The Life and Thought of William Godwin* (London, Routledge and Kegan Paul, 1980).

*Clark, J.P., *The Philosophical Anarchism of William Godwin* (Princeton, Princeton University Press, 1977).

*Martin, J.J., *Men Against the State: The Expositors of Individualist Anarchism in America, 1827–1908* (DeKalb, Ill., Adrian Allen, 1953).

Paterson, R.W.K., *The Nihilistic Egoist: Max Stirner* (London, Oxford University Press, 1971).

*Woodcock, G., *Pierre-Joseph Proudhon* (London, Routledge and Kegan Paul, 1956).

Ritter, A., *The Political Thought of Pierre-Joseph Proudhon* (Princeton, Princeton University Press, 1969).

Kelly, A., *Mikhail Bakunin: A Study in the Psychology and Politics of Utopianism* (Oxford, Clarendon Press, 1982).

Carr, E.H., *Michael Bakunin*, 2nd ed. (London, Macmillan, 1975).

*Pyziur, E., *The Doctrine of Anarchism of Michael A. Bakunin* (Milwaukee, Marquette University Press, 1955).

*Fleming, M., *The Anarchist Way to Socialism: Elisée Reclus and Nineteenth-Century European Anarchism* (London, Croom Helm, 1979).

Woodcock, G., and Avakumović, I., *The Anarchist Prince: A Biographical Study of Peter Kropotkin* (New York, Schocken Books, 1971).

*Miller, M.A., *Kropotkin* (Chicago, University of Chicago Press, 1976).

Drinnon, R., *Rebel in Paradise: A Biography of Emma Goldman* (Chicago, University of Chicago Press, 1961).

Anarchist Movements in Different Countries

France

*Maitron, J., *Le Mouvement Anarchiste en France* (Paris, Maspero, 1975).

*Ridley, F.F., *Revolutionary Syndicalism in France* (Cambridge, Cambridge University Press, 1970).

Italy

Hostetter, R., *The Italian Socialist Movement I: Origins (1860–1882)* (Princeton, Van Nostrand, 1958).

Spain

*Bookchin, M., *The Spanish Anarchists: The Heroic Years 1868–1936* (New York, Free Life Editions, 1977).

*Brenan, G., *The Spanish Labyrinth* (Cambridge, Cambridge University Press, 1969).

*Dolgoff, S., (ed.), *The Anarchist Collectives* (Montreal, Black Rose Books, 1974).

Leval, G., *Collectives in the Spanish Revolution* (London, Freedom Press, 1975).

Germany
*Carlson, A.R., *Anarchism in Germany (Vol. I: The Early Movement)* (Metuchen, N.J., Scarecrow Press, 1972).

Russia
*Avrich, P., *The Russian Anarchists* (Princeton, Princeton University Press, 1967).

U.K.
Quail, J., *The Slow Burning Fuse* (London, Paladin, 1978).

U.S.
*DeLeon, D., *The American as Anarchist: Reflections on Indigenous Radicalism* (Baltimore, Johns Hopkins University Press, 1978).
Brissenden, P.F., *The I.W.W.: A Study of American Syndicalism* (New York, Columbia University, 1920).

Index

Anarcho-communism, 45–59,
    157–60, 163, 165, 166–8, 171–3,
    176–7, 178, 191n
Anarcho-individualism, 4–5, 30–44,
    58–9, 67–9, 155–7, 169–73, 176,
    177–8, 191n, 194n
Anarcho-syndicalism, 97, 124–40,
    166, 203n
Andrews, S.P., 68, 187n
Angry Brigade, 113, 115
Arbitration, 39–40, 177–8
Authority, 15–18, 23, 25, 26–9,
    56–7, 92, 185n
Autonomy, moral, 26–9

Baader, A., 114, 116
Baader-Meinhof group, 113, 114,
    118
Bakunin, M., 9, 10, 45–6, 70–1, 76,
    79ff., 88ff., 95, 98, 100, 189n,
    190n, 192–3n
Benevento insurrection, 100–1
Berkman, A., 56, 85, 89, 90, 112,
    118, 189n, 190n, 191n
Blanc, L., 10, 11
Bologna insurrection, 92, 99–100
Bolsheviks, 87, 89, 90–2, 97
Bonaparte, L., 86
Bookchin, M., 85, 139, 189n, 190n,
    204n
Borkenau, F., 106, 162, 164
Brigate Rosse, 113, 114–15
Brousse, P., 99, 100

Cafiero, C., 99
Capitalism, 9–10, 31–6, 46–9, 83–4,
    141, 143
Capitalist class, 9, 43, 48–50, 116–18,
    125–7

Cohn-Bendit, D., 146–7, 149
Collectives (Spain), 155, 160–7
Collectivism, 46, 53–4
Comfort, A., 204n
Communes, 54–5, 91, 99, 102, 104,
    105–6, 159–60, 171
Communities, 155–60, 166–8, 173,
    206
Confederación Nacional de Trabajo
    (C.N.T.), 128, 136–9, 161, 164,
    165
Confédération Générale du Travail
    (C.G.T.), 129, 133–5, 147, 202n
Contract, see Exchange and Social
    Contract
Crime, 55–6, 117, 176–7

Darwin, C., 72, 193n
Darwinism, social, 72, 193n
Debord, G., 204n
Decentralization, 52–3, 88–9, 165–6,
    171–2, 173, 205
de Gaulle, C., 148
Delesalle, P., 133
de Ligt, B., 122
Democracy: direct, 20, 24, 27;
    parliamentary, 12–13, 38, 50,
    87–90, 128
Dictatorship of the proletariat, 13,
    90–3
Direct action, 126–7

Economic organization, 11–12, 32–5,
    41–2, 51–4, 58, 162–6, 167–8,
    169–73
Egoism, 22–5, 31, 67–8, 69–70,
    186n, 208n
Elitism, 80, 95–6, 120
Engels, F., 78, 82, 83, 92–3

Enlightenment, mental, 21, 63, 64–9
Ensslin, G., 114
Equality, 33, 34, 51–2, 163–4, 165–6, 167, 173
Exchange, 12, 30–1, 32–5, 38–9, 51, 58, 156, 163, 171

Federación Anarquista Ibérica (F.A.I.), 107, 137, 139
Federalism, 52, 54–5, 96–7, 126
Feuerbach, L., 23
Free association, 7–8, 51, 54–5, 56–7, 96–7
Freedom, 2, 45, 58–9, 155, 160, 175
Frick, H., 112, 116, 118
Friedman, D., 151, 187n, 188n

Gandhi, M., 122
General strike, 127, 133, 134, 137–9
Godwin, W., 4, 18–22, 24, 64–7, 150, 190n
Goldman, E., 84, 85, 91, 96, 97–8, 118, 120, 189n, 190n, 191n, 204–5n
Goodman, P., 205n
Gramsci, A., 195n, 197n
Grave, J., 118, 130–2
Griffuelhes, V., 128, 133

Hayek, F.A., 173
Haymarket affair, 110
Hegel, G.W.F., 70–1
Henry, E., 112, 116–17
Historical materialism, 63, 79–82, 192–3n
History, theories of, 63–76
Hobbes, T., 184n
Human nature, 40, 41, 45, 55–6, 58–9, 62–77, 169, 180

International situationists, 143–6, 148–9
International Workers of the World (I.W.W.), 134–5, 138

Jouhaux, L., 133

Jura Federation, 97, 99, 101
Justice, distributive, 32–3, 35, 47, 51–2, 58–9, 69–70, 162, 172–3. *See also* Equality *and* Law

Kant, I., 186n
Kanter, R.M., 160
Kropotkin, P., 46, 48–50, 53ff., 73–6, 79, 80–1, 85, 89ff., 95–6, 98ff., 119–20, 125, 130, 160, 189n, 190n, 191n, 193n, 198n, 205n

Landauer, G., 151, 208n
Law, 6–7, 23–4, 27, 40–1, 175–9, 208n
Lefebvre, H., 143
Lenin, V.I., 13, 90–1, 93, 195–6n
Leval, G., 164
Liberalism, 23, 30, 50, 59, 68
Locke, J., 6

Machajski, J.W., 81
Mackay, J.H., 191n
Makhno, N., 102–4, 107
Malatesta, E., 45, 46, 48, 50, 54–5, 75, 76, 85, 89, 99ff., 120, 130, 189n, 190n, 194n
Marcuse, H., 143
Marx, K., 13, 33, 45, 78ff., 88, 92, 93, 95, 194n
Marxism, 3, 45–6, 78–93, 141–2, 143, 194n
Maximov, G.P., 91
May–June events (1968), 142, 144, 146–9
Milgram, S., 185n
Military organization, 102–3, 106–7
Monatte, P., 129
Most, J., 90, 118
Mutual aid, 50, 72–3
Mutualism, 11–12, 172, 184

Nationality, 179–81, 208
Natural rights, 31, 39
Nechaev, S., 92, 197n

New Left, 141–4, 146, 148–50, 151
Non-violence, 121–3
Nozick, R., 40, 172

Orwell, G., 107, 165, 199n

Parliamentarianism, *see* Democracy, parliamentary
Pataud, E., 134
Plekhanov, G., 93
Pouget, E., 128, 130, 133, 134
Propaganda by the deed, 98–101
Protective associations, 39–41, 58, 59, 176
Proudhon, P.-J., 6, 10, 11–12, 33, 69–71, 76, 80, 81, 99, 172, 184–5n, 193n
Public goods, 41–2, 55, 170–1, 188–9n, 190n

Rand, A., 187n
Ravachol, F.-C., 111–12, 116
Reclus, E., 46, 72–6, 117, 120
Religion, 8–9, 22–3, 180
Revolution, 62, 66–7, 70, 71, 74–6, 84–9, 92–3, 94–6, 98, 123, 126, 127, 131, 139, 145, 148–51
Revolutionary organization, 95–8, 103–4, 105–6, 121–2, 125–6, 129–32, 136–7, 138
Richards, V., 139
Ritter, A., 185n, 191n, 192n
Rocker, R., 129
Rothbard, M.N., 35, 38–9, 43, 67–9, 187n, 188n
Rousseau, J.-J., 69
Russian Civil War, 102–4
Russian Revolution, 91–2, 97–8

Schumpeter, J., 38
Segui, S., 136, 137
Social contract, 5, 20, 37
Social control, 55–7, 160, 166, 173–9
Social Democratic Party (S.P.D.), 87, 90, 111

Social organization, 7–8, 39–42, 50–9, 151, 154–5, 158–60, 161–8, 172–9, 182–3
Social solidarity, 45, 50, 53, 55, 58–9, 72–3, 174–5
Socialism, 4–5, 31–2, 33, 59; state, 10–11, 51, 87–92. *See also* Marxism
Sorel, G., 201n
Spanish Civil War, 105–7, 110, 124, 155, 161
'Spectacle', 144–5, 148
Spooner, L., 37, 39, 67, 188n
Stafford, D., 100
State, 5–10, 15–16, 23–4, 26–7, 36–40, 42–3, 48–50, 82–4, 87–9, 123, 143, 151, 154, 172–3, 179–81, 184n
Stirner, M., 4, 22–5, 29, 186n
Students, 141, 146–8
Syndicalism, revolutionary, 125–9, 132, 133, 136, 201, 203. *See also* Anarcho-syndicalism

Terrorism, 92–3, 109–16; justifications of, 116–21
Thomas, H., 162, 164
Thomas, P., 194n
Thoreau, H.D., 15, 185n
Time stores, 156
Tolstoy, L., 121
Tucker, B., 31, 33–5, 39, 43, 68, 191n, 194n

Unión General de Trabajadores (U.G.T.), 136, 137
Utilitarianism, 18–19, 21–2, 31

Vaillant, A., 112, 117
Violence, 2, 109–10, 120–3, 127. *See also* Terrorism

Walter, N., 75, 76, 189n
Ward, C., 205n
Warren, J., 32–3, 35, 155–6, 187n
Weathermen, 200

Weber, M., 64, 185n
Wolff, R.P., 26–9
Woodcock, G., 190n, 191–2n
Workers' control (of industry),
    147–8, 164–5, 171–2
Working class, 4, 78, 84–7, 93, 125,
    132, 143, 147–8, 165

Yvetot, G., 133